KEYS
to the
CELLAR

KEYS
to the
CELLAR

~~~~~~~~

STRATEGIES AND SECRETS
OF WINE COLLECTING

PETER D. MELTZER

WILEY
John Wiley & Sons, Inc.

To the vintages of my favorite people: 1955 and 1956.

Copyright © 2006 by Peter D. Meltzer

Photography Credits:
Pages ii, xiv and 118 courtesy of Design Build Consultants, Inc.
Pages 46 and 68 courtesy of Acker Merrall & Condit
Pages 73, 85, and 102 courtesy of Zachys
Pages 123 (left) and 130 (top) courtesy of International Wine Accessories, Inc.
Pages 123 (right) and 198 courtesy of Peter Meltzer
Page 130 courtesy of Jacques Bergier
Page 150 © CEPHAS / Joe Partridge
Page 165 courtesy of Christie's
Page 182 © CEPHAS / Ian Shaw

Published by John Wiley & Sons, Inc., Hoboken, New Jersey
Published simultaneously in Canada

For general information about our other products and services or for technical support, please contact our Customer Care Department within the United States at (800) 762-2974, outside the United States at (317) 572-3993 or fax (317) 572-4002.

Wiley also publishes its books in a variety of electronic formats. Some content that appears in print may not be available in electronic books. For more information about Wiley products, visit our web site at www.wiley.com.

Library of Congress Cataloging-in-Publication Data:

Meltzer, Peter D.
Keys to the cellar : strategies and secrets of wine collecting / by Peter Meltzer.
p. cm.
Includes bibliographical references and index.
ISBN-13: 978-0-471-47359-6 (cloth)
ISBN-10: 0-471-47359-6 (cloth)
1. Wine and wine making—Collectors and collecting. I. Title.
TP548.M477 2006
641.2'2075—dc22
2005032318

Printed in the United States of America

10 9 8 7 6 5 4 3 2 1

CONTENTS

~\\\\\\~

ACKNOWLEDGMENTS

∿∿∿

This book would never have happened were it not for Michael and Ariane Batterberry, cofounders of *Food Arts* and *Food & Wine* magazines, who hired me as their twenty-six-year-old wine editor at *Food &Wine* in 1977. Their ongoing friendship and support have been greatly appreciated. Indeed, it was Michael who first suggested the title for this book.

It was on assignment for *Food & Wine* in 1978 that I met a group of passionate, young wine collectors whose large-scale vertical examinations of First Growth Bordeaux and celebrated vintages of claret, such as 1945 and 1959, provided me with a ringside glimpse into the joys of wine collecting. First and foremost among them is Lloyd Flatt, who, with his wife Lauré, remains a very close friend. Other seminal members of The Group (as they liked to call themselves) were Tawfiq Khoury, Lenoir Josey, Barney Rhodes, and Dr. Marvin Overton.

Marvin Shanken, publisher and editor of *Wine Spectator*, gave me my first opportunity to report on the burgeoning wine collecting scene in 1981. A generation later, I remain the auction correspondent for *Wine Spectator*, a beat I altogether relish. Tom Matthews, executive editor of *Wine Spectator*, has provided tremendous support and insight into the fine points of the column, and John Siudut has ably assisted me in interpreting the data he processes for the *Wine Spectator* Auction Index. Senior Editors James Laube and Bruce Sanderson have also conferred a singular perspective on this book, along with former associate editor Ryan Isaac.

Many friends in the auction business have proven invaluable in the compilation of this narrative: Serena Sutcliffe, M.W. and Jamie Ritchie at Sotheby's; Michael Broadbent, David Elswood, Richard Brierley, and Rik Pike at Christie's; Nikos Antonakeas at Morrell & Company; John Kapon at Acker Merrall & Condit; Michael Davis, Paul Hart, and John Hart at Hart Davis Hart; Jeff Zacharia at Zachys (along with auctioneers Fritz Hatton and Ursula Hermacinski); as well as Jerry Zech and Brooke Hilton at WineBid.com.

There are myriad wine retailers who have been of assistance in the preparation of this text. Foremost among them is my close friend Michael Aaron, chairman of Sherry-Lehmann in New York, and his associates Chris Adams and Ken Mudford. Others include Don Zacharia, chairman of Zachys in Scarsdale, New York; Peter Morrell, chairman of Morrell & Company in Manhattan; Chip Cassidy of Crown Wine & Spirits in Miami; Michael Glasby at Premier Cru in Emeryville, California; Jim Knight of the Wine House in Los Angeles; Greg Koslosky of The Wine Club in San Francisco; Lance Storer at Centennial Fine Wine and Spirits in Dallas; and Richard Torin of Clarets in Los Angeles.

Other wine professionals whose refreshing viewpoints have been of great assistance include custom cellar designer Christine Hawley Aaron, importer Adrian Chalk, retailer and sommelier Jean-Luc Le Dû, winemaker John Kongsgaard, Smith & Wollensky vice president and wine expert-at-large Kevin Zraly, and private wine consultants Gorky Rahman, Brian Orcutt, and Kevin Swersey. Wine writers Hugh Johnson and Matt Kramer, along with wine collectors Jacques and Reynita Bergier, Robert Cunningham, Charles Klatskin, Rob Rosania, George Sape, Nicholas Silvers, and Kim Vernon have given me a keen perspective on the current state of collecting.

A host of chefs and food and wine experts have fostered my collecting experience over the years. Foremost among them are Lidia Bastianich, Joseph Bastianich, Philippe Belgrange, Robert Bohr, Daniel Boulud,

Jimmy Brennan, Terry Brennan, Cesare Casella, Jean Denoyer, Wiley Dufresne, Dewey Dufresne, John Fanning, Tony Fortuna, Peter and Penny Glazier, Corinne Guisez, André and Rita Jammet, Daniel Johnnes, Tim Kopec, François and Suzanne Latapie, Ed Lauber, Stephen and Thalia Loffredo, Laura Maioglio, Nick Marzouilla, Tony and Marisa May, Danny Meyer, Eberhard Müller, Julian Niccolini, Drew Nieporent, Wayne Nish, François Payard, Tom Piscicelo, Alfred Portale, Joseph Scalice, André Soltner, Alan Stillman, Larry Stone, Laurent Tourondel, Steve Verlin, Alex von Bidder, Jean-Georges Vongerichten, Jonathan Waxman, and Matt Wilson.

I also want to thank my editors at John Wiley & Sons, starting with Susan Wyler, who commissioned this book. Senior Editor Linda Ingroia and her associate Adam Kowit have shown great enthusiasm—and patience—during the editing process. Also, thanks to Suzanne Sunwoo, the cover designer, and Kate Tyler in publicity and Michael Friedberg in marketing for their efforts.

Too numerous to mention are all the friends who have been subjected to my informal wine tastings—good and bad—which enabled me to forge my cellar "keys." Nevertheless, I'd like to single out Peter and Lynne Bienstalk, Lenny and Judy Borger, Peter Caudwell, Peter C. Jones and Charlotte Frieze, Josh Josephson, Derek Limbacher, Sacha and Jim MacNaughton, Mark and Nina Magowan, John and Galina Mariani, Jim Marlas and Marie Nugent Head, Melvyn and Janie Master, Gail Monaghan, Arnaud de Vienne, Robert and Liz Whitney, and Fred and Abbie Wyman. And I am especially indebted to Heather Meltzer, without whose presence there would be no keys at all.

PREFACE

As a critic who has had a front-row seat at wine auctions for nearly two decades (during which time I also tracked the ever-evolving nature of New York restaurants and their wine lists as editor and publisher of the guidebook *Passport to New York Restaurants*), I have both observed and actively participated in the burgeoning collecting phenomenon. While it's encouraging that the universe of wine aficionados continues to expand, a surprising number of potentially receptive participants remain on the sidelines, intimidated by misconceptions about the collecting process or fears of auction fever.

I'm drawn to wine collecting because it's the only consumable collectible. You can still buy (and drink) a vintage Latour that was harvested when Lincoln was president, or a Cognac distilled during Napoleon's reign. But collecting is no mere historical odyssey. The breadth of cellar-worthy candidates makes the pursuit a full-fledged challenge. Today's highly sought-after, limited-production labels such as Turley, Harlan, Valandraud, and L'Ermita didn't even exist twenty years ago. For everyday drinking, there is now a host of well-made, well-balanced, and well-priced labels worth quaffing while you wait for treasured new releases to mature.

It is precisely because of the rewarding and relatively risk-free nature of wine collecting that *Keys to the Cellar* was forged. Collecting is an engaging pastime. Auctions may be contagious, but they don't bite. Favorite bottles are ultimately emptied, but the memory of a good one—whether it was a $12 Alycastre rosé from Provence or a priceless Château Lafite Rothschild 1799—lingers forever.

Whether your goal is to set aside a tightly knit selection of a few dozen bottles for special occasions or to fill an extensive underground cellar, *Keys to the Cellar* will unlock the secrets of wine collecting. Comprehensive buying strategies are complemented by detailed insights into storing, serving, and enjoying fine wine. Price charts from the *Wine Spectator* Auction Index quantify the performance of hundreds of wines, simplifying the purchasing process and establishing a reliable going rate for collectible wine. Other sections cover prominent wine collectors, tasting notes, and a range of wine storage equipment and accessories.

INTRODUCTION

It's often said that in America, most wine is consumed within a day or two of its purchase. So why collect wine when you can get a good bottle almost anywhere, any time? It's true that for some people, wine will always be just another alcoholic beverage; yet for others, it's an endless source of enjoyment, even an outright passion. The moment you start buying wine for no purpose other than to discover what a specific bottle tastes like, you've made the first tentative steps toward joining the collectors' circle.

The process may end there or take you down a path that leads to a bona fide cellar containing hundreds or even thousands of bottles. It may not be an instant transformation, but eventually most wine lovers evolve into wine collectors. No matter what the scope or size of your collection, there are essential keys that will ensure the undertaking is a success.

Creating a wine collection is a little like assembling a wardrobe; you want to be able to accommodate most foreseeable occasions. From a practical standpoint, it makes sense to have a stash of your favorite bottles on hand. Why run to the local liquor store every time someone drops by for a drink or dinner? A well-stocked cellar not only enables you to plan ahead and enhance your meals, but also lets you transform an ordinary evening into an instant celebration simply by opening a special bottle.

It is monotonous to eat the same food day in and day out, and there is no excuse for serving the same wine all the time, either, especially considering the wealth of top-quality wine produced worldwide. A wine cellar provides breadth of choice. It can also serve as an opportunity to experiment, to finesse your personal tastes, and to learn about different wine regions. There's a virtually unlimited supply of taste experiences awaiting you at a well-sourced wine merchant or auction house. Regardless of how you assemble it, creating a wine cellar is a source of perpetual pleasure.

There's also a potential economic benefit to owning a wine cellar. Fine wine tends to appreciate in value as it matures: the replacement costs of your favorite bottles are likely to escalate over time. By purchasing wines upon their initial release, you can assure their future availability at a fixed cost. Since you will also be overseeing the aging process (ideally in a temperature- and humidity-controlled storage unit), you'll guarantee pristine storage and avoid the risk of uncorking a badly stored bottle.

Although buying fine wine for investment is a somewhat risky undertaking, select wines do have major investment potential. The average price of the wines tracked by the *Wine Spectator* Auction Index (see page 247) has more than doubled since its creation in 1995. Even more dramatic are the First Growth Bordeaux from the 1982 vintage, some of which have appreciated by as much as 1,000 percent since they were offered as futures in 1983.

Compared to the cost of many other collectibles, such as modern art, antique silver, or furniture, wine is relatively inexpensive. For $5,000 to $10,000, you can assemble enough wine to provide at least a year's worth of drinking pleasure. Of course, if you are planning to put together a well-balanced cellar with enough wines to cover near-, mid-, and long-term imbibing, you are embracing a much more serious expenditure (see page 36), but even a lifetime's worth of fine wine falls short of the price of an Andy Warhol silk screen. Conversely, if you only drink wine at home a few nights a week, your outlay will be considerably less. But whether you consume your cache in six months or six years, you should understand that a collection is never static. It has to be replenished or redefined as it is depleted: you are not buying bottles to hoard, after all; you are buying wine to drink.

Those bitten by the wine-collecting bug know how dramatically their hobby differs from other kinds of collecting. Collectible paintings hang on a wall for all to enjoy unless their owner decides to dispose of them; fine wine normally reposes out of sight in a cellar until it is systematically disposed of in order to be enjoyed. Until that moment, the bottle has value, but no definition—merely potential. But in the very act of discovering a wine's essence and quality, the collector must empty the bottle, rendering it worthless.

While it would be highly unusual for a stamp or baseball-card collector to intentionally destroy a prized item in his or her portfolio, wine collectors effectively do so every time they uncork treasured bottles in the company of friends. This purposeful act of sharing presupposes a special temperament that separates wine collecting from other pursuits.

So why create a collection which by definition can only be savored by depleting it? For true wine aficionados, it's all in the bottle. They buy in order to drink and to share their prized labels with kindred palates. They are passionate about the experience of wine, not simply the possession of wine. And, in most cases, it's an experience of fine or rare wine that turns the occasional drinker into a passionate collector.

A CELLAR TO FIT YOUR LIFESTYLE

~\\\\\\\~

~~~~~~

WHEN DOES AN ACCUMULATION OF WINE BECOME A COLLECTION? It's a bit like asking when a selection of paintings becomes an art collection. There's no clear answer, and it's a perception usually made in hindsight. Matt Wilson, a Manhattan wine retailer and an extremely astute wine collector, states simply, "a collector is someone who deeply appreciates fine wines and has enough in stock to enable regular access." But wine collecting is also about a state of mind, not just about having a certain number of cellar-worthy bottles. It presupposes a commitment to the collecting process and to learning about wine in general. Most collectors also have an enthusiasm (if not a passion) for learning about the history of specific regions and growers.

A person's critical leap into wine collecting can be difficult to pinpoint, but there are telltale signs. It might begin when you have more wine than any freestanding shelf in the kitchen can accommodate, or when your storage room brims with unopened wine crates. Or the day you realize you have more wine on hand than you could possibly drink during the ensuing year. For truly impassioned enophiles, collection status may only be achieved when they have enough wine on hand to last a lifetime.

Generally speaking, though, a functional collection entails having at least enough wine to last a year. For the developing wine collector, that means roughly 250 bottles—more still unless you plan to replenish your stock as it dwindles. At the other end of the spectrum, some serious collectors have cellars that number in the thousands of bottles. Initially, you'll want to achieve a balance between everyday wines and cellar-worthy wines that will improve as they age. Over time, by cellaring new releases that represent good value, along with more substantial collectibles, you'll achieve a perfect mix.

Not just any bottle qualifies as a wine collectible. Normally, it must possess a heightened level of complexity along with an extended shelf life. For this reason, simple Beaujolais, Zinfandels, or Pinot Grigios, and wines from unexceptional vintages, however pleasant to serve on an everyday basis, won't improve much over time, nor will they have any resale value, whereas a Bordeaux or Cabernet Sauvignon from a good vintage is an ideal candidate for aging.

That doesn't mean that collectible wines are always very expensive ones. Even among cellar-worthy bottles, there is a considerable range in price and quality. In 2005, I picked up a case of Corton Chandon de Briailles 1999 at auction for under $400, along with a dozen bottles of Charlopin-Parizot Gevrey-Chambertin Cuvee Vieilles Vignes 1998 for $240, and quality white wines such as William Fèvre Chablis Fourchaume Vignoble de Vaulorent 2002 (an excellent vintage) for an average of $33 a bottle. Of course, specific price points are up to the individual buyer. I know some collectors who only go after bargains: wines that, in their estimation, are undervalued or under-priced. This approach requires considerable legwork, but part of the pleasure is in the pursuit. Others, having sampled a broad array of wine over time, conclude that they only want to cellar—and drink—the best. That might mean Screaming Eagle Cabernet Sauvignon, the preeminent California cult wine, classic Bordeaux like Château Pétrus 1989, or the best Burgundies, like Domaine de la Romanée-Conti (DRC) Romanée-Conti 1990, which cost in the thousands of dollars per bottle. It's an expensive undertaking, but one that pleases at the highest level.

Most new collectors will only be filling a cellar with wines they intend to drink at some point, yet as auction correspondent for *Wine Spectator*, I always get letters from readers who instead want to know about buying wine as an investment. For decades, English collectors have financed future wine purchases by bulking up their inventory and eventually selling off the overage. Second-guessing a wine's investment potential is inherently risky. Several highly praised vintages have turned out to be less than stellar. Investors who speculate on wine's resale potential focus on hard-to-come-by, limited-production labels with a proven track record. Quality should take precedence over quantity: there's no point in stocking up on lesser labels that are unlikely to appreciate significantly. Investing is a tempting process for enophiles with a gambling spirit, but if speculation is your goal, always be prepared to drink your investment in the event of a market collapse. (For more information, see "*The Investment Cellar,*" page 12.)

PLANNING YOUR CELLAR

∧∖∖∖∖∖∖

Before combing retail stores, surfing the internet, or pouring over auction catalogs, take a very close look at your lifestyle to determine which wines will fit best with your present and anticipated drinking requirements. Without a concrete plan, you run the risk of picking up a bit of this and a bit of that and never developing any sense of direction or cohesion. There are hundreds if not thousands of labels worth collecting. The task is to find the right ones for you.

The most important step is to try to project the occasions at which your wines will be poured. Most collectors don't spend their lives hosting a procession of wine tastings, and there isn't much pleasure in sampling a bottle all by oneself. Most often, collectors serve wine in the company of friends. Extrapolate from your present drinking patterns so you don't find yourself top-heavy with wines that don't fit into your lifestyle.

There's no point, after all, in stocking up on $100+ bottles if you don't foresee many opportunities to serve them, no matter what their appeal or score. More wine goes bad for not being drunk than for any other reason. Too often, people put away a "special" bottle in anticipation of a "special" moment that never arrives.

DRINKING YOUR TREASURES

Fine wine is one of the few things that gets better as it gets older, but you can ruin a good thing by waiting too long to uncork a vintage classic. I have sampled 1900 Margaux and 1870 Lafite Rothschild, 1947 Pétrus and 1911 Cheval-Blanc, and they were all more than holding their own—some of them quite beautifully. I wouldn't hesitate to buy them again, assuming they had been stored properly. But I also recall the disappointment of uncorking much younger wines, like Château La Mission Haut-Brion 1966, Château Mouton-Rothschild 1966, and Beaulieu Vineyards Private Reserve Cabernet Sauvignon 1968, which were past peak because I had held on to them too long. If you have multiple bottles of the same wine, open one periodically to see how it's coming along. Don't wait until it reaches the maturity date specified in some vintage chart only to find out the "expert" was wrong. Don't expect miracles from a charming but relatively simple *cru bourgeois* that was never meant to be kept more than a decade.

Sometimes it's hard to take a corkscrew to a valuable bottle of wine, especially if it's the only one you own. In 2001, I served a magnum of the spectacular Haut-Brion 1961 at my birthday. We were three couples at dinner, and all of us were extremely fond of fine wine. The wine fully lived up to its reputation—yet I was almost sorry to see it go. In truth, I had agonized over opening it at all, as I had owned the wine for nearly twenty years. But I was thrilled with everyone's reaction to the wine and the thought that we were drinking a $5,000 bottle that had originally cost around $100. I recalled a poem about wine by the late and legendary Baron Philippe de Rothschild (owner of Château Mouton-Rothschild) in which he wrote, "Wine never dies. Instead, it lives in the soul of the person who consumes it." If you hesitate to open something special when the occasion merits it, you are better off selling it than letting it die a slow death in your cellar.

5

Assess the level of wine interest on your typical guest list and reserve your treasures for serious rather than social drinkers. You don't want to find yourself in the position of calculating whether a particular guest is worth the wine you're serving. Unless you want to turn an average dinner into a didactic exercise, you'll be frustrated if no one wants to hear about the bottles' salient characteristics. Don't load up on expensive, rarified treasures if the majority of your friends display only a passing interest in what's being poured. Most collectors relish comparing their thoughts on a specific bottle—the average dinner guest may not.

Ultimately, a wine cellar should reflect your personal taste—not some abstract notion of an ideal cellar crafted by others. There's a story about a man who returned a case of wine to his wine merchant because he didn't like the way it tasted. Shortly thereafter, the wine received rave reviews in the professional wine press, and he sheepishly returned to the merchant to buy back the same case. Trust your palate; after all, you, not a critic, will be serving the wine at your house.

A Year of Good Drinking

Unless possessed of unlimited resources, the beginning collector should focus on cellaring wines for the upcoming calendar year, rather than the ensuing decade. That entails an assessment of projected drinking requirements (best calculated on a monthly basis), specific wine types, and quality levels. The actual amount of wine to lay down also depends on the available storage capacity, because fine wine should be stored in a climate controlled environment.

For most collectors, it's unrealistic, not to mention prohibitively expensive, to open a fine or rare bottle every time they reach for a corkscrew. A practical solution is to break down your shopping list into three categories: "good," "better," and "best." The exact price range for each will vary according to your budget. For the sake of argument, "good" wines might cost around $20. "Better" might be between $20 and $50, and "best," over $50.

DRINKING FINE WINE THE FIRST TIME

While I don't recommend it, I have served great wines such as Châteaux Lafite Rothschild 1953, Latour 1955, and Haut-Brion 1989 to total neophytes with tremendous success. (You have to feel confident as a "tour guide" to pull it off.) Although my guests were casual wine drinkers, they immediately perceived the complex nature of what they were consuming, even though they lacked the vocabulary to describe it. At the most basic level, many of them were wowed by the age of the wines alone.

Anyone who has mastered the basics of wine tasting (see page 135) is ready to experiment with something great. But it's unwise to do it in the abstract, because without some reference points, the experience can potentially be wasted. One good approach is to organize a vertical selection (different vintages of the same wine), and include an OK vintage alongside a great one. You might, for instance, compare two bottles of Robert Mondavi Cabernet Sauvignon Reserve (a premium California label), such as the stellar 1997 and the more average 1998. The same process might apply to contrasting the 1999 vintage of Château Léoville-Barton with the highly rated 2000.

Another approach would be to conduct a mini-horizontal tasting (different wines of the same vintage). You could examine the characteristics of three Pauillacs: Château Pichon Lalande, Château Grand-Puy-Lacoste, and Château Duhart-Milon from the 1995 vintage. If you prefer, examine some Napa wines from the excellent 1994 vintage: Pride Mountain Cabernet Sauvignon Reserve, Silver Oak Cabernet Sauvignon, and Chateau Montelena.

While it's paramount that you store your "better" and "best" wines in a temperature- and humidity-controlled facility, "good" wines, which you are likely to consume within a year, are unlikely to spoil if left in a cool space, thereby freeing your storage facility's capacity for the better stuff.

It's impossible to predict the exact amount of wine a collector will require on an annual basis, but as the chart on page 9 shows, an average couple could easily go through thirty cases a year—more if they entertain a lot, less if they dine out more often or drink wine infrequently.

Plotting Your Year of Drinking

By dividing your projected consumption into these categories suggested in these sample and blank charts, you can approximate the amount of wine you'll need and see how it divvies up between the three basic quality levels. It will then be easier for you to decide whether to purchase by the case, the six-pack, or the bottle—and at what price point. If you want to plan your cellar with long-term as well as short-term consumption in mind, multiply the annual total by the number of years for which you are cellaring, and make sure your "better" and "best" wines include a number of younger vintages that will last.

If you are just testing the waters, or if the prospect of buying thirty cases of wine seems daunting, assemble six mixed cases (seventy-two bottles) consisting largely of everyday ("good") wines from the world's major wine-producing regions. Don't worry about wines that require aging, but do allocate a portion of your purchases to "better" wines and at least one or two bottles of "best" wines for special occasions. Plan to consume this starter's kit over a three- to six-month period to determine whether you want to pursue a more serious collection. It's a less committal, instructive entry into the world of collecting wine.

Because of their cost, investment-grade wines priced in excess of $300 per bottle are largely out of the question for the beginner. If your sights are set on a cellar that consists exclusively of rare wines, you'll simply have to cut back on quantity to stay within your budget. However, at some point, it is worth springing for at least one or two great bottles that can serve as a benchmark against which other wines can be judged: you cannot say, "This is the best bottle of wine on the market," if you haven't ever sampled the market's best.

As long as you take the "good," "better," "best" approach to the wines you select, there is no end to the range of possibilities, or the didactic potential, of your cellar.

The following chart projects an average couple's monthly and annual wine consumption at the rate of half bottle per person per meal.

no.	occasion	"good"	"better"	"best"	total bottles
16	Family dinners at home	10	4	2	16
2	Casual dinners for four	2	2		4
1	Dinner party for eight		2	2	4
4	Impromptu visits	3	1		4
	monthly totals	15	9	4	28
	annual totals	180	108	48	336

This sample chart shows how to calculate your projected annual wine consumption; break down the number of "good," "better," and "best" bottles by month for various occasions, then tally annual totals.

no.	occasion	"good"	"better"	"best"	total bottles
	Family dinners at home				
	Casual dinners for four				
	Dinner party for eight				
	Impromptu visits				
	monthly totals				
	annual totals				

Photocopy this blank chart to calculate your own projected wine needs.

Fine Tuning the Cellar to the Dining Room

While some of your treasures may be best enjoyed on their own, you'll probably want to make sure that a sizable portion of your cellar matches the kinds of food you usually eat at home. A home cook who prefers recipes from the American Southwest will want a different roster of wines than someone who sticks to classical French cooking—or doesn't cook at all. The *red wine with meat, white wine with fish* adage was debunked long ago. Certain reds, like Pinot Noirs and Côtes du Rhônes, marry well with seafood, whereas, in general, more tannic Bordeaux do not.

If you have eclectic food tastes or are not sure about the perfect fit, the best and most enjoyable recourse is to stock your cellar with an assortment of different varietals, ranging from Chardonnay to Riesling and Pinot Noir to Syrah, and systematically test them with your favorite dishes—for example, against grilled fish, chicken, and beef. Record your impressions in a notebook or computer file. Then break the wine categories down and try an array of different vintages of a particular wine to discover how they combine with a certain dish. It's surprising how quickly you'll make the ideal match (see page 146, "Pairing Wine with Food").

No matter what your drinking preferences, don't ignore your white wine quotient. Most collectors concentrate on red wines because they have a longer shelf life and develop more nuances in flavor as they mature than the average white. As a result, they tend to underestimate their everyday consumption of white wine and often find themselves running out.

10

Storing It All

Before you start buying in quantity, consider how much space you can allocate to storage. Wine is bulky. A simple cellar with a 100-case capacity will take up roughly 250 cubic feet of space (see page 124 for more details). While there are no hard and fast rules about the composition of a wine cellar, it is essential to store your collection correctly. Fine wines require temperature and humidity-controlled storage. There is no point in assembling a cache of fine wine without the ability to prevent the onset of premature oxidation that proper storage facilities afford.

Even if you have access to a naturally cool and damp basement where you can conveniently install wine racks, you're better off equipping the room with temperature and humidity controls. (While a naturally or *passively* cooled basement may keep your wines in good condition for years, it's a risky and less-than-perfect means of storing wine—especially if you have any intention of selling a portion of your collection down the road, as auction houses prefer consignments from facilities equipped with climate controls.) An excellent alternative is to invest in either a modular cellar equipped with a refrigeration unit or a freestanding cabinet with temperature and humidity controls. Buy a unit that exceeds the present capacity of your inventory so you have room to expand. If you're starting out your collection, a 250-bottle unit should be sufficient to accommodate your higher-end "better" and "best" selections. See "Storing and Enjoying Your Wine," pages 119–149, for more detailed information on finding the right storage system for your collection.

"Good" wines that you plan to consume within a year can be safely stored on their sides (to keep the corks moist) without risking damage. But, remember that Pinot Noirs are less sturdy than Cabernets and Nebbiolos; white wines are more sensitive still. If possible, store these wines in a cool space, away from your stove, refrigerator, and heating units. Expensive wines that you plan to drink soon are unlikely to spoil in the short term if left in a natural environment, but if you want to preserve them in pristine condition, why take the risk?

11

As an alternative, many retailers will store your wine for a monthly fee of about $2.00 per case. Tip: hold back on two or three bottles from every case destined for deep storage so that you can taste them periodically and chart their progress.

FOUR STYLES OF CELLARS

There's no unequivocal approach to creating a wine cellar. Nothing prevents you from focusing on a vertical or horizontal array of your personal favorites, no matter what they are—Zinfandels, Riojas, Barbarescos, or Shiraz. No matter what you want the specific contents of your cellar to be, however, it's essential to have a working strategy for assembling it that reflects your drinking needs.

Most wine collections are structured along one of these lines:

THE BALANCED CELLAR: The proportional approach to creating a wine cellar involves buying a mixture of wines of different vintages and at varying price points that will mature at different times. (You don't want all your wines to reach their peak at once.) That might mean a range of quality labels spanning the past twenty years along with quality wines from off-vintages, such as 2002 Bordeaux, which represent good value. This format allows you to oversee the aging process and assure proper provenance and condition.

THE INSTANT GRATIFICATION CELLAR: This involves putting together a small cellar full of fine wines that are ready to drink right away. Maybe you don't have the space to store a lot of wine. Maybe you're not yet interested in buying wines that won't be ready for another ten to fifteen years. Whatever your reason, an instant gratification cellar consists of approximately two hundred bottles, which could fit into a small storage unit. Replenish the cellar every few months, as it is depleted.

THE TASTING CELLAR: For some wine collectors, a taste is all that counts. Similar in size to the instant gratification cellar, the tasting cellar functions as a learning tool. It's a tightly focused selection of wines (often as few as one or two bottles per winery) meant to be compared and contrasted, both for educational purposes and to assess the aging potential of a wine before buying a whole case.

THE INVESTMENT CELLAR: Investing in wine for future profit is a somewhat precarious yet potentially rewarding collecting technique. You focus only on the best vintages of top-notch Bordeaux, Burgundy, California, and Italy in the hopes that they will increase substantially in value over a finite period of time. You can concentrate on futures and recently released labels, or older wines that are likely to have continued elasticity. Most investor-collectors ultimately sell half or all of their cellars to finance future acquisitions.

12

The Balanced Cellar

It's theoretically possible to have a cellar full of wine and still have "nothing" to drink, either because the contents consist of newly released wines that require additional bottle aging, or because the selection is skewed toward expensive, blue-chip labels that are not suitable for everyday dining. For most collectors, the goal is to achieve a balanced mix of different price points, pairing recent releases with mature bottlings. You can thereby accommodate acquisitions for your projected short-, mid-, and long-term requirements.

Prioritize your purchases according to your individual drinking schedule and your pre-existing collection. And be flexible. If you've already amassed a broad array of everyday wines, then concentrate on special-occasion purchases—and vice versa. If you haven't laid away wines for future consumption, check out current offerings. A practical way to build a long-term selection of wines to serve on special occasions is to put away at least one case of a special vintage every year.

If you are starting from scratch, you will initially have to tip the balance in favor of older vintages. Otherwise you'll run short on mature bottlings, leaving you with bottles that are not really ready to drink. There's no point in committing "vinocide." Alternatively, you can compensate for a lack of older vintages by focusing on "good" wines that are approachable in youth such as Morrelino di Scansanso from Tuscany, Guigal Côtes du Rhône, or select Merlots, like Chateau St. Jean Sonoma County. They won't deliver the same depth of flavor as their older, more complex counterparts, but at least you won't confront the unpleasant overload of tannin that young Bordeaux or Cabernet Sauvignons may impart.

As your younger wines mature and reach drinkability, you won't need to buy as many mature wines because they will have aged in your very own cellar. When I first started collecting wine more than 25 years ago, I went overboard on California Cabernet Sauvignons and Bordeaux classified growths from the then-heralded 1978 vintage. Having almost filled my

13

storage cabinet to capacity, I quickly realized that few of my acquisitions were ready to drink. Luckily I was able to avail myself of older wines at the annual Heublein auction of rare wines (see page 163) and at retail.

Anyone can assemble a creative, balanced cellar based on a systematic approach to wine regions, styles, and vintages. To facilitate the acquisition (and learning) process, many auction houses offer mixed lots that are structured either horizontally or vertically. For instance, at an Acker Merrall & Condit sale, bidders had an opportunity to snap up four bottles each of the acclaimed Silver Oak Cabernet Sauvignon from the 1995, 1996, and 1997 vintage for $800–$1000. At Aulden Cellars-Sotheby's, a mixed lot consisting of five bottles of Cornas Domaine de Saint Pierre 1994 and six bottles of Jaboulet Côte Rôtie Les Jumelles 1997 was offered for $150–$225.

If you are relatively new to wine and want a quick immersion course in putting together a balanced cellar, acquaint yourself with collectibles that are readily available in the marketplace. Since your goal is to create a lasting collection, focus on wines that have an extended shelf life. If you are unsure of how to start, find a trustworthy wine merchant who can provide assistance in assembling mixed cases at different price points so that you can begin to develop personal preferences (see page 46, "Relating to Your Retailer"). Avoid buying the labels you commonly drink. The point of the exercise is to discover and diversify.

Even seasoned collectors can benefit from this approach. In the fall of 2005, Jean-Luc Le Dû, the former sommelier at four-star restaurant Daniel, opened a wine shop in Manhattan's West Village called Le Dû's Wines. Le Dû is well connected in the wine trade and showcases hard-to-come-by producers. At my request, he put together a stunning array of white Burgundies priced under $30. Jean-Marc Pillot Bourgogne Grands Champs 2003 and Chateau de Puligny-Montrachet Monthelie Blanc 2002 emerged as personal favorites.

When choosing collectible reds, set your sights on the noble grape types, such as Cabernet Sauvignon (or related blends), Pinot Noir, Syrah, and

Nebbiolo. You might consider Le Vieux Donjon 2003 from Châteauneuf-du-Pape, Château Calon-Ségur 2000 from Saint Estèphe, I Sodi di San Niccolò 1997 from Tuscany, or Dunn Cabernet Sauvignon Howell Mountain 1997 from Napa Valley. These are just a handful of labels among hundreds of possibilities and certainly not obligatory acquisitions. They are examples of wines commonly found at auction and in the rare wine sections of retail stores, and represent good starting points.

You might also want to include some white Burgundies and premium California Chardonnays. Apart from dessert wines like Sauternes, these are the most age-worthy whites on the market—the best can last for decades. Labels worth sampling include Beringer Chardonnay Napa Valley Private Reserve 2001, Saintsbury Chardonnay Carneros Reserve 2001, and Verget Chablis Vaillons 2002. If you are ready to reach for something more complex, consider a Vincent Girardin Gevrey-Chambertin Vieilles Vignes 2002. Do reserve space for a couple of Rieslings from highly regard Austrian wineries such as Josef Jamek, Hirsch and Nigl, along with Dr. F. Weins-Prüm from Germany.

In order to make sense of your purchases, it is essential to keep some sort of log of your tasting notes and impressions. A small spiral binder will always do, as will a Palm Pilot or a laptop outfitted with a basic spreadsheet. There are elaborate wine storage programs on the market that can further simplify the procedure. Don't rely on memory alone. Professional tasters always take detailed notes, but if you are tasting on the run (at a dinner party or in a restaurant), come up with some simple icons such as a ☺ or a ☹ to quickly register your impressions until you can write more. It's a fool-proof reference.

The next step is to start sampling varietals from different wine regions—especially those you're less familiar with—so that you learn the differences between a blue-chip California Cabernet Sauvignon such as Ridge Monte Bello Santa Cruz Mountains and a classified Bordeaux such as Château Gruaud Larose. Once you develop distinct favorites, start cellaring your preferences. Finally, move on to creating vertical samplings,

15

VINTAGE CHAMPAGNE

Every wine cellar should house at least a small supply of Champagne in order to accommodate an impromptu celebration or festivity. A stash of four to six bottles of nonvintage Champagne should suffice, plus a couple of bottles from a top vintage that will have extended aging potential.

Nonvintage Champagnes are meant to be consumed within a year or two of release, although they may withstand anywhere from five to ten years additional aging if stored properly. From a collector's standpoint, vintage Champagnes pack greater interest. In Champagne, a vintage is declared only when a harvest is of exceptional quality. Vintage Champagnes are normally aged for a longer period than their nonvintage counterparts, and can continue to mature for decades after release.

At an Aulden Cellars-Sotheby's 2005 sale, top vintage Champagnes ranged from Veuve Cliquot Grande Dame 1985 at $132 per bottle to six bottles of Dom Perignon 1995 at $995. Veuve Clicquot Brut Champagne Gold Label Vintage Reserve 1996 averaged a more modest $60 per bottle.

One sought-after category of vintage Champagne is labeled "recently disgorged," or "R.D.," or as a "Library" or "Collection" release. In order to enhance complexity, they are aged for a prolonged period of time on their lees (dead yeast), and the lees are only disgorged (or expelled) prior to release. In theory a vintage Champagne from 1990 that is disgorged in 2001 is much fresher than one that went on the market shortly after its lees were disgorged in 1993, because the yeast lees act as a preservative. At Aulden Cellars-Sotheby's in Fall 2005, a 1953 magnum from the Krug Collection commanded $12,925. In the first half of 2005, the *Wine Spectator* Auction Index average for Bollinger Brut RD 1990 was $150 per bottle.

Older vintage Champagnes can be an acquired taste, as they may develop rich and concentrated flavors not associated with younger varieties. Buy by the bottle before you spring for a case. Study condition reports carefully; it's not worth taking a risk on bottles showing low levels as the contents may have Maderized and the bubbles may have dissipated. There's no point in uncorking a flat vintage.

VINTAGE PORT

Vintage Port first entered the English market in the late eighteenth century and still enjoys an international following. Unlike most collectible wines, Port is fortified with brandy, which stops the fermentation process, resulting in a sweeter wine with higher alcohol content. Vintage Port should not be confused with Tawny or wood Ports, which are aged exclusively in cask and do not improve once bottled. Vintage Port is aged in barrel for roughly two years and then bottled, where it will continue to mature for decades. As a rule, vintage Port throws off sediment as it ages, and will consequently require decanting before serving.

As with vintage Champagne, vintage Port is only made in top years, which a shipper "declares" the second spring after the harvest. Because of quality variations among producers, not all Port shippers will declare a vintage from identical harvests. There have been just over two dozen major vintage Port declarations during the past century.

Until the last decade, vintage Port was largely the preserve of seasoned collectors because it took so long for the wine, once released, to reach maturity, which called for considerable storage facilities—and patience. Thanks to recent changes in the vinification process, vintage Ports are now more approachable in their youth, although they will still benefit from up to fifteen to twenty years of bottle age. From an investment standpoint, vintage Ports do not represent a quick turnaround, but instead tend to rise in value only as they reach maturity.

Two of the best recent vintages for Port are 1994 and 1997. Top-scoring vintage Ports from 1994 include Fonseca ($148 per bottle at auction), Quinta do Noval Nacional ($563 per bottle at auction), and Taylor Fladgate ($183 per bottle at auction). Among the highest rated 1997s are Dow ($37 per bottle at auction), Graham ($33 per bottle at auction), and Warre ($73 per bottle at auction). Classics like Taylor Fladgate 1963 average $255 a bottle at auction. In contrast, the highly rated 1985 vintage Ports, now eminently drinkable, range from $34 to $70 per bottle.

17

which you can use to teach yourself the differences between vintages. From California, try to obtain Cabernet Sauvignons from stellar vintages, such as 2002, 2001, 1999, 1997, and 1994. From Bordeaux, look for examples from the great harvests of 2003, 2000, 1995, and 1990. To fine-tune your quest, seek out examples from a single winery or château.

By carefully examining wines from great years such as these, you'll determine which ones you like best and which ones you might want to acquire in multiple quantities. Instead of buying by the case, look for mixed lots at auction, or auction websites featuring small quantities of premium listings. That way, you can indulge in a couple of memorable bottles without tying up space or capital.

More seasoned collectors should branch out to experiment with unfamiliar wine regions, varietals, or vintages. Everyone has a weak spot, whether it's Barolo, Ribera del Duero, Syrah, or Shiraz. If your tasting experience has been limited to relatively recent releases, then pick up some older vintages of the wines you favor. Apart from the dozens of how-to guides to various wine regions, there are a host of online resources: the *Wine Spectator*'s online database of tasting notes (winespectator.com), which contains over 140,000 wine reviews, is an excellent source of information. *Decanter* magazine (decanter.com) also posts lengthy reviews, as does Robert Parker, the internationally reknowned wine authority (erobertparker.com).

You may also want to experiment with wines from quality wineries produced in off-years. They will be much less expensive, and generally more approachable in their youth. Burgundies from 1997 and 1998, Rhônes from 1996 and 1997, Bordeaux from 2002 and 1999, Tuscan estate bottlings from 1996, and California labels from 1998 and 2000 are some good examples.

BALANCED CELLAR

The sample cellar depicted below contains a representative selection from the world's major wine producing regions, which I suggest as a model for someone starting their cellar. Nothing is engraved in stone, however, and collectors are encouraged to mix and match depending on their pre-existing inventory.

The Average Cost represents the average price these bottles fetch at auction, and reflects a balance of "Good," "Better," and "Best" price levels. The number of bottles is merely a suggestion as to quantities to stock up on. For example, the case of Château Sociando-Mallet 1995 represents a well-priced but age-worthy Bordeaux that might have come up as a case lot at auction, whereas the more expensive Sauternes or Chateau Lynch-Bages might have come up as single bottle sales or as part of a mixed lot.

This cellar represents a balance of short- (S), medium (M), and long-term (L) drinking, as indicated in the final column. Although I have projected consumption times, it's a good idea to try a medium- or long-term bottling well in advance of its theoretical maturity date in order to determine *your* personal preferences. There's no law that says a Château l'Arrosée 2000, designated as a long-term pour, can't be enjoyed now if you like the way it is showing.

wine	average cost	bottles	total cost	term
CHAMPAGNE				
Deutz Brut Champagne Classic NV	40	6	240	S
Veuve Clicquot Brut Champagne Gold Label Réserve 1996	59	3	177	M
BORDEAUX				
Château Péby-Faugères 2000	40	3	120	M-L
Château Haut-Bailly 1989	41	3	123	M
Château La Lagune 1989	32	4	128	M
Château Langoa-Barton 1996	29	12	348	M-L
Château Lynch-Bages 1985	129	2	258	S-M
Château Potensac 2001	17	9	153	M-L
Château Suduiraut (Sauternes) 1995	49	4	196	M-L
RED BURGUNDY				
Anne Gros Chambolle-Musigny La Combe d'Orveau 1996	47	3	141	S-M
Dominique Laurent Clos Vougeot 2000	42	3	126	M
Tollot-Beaut Chorey-lès-Beaune 2001	22	3	66	S-M

wine	average cost	bottles	total cost	term
WHITE BURGUNDY				
Domaine du Château de Puligny-Montrachet Monthélie Blanc 2002	33	6	198	S
Verget Chablis Montée de Tonnerre 2002	32	4	128	S-M
RHÔNE				
E. Guigal Châteauneuf-du-Pape 1999	34	9	306	M-L
Le Vieux Donjon Châteauneuf-du-Pape 2001	34	3	102	M
OTHER FRANCE				
Hugel Riesling Alsace Jubilée Réserve Personnelle 2001	32	6	192	S-M
CALIFORNIA CHARDONNAY				
Au Bon Climat Chardonnay Sanford & Benedict 2002	32	6	192	S-M
Aubert Chardonnay Ritchie Vineyard 2001	50	3	150	S
Matanzas Creek Chardonnay 2002	30	3	90	S
CALIFORNIA CABERNET SAUVIGNON				
Beaulieu Vineyard Cabernet Sauvignon Georges de Latour Private Reserve 1999	42	3	126	M-L
Beringer Cabernet Sauvignon Knights Valley Appellation Collection 1997	23	3	69	M
Clos du Bois Cabernet Sauvignon Briarcrest Vineyard 1996	29	6	174	M
Forman Cabernet Sauvignon 1999	31	6	186	M
Freemark Abbey Cabernet Sauvignon Bosché Estate 1999	37	6	222	M
Silver Oak Cabernet Sauvignon 1999	79	3	237	M
Sterling Cabernet Sauvignon Diamond Mountain Ranch 1999	26	6	156	M
CALIFORNIA AND OREGON PINOT NOIR				
Argyle Pinot Noir Reserve 2002	28	6	168	S-M
Chalone Pinot Noir Chalone 2002	25	3	75	M
Domaine Drouhin Pinot Noir 2000	40	3	120	M
Saintsbury Pinot Noir Carneros Reserve 1997	38	6	228	M
Sanford Pinot Noir 2002	27	6	162	M
Williams Selyem Pinot Noir 2002	39	6	234	M-L
OTHER CALIFORNIA				
Pride Merlot 2001	48	6	288	S-M

wine	average cost	bottles	total cost	term
ITALY				
Antinori Tignanello 2000	44	3	132	L
Barone Ricasoli Casalferro 1997	45	3	135	M
Beni di Batasiolo Barbaresco 2001	38	3	114	L
Casisano-Colombaio Brunello di Montalcino 1999	40	3	120	M
Castello di Neive Barbaresco Santo Stefano 2001	41	3	123	M
Marcarini Barolo Brunate 1997	51	3	153	M
Renieri Rosso di Montalcino 2003	25	6	150	S-M
Sette Ponti Crognolo 2001	35	3	105	M
SPAIN				
Condado de Haza Ribera del Duero 1996	25	3	75	M
Dominio de Pingus Ribera del Duero Flor de Pingus 2000	45	3	135	M-L
ARGENTINA				
Bodega Catena Zapata Chardonnay Mendoza 2004	19	12	228	S
Bodegas Esmeralda Malbec Mendoza Catena Lunlunta Vineyards 2002	20	6	120	M-L
Tikal Malbec Altos de Mendoza Amorío 2002	31	9	279	M
CHILE				
Concha y Toro Cabernet Sauvignon Puente Alto Don Melchor 2000	41	3	123	M
AUSTRALIA				
Penfolds Shiraz South Australia St. Henri 1999	40	6	240	M
Barossa Valley Estate Shiraz Barossa Valley Ebenezer 2000	30	6	180	M
VINTAGE PORT				
Warre Vintage Port 1985	53	2	106	M-L
Niepoort Vintage Port 1997	45	4	180	L
total		245	$8,577	

All data obtained from the Wine Spectator Auction Index

The Instant Gratification Cellar

An instant gratification cellar consists of a tightly knit selection of mature wines meant for near-term consumption. Rather than focusing on an all-encompassing collection that includes wines for aging, this is a rotating selection of bottles based on your upcoming drinking and entertaining patterns, predicated, of course, on your budget. Thanks to the proliferation of wine auctions and fine wine websites, it's possible to buy mature vintage wines on an as-needed basis, projecting no more than a few months ahead.

Those who go the instant gratification route usually do so because their storage space is limited or because they've made a conscious decision to skip the wine's aging process and focus on classic vintages readily available in the auction or retail pipeline that are ready to drink. (If you choose this route because of space constraints but do want to lay down a stash of futures or new releases, you can always store them in a wine warehouse; see page 123.)

A two-hundred-bottle cellar, which roughly matches the capacity of a small or mid-sized storage unit, can provide a year's worth of challenging wine experiences, as long as you replenish what you drink before you deplete the entire stash. Once your supply begins to dwindle, consult your tasting notes and either seek out more of the same wines or move on to others.

Remember, two hundred bottles translates into just over sixteen cases, so unless you intend to serve the same wines on a regular basis, you are better off diversifying by purchasing smaller parcels, which assures you a greater variety. Most auction houses do the guesswork for you by assembling mixed lots that include an assortment of Californian, French, or Italian wines in quantities as small as four bottles. Another expedient is to buy six-packs or browse websites such as WineBid.com that offer smaller lots. Alternatively, you can customize your vertical or horizontal cache yourself by sourcing fine wine retailers.

As with a standard wine collection, the actual selection procedure should be entirely personal. Choose wines that reflect the way you like to entertain, the foods you like to cook, and the company you keep. But avoid stocking up on wines that you don't expect to consume in the near term, because you won't have the luxury of time and space. For the same reason, wines that haven't reached maturity, no matter what score they may have received in professional wine journals, don't have a place here.

Assembling mini-verticals of two or three vintages of a wine lends itself particularly well to the instant gratification approach. Contrast a Dominus 1987 with a 1994 and 1999 (some of its best years) to discover firsthand how the wine has evolved over time. The number of bottles to procure from each vintage will depend on the size of your cellar. As a rule, pick up at least three bottles of each, so you can serve them on more than one occasion. Twin vintages of classified Bordeaux like 1989 and 1990 or 1995 and 1996 have been the subject of considerable discussion. Determine your own position. For example, compare bottles of Château Pichon Longueville-Baron and Château Pichon Longueville-Lalande from either 1989 and 1990 or 1995 and 1996. Alternatively, put Château Léoville-Barton and Château Langoa-Barton through the same exercise. You'll be amazed how the salient characteristics manifest themselves when you conduct your own small examinations.

At auction, many mature wines can be snapped up for less money than recent releases, so assembling an instant gratification cellar needn't be outrageously expensive. For example, at retail, Spottswoode Cabernet Sauvignon 2002 can cost as much as $150 a bottle whereas, at auction, the highly acclaimed 1994 vintage averages $91 and the 1992 averages $64 per bottle. But for special occasions, there's nothing like uncorking a true classic, such as a bottle of Heitz Cellars Martha's Vineyard Cabernet Sauvignon 1974 or Emmanuel Rouget Vosne-Romanée Les Beaumonts 1990 (both about $500 at auction). The memory of the occasion will endure long after the wine has been drunk.

23

INSTANT GRATIFICATION CELLAR

This broad-based list of suggestions is meant to be as didactic as it is pleasurable, enabling the collector to sample an extensive array of labels from diverse wine regions. It mirrors the composition of the average auction, and is weighted toward Bordeaux. Since the total amounts to just over 200 bottles, this collection will have to be replenished or upgraded as it is depleted.

wine	average cost	bottles	total cost
BORDEAUX			
Château Calon-Ségur 1989	56	3	168
Château Canon-La Gaffelière 1982	36	3	108
Château Canon-La Gaffelière 1988	42	3	126
Château Pavie-Decesse 1995	25	4	100
Château Clinet 1988	59	2	118
Château Chasse-Spleen 1995	25	6	150
Château Haut-Bailly 1995	54	4	216
Château Haut-Bailly 1996	31	4	124
Château Haut-Batailley 1982	59	2	118
Château Lafite Rothschild 1995 375-ml	127	4	508
Château Langoa-Barton 1982	55	3	165
Château Langoa-Barton 1989	41	4	164
Château Langoa-Barton 1990	46	4	184
Château Lascombes 1995	27	6	162
Château Le Roc de Cambes 1996	25	6	150
Château Léoville Barton 1990	98	3	294
Château Léoville Barton 1996	52	3	156
Château Latour 1995 375-ml	137	2	274
Château Mouton-Rothschild 1995 375-ml	120	2	240
Château Pape Clément 1982	59	2	118
Château Pichon-Longueville-Baron 1995	55	3	165
Château Pichon-Longueville-Baron 1996	50	3	150
Château Pichon-Longueville-Lalande 1989	154	3	462
Château Pichon-Longueville-Lalande 1990	121	3	363
Château Gruaud-Larose 1995	43	6	258
Château Rieussec 1990 375-ml	28	6	168
Vieux-Château-Certan 1989	67	2	134

wine	average cost	bottles	total cost
RED AND WHITE BURGUNDY			
Anne Gros Clos Vougeot Le Grand Maupertui 1998	54	4	216
Comte Lafon Mâcon-Milly-Lamartine 2004	18	12	216
Emmanuel Rouget Vosne-Romanée 1996	73	2	146
Marquis d'Angerville Volnay Champans 1996	34	6	204
Jean-Marc Pillot Les Grands Champs (blanc)2004	30	12	360
RHÔNE			
Pierre Usseglio & Fils Châteauneuf-du-Pape Cuvée de mon Aïeul 1999	56	6	336
ITALY			
Argiano Solengo 1997	54	4	216
Bruno Giacosa Barbaresco 1989	64	4	256
Pio Cesare Barolo 1998	60	4	240
CALIFORNIA			
Arietta 1998	41	4	164
Arietta 1999	60	4	240
Dominus 1987	98	2	196
Dominus 1997	136	2	272
Etude Pinot Noir Carneros 2001	26	6	156
Merry Edwards Pinot Noir 2002	32	4	128
Spottswoode Cabernet Sauvignon 1992	64	2	128
Steele Chardonnay Goodchild Vineyard 2002	28	12	336
Talley Chardonnay 2002	25	12	300
AUSTRALIA			
Clarendon Hills Shiraz Clarendon Liandra Vineyard 1998	46	2	92
VINTAGE PORT			
Warre Vintage Port 1985	52	2	104
total		202	$9,649

All data obtained from the Wine Spectator Auction Index

The Tasting Cellar

Even more focused than the instant gratification cellar, the tasting cellar is a learning tool, meant to compare similar wines and assess their aging potential.

A tasting cellar will vary dramatically in composition and size according to the objectives of its owner. Some collectors systematically set aside dozens of different bottles simply to assess whether they're eventually worth cellaring as case-lots for future drinking. Others use a tasting cellar as an educational tool to learn the salient characteristics of a specific wine, vintage, or region and stop there. Still others assemble a tasting cellar solely to conduct formal vertical or horizontal examinations of a winemaker's output.

Whereas collectors who seek to amass a balanced cellar tend to buy by the case or the six-pack in order to have sufficient quantities for entertaining, the taster can settle for one or two bottles of a specific wine at a time, because the point of the exercise is to achieve breadth or depth of selection for comparison's sake, not to slake the thirst of a roster of dinner companions. Depending on the age of the wine, you can accommodate twelve to fourteen tasters per bottle, assuming a two-ounce pour, and a minimum of sediment. (For more information on organizing a tasting, see Holding a Horizontal or Vertical Tasting, page 139.)

The cost of creating a tasting cellar will vary according to your personal goals. If you are looking to sample an array of basic Châteauneuf du Papes, your outlay for a dozen different labels could run less than $400. However, if you are curious about discovering the nuances of a Château Rayas Châteauneuf du Pape Réservé 1990 and a Château de Beaucastel Hommage à Jacques Perrin 1990—both exquisite estate bottlings—the tab for just two bottles would run about $1,125 at auction.

You could craft a tasting cellar around regional standouts. If, for example, you want to learn more about the fine wines of Sicily, Puglia, or Campania, seek out a retailer who stocks a substantial inventory of southern

Italian wines. You might want to consider some of the newer labels in the marketplace that have gained critical acclaim, such as Antinori's Aglianico-Cabernet Sauvignon Tormaresca 2000, Castel del Monte Rosso "Il Falcone" Riserva 1997, or Primitivo di Manduria "Archidamo" Peruini 1998.

Auctions can be an effective means of bolstering your tasting cellar because they regularly feature a wide array of mixed lots, which can translate into a horizontal or vertical flight. At a recent Acker Merrall & Condit auction, a ten-bottle mini-tasting of Turley Zinfandel from four different vineyards spanning vintages from 1997 to 2000 fetched $696.

Since the minimum value of a consignment tends to run well in excess of $1,000, few brick-and-mortar auction houses offer inexpensive single-bottle lots. They are, however, an ideal source for treasures like Beaulieu Vineyards Private Reserve Cabernet Sauvignon 1951 or Domaine de la Romanée-Conti 1969, which average $1,275 and $3,300 per bottle, respectively, in the event you want to spring for a truly special taste. In contrast, several Internet auction houses have developed business models that favor small lots. At the time of writing, for example, several cellar-worthy candidates were on the block including a bottle of Beringer Bancroft Ranch Merlot 1997 at WineBid.com for a minimum bid of $60. Clos du Bois Reserve Malbec 1997 was offered for a minimum bid of $30 per bottle. At the same time, MagnumWines.com was offering a bottle of Tenuta San Guido Sassicaia 1985 for $750—well below the *Wine Spectator* Auction Index average of $1,011.

27

TASTING CELLAR

The basic tasting cellar described below amounts to thirty-two individual bottles and costs $3,200. Adding twenty-four more expensive alternates bring the total to just over $10,000. Since you get approximately twelve two-ounce pours to a bottle, there's no reason why your fellow-tasters shouldn't contribute to the pot.

wine	*average cost*
BORDEAUX	
Château Grand-Puy-Lacoste 1982	131
Château Grand-Puy-Lacoste 1996	78
Château Grand-Puy-Lacoste 2000	63
Château Pavie 1998	133
Château Pavie 2000	268
Château Pavie 1990	128
Château Lynch-Bages 1990	145
Château Lynch-Bages 1995	68
Château Lynch-Bages 2000	99
Vieux-Château-Certan 2000	122
Vieux-Château-Certan 1998	150
BURGUNDY	
Dominique Laurent Savigny-lès-Beaune 1996	49
Dominique Laurent Nuits-St.-Georges Les Cailles 1996	78
Daniel Rion & Fils Vosne-Romanée Les Beaux-Monts 1996	48
Daniel Rion & Fils Vosne-Romanée Les Beaux-Monts 1990	70
RHÔNE	
Château Rayas Châteauneuf-du-Pape Réservé 1998	114
Château Rayas Châteauneuf-du-Pape Réservé 2000	117
Le Vieux Donjon Châteauneuf-du-Pape 1998	25
Le Vieux Donjon Châteauneuf-du-Pape 2001	32
CALIFORNIA	
Colgin Cabernet Sauvignon Herb Lamb Vineyard 2000	223
Colgin Cabernet Sauvignon Tychson Hill Vineyard 2000	174
Pride Cabernet Sauvignon 2001	99
Pride Cabernet Sauvignon 1997	72
Paloma Cabernet Sauvignon Spring Mountain District 2001	45
Paloma Merlot Spring Mountain District 2001	45
ITALY	
Antinori Solaia 1999	127
Antinori Tignanello 1999	83

wine	average cost
Fattoria Le Pupille Morellino di Scansanso 1999	14
Fattoria Le Pupille Morellino di Scansanso Poggio Valente 1999	45
Tenuta San Guido Bolgheri-Sassicaia Sassicaia 1998	115
VINTAGE PORT	
Taylor Fladgate Vintage Port 2000	102
Taylor Fladgate Vintage Port 1994	183
Fonseca Vintage Port 2000	59
Fonseca Vintage Port 1994	148
total 34 bottles	$3,452

More Expensive Alternatives

BORDEAUX	
Château Cheval-Blanc 2000	588
Château Haut-Brion 1998	162
Château Angélus 1990	227
Château Lafite Rothschild 1995	198
Château Lafite Rothschild 1996	303
Château Lafite Rothschild 2000	433
Château Lafite Rothschild 2001	132
Château Latour 1996	239
Château Margaux 1995	276
Château Margaux 1996	278
Château Mouton-Rothschild 1996	164
Château Pétrus 1998	1457
BURGUNDY	
Comte Georges de Vogüé Musigny Cuvée Vieilles Vignes 2002	361
Comte Georges de Vogüé Musigny Cuvée Vieilles Vignes 1996	259
Domaine Leroy Richebourg 1999	411
Domaine Leroy Romanée St.-Vivant 1999	407
Ramonet Bâtard-Montrachet 2002	286
Ramonet Bâtard-Montrachet 1996	290
Emmanuel Rouget Vosne-Romanée Cros Parantoux 1999	316
Emmanuel Rouget Vosne-Romanée Cros Parantoux 1996	316
CALIFORNIA	
Bryant Family Cabernet Sauvignon 2002	356
Bryant Family Cabernet Sauvignon 1999	329
Harlan Estate 2001	573
Harlan Estate 1999	380
total 24 bottles	$8,741

All data obtained from the Wine Spectator Auction Index

┌───┐

Restaurants as Learning Tools

The best thing about the tasting approach is that you can take the concept with you when you dine out. Restaurants aren't usually the best places to experiment with cellar-worthy wines because markups tend to be outrageously high—often as much as 300 percent above cost. For that reason, many serious collectors I know tend to read a wine list from right to left, basing their final selection on the bottle's price more than any other criteria.

However, an increasing number of wine destination restaurants are lowering their markups below 200 percent on upper-end wines, both to curry favor with customers and to move their inventory. Cru and Veritas in New York are but two examples. As the late Paul Kovi, co-owner of Manhattan's prestigious Four Seasons, once said, "We want our restaurant to be a wine celebration, not a wine cemetery."

One obvious advantage a restaurant has over a retail wine store is that it provides the chance to taste a wine in the context of a meal. It's an opportunity to let your curiosity run wild by pairing wines from diverse regions or vintages with different dishes to see what marries best. There's clearly no point in ordering something you regularly drink at home, so take advantage of a wine list's breadth or depth. (Do remember to bring along a notebook so that you can recall the label the next day.)

A good sommelier or wine director won't necessarily steer you toward the upper echelons of the list. In theory, a sommelier knows the inventory backward, and should familiarize you with some of the cellar's hidden treasures. That might mean an obscure but first-rate Chardonnay, a little known Châteauneuf du Pape, or a Bordeaux or Burgundy from an off-vintage that shines brighter than the rest. Skilled sommeliers are as current with the contemporary wine scene as any retailer or auctioneer. What's more, they get feedback nightly on their recommendations, so they're in a good position to inform you about recent releases and vintages that are showing particularly well. Take advantage of their expertise. If you are relatively new to collecting, they can answer your questions about aeration, decanting, and even glassware.

└───┘

Many restaurants organize regular tasting events under the supervision of their sommeliers or visiting winemakers. These wine-and-food parings, during which every entry on the menu is matched with a specific wine, can be an invaluable (and tasty) experience.

Anyone contemplating a major purchase at auction, be it a California cult wine or a highly touted Burgundy from Leroy, can turn a well-stocked restaurant wine cellar into an educational experience. It's far better to discover that you dislike a single bottle before you have invested in a full case. And if you want to know how your Château Léoville-Barton 2000 or Shafer Cabernet Sauvignon Hillside Select 2001 is coming along, locate a restaurant that stocks it and find out for yourself without depleting your own inventory.

Many major collectors have singled out a restaurant experience as their original wine awakening because their host had selected an extraordinary bottle that they otherwise would not have contemplated buying. That doesn't mean you have to spring for a bottle of Château Le Pin 1990 or a Colgin Cabernet Sauvignon 1997, but there's every good reason to treat yourself to something special from time to time. I remember having a bottle of the legendary Jaboulet Hermitage La Chapelle 1961 at Restaurant Pic in the Rhône Valley in 1983 for what was then the exorbitant sum of $200. It now sells for about $4,000 at auction.

No matter what you order, make a note of the wine and food affinities that worked—or didn't. Did the Cabernet Sauvignon go well with the grilled tuna? Was Sauvignon Blanc an ideal match with the salmon tartare? Ultimately, you'll build your own set of combinations to use in your home kitchen, reflecting your personal tastes.

Finding a wine-friendly restaurant is fairly easy thanks to the proliferation of restaurant guides that also focus on wine service. You can find hundreds of restaurants with good wine lists in cities around the country at www.zagat.com, the website for the Zagat Survey. More than twenty years ago, *Wine Spectator* initiated a restaurant awards program that honors a restaurant's commitment to a fine wine list. There are now more than 3,300 recipients of its basic award. At the top, there are some 60 "grand award" winners: restaurants with wine lists of outstanding breadth and depth, boasting a total of more than 1,250 listings.

Tip: If you have ordered something extremely special (or even if you have brought a great wine from your own cellar, if the restaurant permits you to BYOW), offer a glass to the sommelier. It's not only a pleasant gesture, but one that might bring you future rewards as well.

The Investment Cellar

I have always believed that wine is best appreciated in the glass. Despite the dramatic gains that select wines have made since the legalization of wine auctions in New York in 1994, the *Wine Spectator* Auction Index still lags slightly behind the Dow Jones Industrial average. If you are looking for profit, there are far better investment instruments than wine (although a collector who purchased a case of Château Mouton-Rothschild 1982 as a future in 1983 for $400 and sold it for $9,440 in 2006 may disagree).

The mechanics of creating an investment-grade cellar are simple enough. Buy a highly rated wine, either as a *future* (an offering made by wine retailers in advance of a wine's release) or immediately upon release. Store it carefully for several years until it approaches maturation, and then sell it at auction. You can also take advantage of periodic lulls in the salesroom and snap up lots that are trading below recently realized price levels.

Either way, you have to know what to buy and how much to pay for it, because not all wines appreciate equally. Lesser classified growths, minor Burgundies, and bottlings produced in large quantities do not qualify. First growth clarets, select super seconds, and premium Burgundies are all good bets. California cult wines and select vintage classics such as Heitz Martha's Vineyard Cabernet Sauvignon 1974 continue to escalate in value. While the performance of Italian estate bottlings has been erratic, high-end labels from Antinori or Tenuta San Guido Sassicaia have a strong following.

Understanding the correlation between vintage quality and resale price goes beyond a wine's individual tasting score. With the exception of a handful of treasures such as Châteaux Lafite Rothschild 1900, Mouton-Rothschild 1945, and Cheval-Blanc 1947, other wines from those vintages are mostly past peak and unlikely to appreciate, regardless of their initial scores. In contrast, it may take considerable time for cult or *garage* wines that arrive in the marketplace with a hefty price tag to show a return on their investment. The same is true for a classic such as DRC Romanée-Conti 1999 for which you pay top dollar today at auction.

The list of investment-grade candidates is fairly narrow: First Growth Bordeaux; equivalents such as Châteaux Pétrus, Le Pin, Cheval-Blanc, Lafleur, and Latour-à-Pomerol. The performance of trendy new garage wines such as Châteaux Valandraud, La Mondotte, and Tertre Rôteboeuf can be unpredictable. Although prices may be prohibitive, Burgundies from Domaine de la Romanée-Conti and other top producers such as Leroy, Dujac, Dugat, Jayer, Ramonet, and Roumier have enjoyed dramatic appreciation. California cult wines such as Screaming Eagle, Harlan Estate, and Bryant Family have outperformed the cult wine pack. Other rising California stars include Pride Reserve, Foley, Switchback, Sloan, Bryant, and Abreu. Among Côtes du Rhônes, Jean-Louis Chave and Château Rayas lead the category.

The most reliable source of information for the prospective investor is the *Wine Spectator* Auction Index, a biannual database published in the magazine that tracks the performance of 160 frequently traded wines, listing their average price, high and low bids, and the percent change in their prices. The online version of the index, a by-subscription-only service found in the Collecting section of *Wine Spectator* online (www.winespectator.com) covers ten thousand entries. The data tracks which wines have performed best during the most recent six-month period, providing a realistic indication of actual worth and growth potential.

It is equally important for the wine investor to understand how provenance and condition affect a wine's resale possibilities. When a wine is consigned directly from the winery or the cellars of a celebrated collector, hammer prices can exceed normal levels by more than 100 percent.

In May 1997, the collection of Sir Andrew Lloyd Webber witnessed sky-high bids at Sotheby's London. So did the collection of famed heiress Doris Duke, which was sold at NYWinesChristie's in June 2004. Consignments direct from Châteaux Latour and Haut-Brion produced similar results because of their pristine condition. As New Jersey collector Charles Klatskin likes to say, "Provenance is paramount. There's no point in cellaring inferior wine." In other words, a 1961 Château Latour from an undisclosed consignor with obvious signs of evaporation is an unwise investment at any price because it won't likely find another cellar. It might still be great drinking, however, if you are willing to take the risk.

Be sure the wine comes from reliable auction houses and merchants who vet their merchandise. Retailers who receive special allocations from limited-production wineries are worth cultivating. If you are on good terms with your wine merchant, you are likely to get advance notice of special shipments or closeouts. In the event of hot futures offerings like Bordeaux 2000, 2003, or 2005, preferred clients tend to head the list of recipients. Another means of securing top wines at the best price is to subscribe to a winery's mailing list.

Remember that investing in wine differs substantially from investing in stocks or bonds. Fine wine is not an efficient market. The spread in asking prices for a specific vintage may be considerable, and projecting a wine's ultimate appreciation can be problematic, as vintage scores are subject to revision. Remember to factor in the cost of storage, insurance, breakage, and interest charges. In other words, do the math before you buy.

When your primary goal is to achieve a return on your wine investment, the old adage *less is more* applies. If you are contemplating a $10,000 investment, you are generally better off buying four $2,500 cases (or two $5,000 lots) than diversifying your capital and purchasing ten $1,000 cases. Wines in the upper echelon of the price spectrum tend to appreciate by a greater factor than those in the lower ranks.

One variation on investing is to seek out wines that are currently undervalued in the auction marketplace and portend future value. Serena Sutcliffe, head of Sotheby's international wine department, says that Vieux Château Certan, Clos L'Eglise, and Château La Tour Haut-Brion represent particularly good value. Similarly, Richard Brierley, Christie's North American wine director, feels that recent vintages of Châteaux Lynch-Bages and Rauzan-Ségla are good bets, along with Chablis from Raveneau and Dauvissat. He also recommends considering recent releases of Bonneau de Martray Corton Charlemagne. John Kapon, the auction director for Acker Merrall & Condit, believes that the highly rated Château L'Evangile 1990 (which received a 95 out of 100 score from the *Wine Spectator* tasting panel) is a relative bargain at $175 per bottle. He also feels that assortment cases from Domaine de la Romanée-Conti are worth cellaring.

Sotheby's Sutcliffe adds that the lofty prices for 2003 and 2005 Bordeaux futures make mature wines offered at auction look particularly attractive. "Collectors definitely love the idea of buying ready-to-drink claret, and they can immediately fall on 1985s, 1989s, and 1990s," she says. Like Sutcliffe, Kapon also feels that the 2003s will have an impact on the prices of older vintages in the auction pipeline. He believes that the gradual entrance of expensive Bordeaux 2000s into the marketplace has strengthened the prices of older Bordeaux from 1982 through 1990 and, to a lesser extent, 1995 and 1996. "Collectors are realizing that these older wines are accessible for the same price or less than the 2000s, and ready for instant drinking pleasure," Kapon notes. "In the context of the 2000s, they're simply undervalued."

Auction prices for the highly acclaimed Bordeaux 2000s remain erratic, making it difficult to judge whether or not they will constitute a good investment. Yields were large in 2000 and *en primeur* (the French expression for futures) prices were expensive. Both factors weigh against instant appreciation. Collectors who acquired futures simply to dump their cache for a quick profit may be disappointed. A large quotient of the 2000s is

35

selling for less at auction than the retail release prices set in 2003. But odds are that as they approach maturity, those prices will rise dramatically.

In contrast, Kapon observes that 2001 and 2002 California Cabernet fever is taking hold, and as a result, it has "brought a little sizzle back to some of the older vintages, like 1994 and 1997, and boosted the entire segment of the market." Australian wines have terrific appeal, but at auction, their performance has been quixotic. Bidders seem to focus on labels such as Three Rivers, Greenock Creek Roennfeldt Roads, and Marquis Philips Shiraz Integrity. Since they can be volatile, it's worth keeping your paddle at the ready in the event of a bargain.

As the following chart illustrates, wine investments are no sure thing, particularly when you take into account the fact that money invested more traditionally will double every seven years. Château Margaux 1961 now sells for less than it did eight years ago, and Lafite Rothschild 1961 has not kept up with the other first growths. The bottom line: Invest if you wish, but be prepared to drink your portfolio.

How Much to Spend?

In the estimation of Acker Merrall's John Kapon, it usually takes six to twelve months for a client to create a serious cellar. Most collectors start out as small buyers, with a focus on California and Australia because they are easier to understand and appreciate. "But eventually," he claims, "all roads lead to France, whether it's Bordeaux or Burgundy." Several collectors I have profiled throughout this book substantiate Kapon's contention. They view it as a natural progression from the big, concentrated style of premium California labels to the more subtle nuances inherent in a fine Bordeaux or Burgundy. Not coincidentally, more than two-thirds of all fine and rare wines offered at commercial auctions are French.

THE INCREASE IN VALUE
OF TOP LABELS OVER A DECADE

wine	vintage	4q 1995 $	2h 2005 $	% change
Château Haut-Brion	1989	201	689	243
	1982	143	378	164
	1961	540	1470	172
Château Lafite Rothschild	1989	88	237	169
	1982	192	701	265
	1961	403	423	5
Château Latour	1989	72	226	214
	1982	247	825	234
	1961	847	2357	178
Château Margaux	1989	99	252	155
	1982	227	606	167
	1961	526	660	25
Château Mouton-Rothschild	1989	94	246	162
	1982	311	746	140
	1961	570	1084	90
	1945	2898	5286	82
Château Pétrus	1989	492	1897	286
	1982	804	2463	206
	1961	2280	5368	135
Château Le Pin	1990	479	1482	209
Château Cheval-Blanc	1989	79	222	181
	1982	396	841	112
	1961	442	708	60
	1947	3260	3776	16
Domaine de la Romanée-Conti	1985	2095	7391	253
Domaine de la Romanée-Conti	1978	2108	6971	231
Screaming Eagle Cabernet Sauvignon (4q 1997)	1992	678	3193	371

All data obtained from the Wine Spectator Auction Index

Investors beware: While the right wine can bring in a return far in excess of more traditional instruments of investing, even the best labels vary erratically in their performance. The only safe bet is to buy wines you'll be happy drinking.

INVESTMENT CELLAR

In the best case scenario, an investment cellar consists of full (12-bottle) cases of an individual wine—with the exception of California cult wines that are often sold by the three-pack. If you wish to diversify your portfolio or limit the dollar value of your expenditure, you might consider buying six-packs instead. Understand, however, that the re-sale value of two 6-bottle lots usually falls below the price of a single 12-bottle consignment of the same wine. Under the circumstances, if the $22,452 price tag on the 90 wines listed below seems daunting, you might be better off cutting back on the number of listings rather than reducing the bottle count.

wine	average cost	bottles	total cost
BORDEAUX			
Château Lafite Rothschild 2000	433	12	5196
Château L'Église Clinet 2000	280	12	3360
Château Lynch-Bages 2000	109	12	1308
BURGUNDY			
Dujac Bonnes Mares 1999	288	12	3456
RHÔNE			
Jean-Louis Chave Hermitage 1998	114	12	1368
ITALY			
Tenuta San Guido Bolgheri-Sassicaia Sassicaia 1998	160	12	1920
CALIFORNIA			
Colgin Cabernet Sauvignon Tychson Hill Vineyard 2001	338	3	1014
David Arthur Cabernet Sauvignon Elevation 1147 2001	249	6	1494
Harlan Estate Cabernet Sauvignon 1999	380	3	1140
VINTAGE PORT			
Taylor Fladgate Vintage Port 1994	183	12	2196
total		96	$ 22,452

All data obtained from the Wine Spectator Auction Index

OTHER INVESTMENT-WORTHY LABELS

Extremely rare Bordeaux from classic vintages such as 1945, 1947, and 1961 vintage may still show some upside potential, but you are better off placing your bets on recent vintages such as 2003, 2000, and 1995. Similarly, select red Burgundies from 1978, 1985, and 1990 continue to escalate in value, but 2003, 2002, and 1999 are better bets from an investment standpoint. Recent California vintages most likely to appreciate are 1999, 2001, and 2002. Be prepared to drink your wine if the market tumbles.

Bordeaux

(All First Growths, see page 155)

Château Cheval-Blanc
Château Lafleur
Château Latour-à-Pomerol
Château Le Pin
Château Pétrus

Burgundy

Armand Rousseau Chambertin
Comte Georges de Vogüé Musigny
    Cuvée Vieilles Vignes
Domaine Leroy Musigny
Domaine de la Romanée-Conti La
    Tâche
Domaine de la Romanée-Conti
    Romanée-Conti
Domaine des Comtes Lafon
    Montrachet
Domaine Ramonet Montrachet
Henri Jayer Vosne-Romanée Cros
    Parantoux

Rhône

Château Rayas Châteauneuf-du-Pape
    Reserve
E. Guigal Côte-Rotie La Mouline
Paul Jaboulet Ainé Hermitage La
    Chapelle

California

Abreu Cabernet Sauvignon Napa Valley
    Madrona Ranch
Bryant Family Cabernet Sauvignon
Screaming Eagle Cabernet Sauvignon
Shafer Cabernet Sauvignon Stags Leap
    District Hillside Select

Italy

Gaja Langhe Sorì Tildìn
Luciano Sandrone Barolo Cannubi
    Boschis
Tenuta dell'Ornellaia Bolgheri
    Ornellaia

Spain

Bodegas Vega Sicilia Ribera del Duero
    Unico Gran Reserva

39

COLLECTIBLE SPIRITS

What goes best after a meal full of high-end wines? For some, the answer is a high-end *digestif.* The pursuit of a fine vintage Armagnac, Cognac, and Single Malt Scotch can be just as challenging—and rewarding— as tracking down a rare bottle of Château Lafleur or Henri Jayer Vosne-Romanée Cros Parantoux. In fact, some vintage spirits cost even more than their vinous counterparts.

As with fine wine, condition, scarcity, and provenance are the prime determinants of a bottle's price. Storage requirements, however, are less stringent. Because of their elevated alcohol content, spirits do not require temperature and humidity controls. However, they should be stored away from sources of heat such as a stove, refrigerator, or dishwasher. Theoretically, spirits do not have to be placed on their side, although serious collectors tend to do so anyhow, as an added precaution against evaporation.

Probably the best way to familiarize yourself with the intricacies of a vintage Armagnac or Cognac (since WWII, the latter is only vintage dated if it was landed at a British distillery in barrel prior to bottling) is to seek the advice of a knowledgeable retailer who carries a wide variety of styles. At Park Avenue Liquors in New York, for instance, owner Mike Goldstein offers an array of Cognac priced between $33 and $6,700 per bottle. Pops Wine & Spirits in Island Park, New York, carries 258 different labels of Armagnac and Cognac.

Sourcing vintage spirits at auction requires patience and acumen, partly because the only state that permits the auctioning of spirits is Illinois. The range of spirits on offer is usually broader at U.K. auctions. Sotheby's sold two bottles of Cognac Napoleon Grande Fine Champagne Reserve 1811 for $2,700 in February 2003. At Christie's in 2004, a 12-bottle case of McBrayer American Bourbon No. 1, 1913 sold for $3,069 and two bottles of Green Chartreuse 1890 (the herbal liqueur) went for $1,346. Recent releases tend to be less expensive. In November 2004, Sotheby's sold eight bottles of Hine Grande Champagne Cognac 1966 for $600. At Edward Roberts International, the Chicago-based auction house, two bottles of Bushmill's Single Malt Irish Whiskey (21 years old) sold for $144.

The most expensive Single Malt Scotch ever sold at auction was a bottle of the Dalmore 62 (a blend of single malt Scotches from the 1868, 1878, 1926, and 1939 vintages): one bottle brought $44,000 at McTear's auction house in Glasgow, Scotland, in 2002; another was purchased by a guest at the Park Hotel in Surrey, England, for $58,000 in 2005. Why the whopping price-tag? Only 12 precious bottles of the highly esteemed Scotch were originally produced in 1942. That means the outstanding ten bottles said to be in private hands may have skyrocketed even further in value.

The Dalmore notwithstanding, the market for rare spirits is far less volatile than the fine wine business. Spirits prices have remained stable over the last four to five years with little fluctuation, with turn-of-the-century Cognacs like 1900, 1904, and 1914 being the most sought-after.

At auction, the average price of a single lot (anywhere from one to twenty-four bottles) is about $1,500. How much you spend on your wine cellar is a function of your budget and entertaining objectives, and is, of course, a personal decision. It's possible to get started on as little as $5,000. I also know of private wine dealers who have been handed seven-figure budgets to assemble a wine collection and retailers who have been given up to $500,000 by a client to create a collection of fine and rare wine. At a single auction the average dollar expenditure per bidder is in the neighborhood of $18,000—a better indication of the average collector's budget. This figure, too, may skew high, as big-time collectors with seemingly unlimited resources will spend far more. At the other end of the price spectrum, there are numerous buyers who zero in on one or two lots per sale worth well under $1,000.

A collector who is starting a wine collection will buy many more bottles than one who is simply maintaining a preexisting wine cellar. Individual wish lists can also tip the scales. If your heart is set on cellaring California cult wines or first growths from celebrated Bordeaux vintages such as 1982 or 2000, the costs involved will soar. A case of DRC Romanée-Conti 1999 alone could set you back $60,000. Yet as Jacques and Reynita Bergier (the husband-and-wife collecting team profiled on the following page) demonstrate, it is possible to assemble a respectable collection without breaking the bank. They pride themselves on uncovering bargain bottlings in the $30 to $50 range.

Along the way, you may want to consider whether a $100 wine is twice as good as a $50 wine. It's not, necessarily. Beyond a certain threshold, you are paying for scarcity, provenance, reputation, and future selling potential. At some point, you encounter the law of diminishing returns. In a blind tasting, would a $1,700 bottle of Screaming Eagle consistently show seventeen times better than a good $100 California label such as Phelps Insignia Napa Valley? Probably not. But then, a $100 bottle doesn't pack the cachet and excitement of uncorking a Screaming Eagle, either.

Economist Richard Thaler, a long-standing wine aficionado, addressed the question of a wine's adjusted cost price to a group of economists. He asked them: if you bought a bottle of Bordeaux for $20, and it is now worth $75, what does it feel like you are spending when you drink it? Most responded, $75—the actual replacement cost. Others answered $20, the original cost price; still others, $0. "My favorite answer," Thaler commented, "was from the respondent who said, 'I feel like I'm saving money, because I'm drinking a $75 bottle for $20.'"

Learning to live with a wine collection is really no different than the photography or art lover who sees his collection appreciate over time. At various points, all collectors are faced with the same dilemma: to sell or not to sell. Lloyd Flatt (a veteran collector profiled on page 179) believes the sensible collector is one who thinks about sharing his finds, not calculating the adjusted cost price per glass. "I mentally expense the cost of my bottles at the moment of purchase. That way, if someone asks me 'what's it worth?' I can honestly say 'nothing.'"

AN IDEAL BALANCE: JACQUES
AND REYNITA BERGIER'S CELLAR

Jacques and Reynita Bergier are proof positive that you don't have to be investment bankers to build a substantial, quality wine collection. This committed couple has created a coherent wine cellar over nine years while adhering to a generous but not open-ended budget. They have strategically assembled an 1,800-bottle cellar conceived for the short, mid-, and long term, balancing their fine and rare acquisitions with a large stash of inexpensive wine for everyday drinking. It's all housed in a climate-controlled cellar they built in their New Jersey home (see photo, page 127).

Although Jacques, 47, and Reynita, 37, are both French by birth, neither of them had any particular affinity for wine until about a decade ago. "We were basically beer drinkers," admits Jacques, vice president of Duchateau U.S., an importer of Leonidas Belgian chocolates. The Bergiers became interested in wine in 1996, when they attended a horizontal tasting of 1986 Bordeaux at Christie's. After that, they picked up some basic textbooks on the wines of Bordeaux, attended every presale tasting they could, and started analyzing auction catalogs and retail price lists.

CREATING THEIR CELLAR: Initially, the couple would spend hours studying and cross-referencing auction estimates against the realized sale results and retail prices to gain an understanding of fine wine pricing. When they felt they had a solid grasp on what the wines were worth, they began to bid, setting a conservative ceiling and sticking to it. This sometimes meant bookmarking as many as 100 items in a 1,500-lot sale, yet coming home empty-handed if the bidding got too heated. "We tended to buy at auction because generally the prices are better than retail," explains Jacques Bergier. "But since we limited our expenditures to a maximum of $3,000 per sale, and often far less, we had to be very selective and equally disciplined."

One of their buying strategies was to focus on the lesser growths of claret, primarily those from the 1989 and 1990 vintages, which were relatively inexpensive compared with the classics or more recent top vintages, such as

1995 and 1996. Reynita stresses, "The main thing is not to become so emotionally involved in the bidding process that you end up overspending. You have to be focused. That way, you make the most of your budget. Our goal has always been to have a quality cellar that is always adequately supplied. It's not collecting in the same manner as one would collect silver or porcelain. It's more like intellectualized drinking."

Now that their cellar has reached a size they're happy with, says Jacques, "we've been trying to maintain the cellar rather than increase it. We are still buying, but we're not going for select, high-end collectibles. Instead, we are focusing more on the middle range and things that we like—whenever we can grab them at bargain prices."

BEST BUYS: Getting the best value for their money translated into buying five or six cases of a basic Burgundy from Leroy (one of the region's top winemakers) for under $14 a bottle, some Côtes du Rhône Guigal 2003 at $11 a bottle, and Syrah Renard (a highly rated Napa Valley vineyard) at $14 a bottle, about half the going rate. Jacques also bought cost-effective Bordeaux futures from 2003, such as Château Sociando Mallet and Château Lagrange, at $450 and $330 per case, respectively. "Over the last five years, our wine spending was anywhere between $6,000 and $12,000 each year. That amounted to a basic $5,000 for a year's worth of "cheapies" for us to consume on our own, plus more for cases of better wines as well as a few futures."

BEST BOTTLES: While they don't list any Château Pétrus or 1982 first growths in their inventory, the Bergiers do have a small vertical of Château Mouton-Rothschild, along with Château Montrose 1990, Château Pichon Longueville-Lalande 1985, and Château Petit-Village 1988. They even own six scarce bottles of Quinta do Noval Vintage Port Nacional 1994, which they picked up for $300 a bottle, a steal compared to the average auction price of $800. "We only look for bargains," explains Jacques, "like the five bottles of Montrose 1990 we once snapped up for an incredible $650 at Christie's at a time when the average for five bottles was $1,220."

In 1998, the year 1996 Bordeaux was first released, Jacques picked up twenty solid cases of first and second growths from that vintage, including Châteaux Lafite, Mouton, Haut-Brion, Ausone, and Cos d'Estournel. They are all still in the cellar in their original wooden cases. "We do not really have a fixed budget; we play it by ear from year to year, depending on the other things that we spend on."

COLLECTING WISDOM: Looking back at his own buying patterns, Jacques has realized that collecting wine is not necessarily a systematic process. "For us, and no doubt for a large majority of committed collectors, exceptional vintages may prompt the acquisition of more wine than weaker vintages. However, other outside events—the performance of the economy and the stock market, buying a home, the birth of a child—all impact greatly on our purchasing ability." Although the Bergier's buying patterns may vary, they feel that one aspect of wine collecting remains constant. "Ever since we began buying fine wine, we have been living better," says Jacques. "We've met some very nice people at wine tastings whom we have enjoyed entertaining. We eat better, and we drink better."

RELATING TO YOUR RETAILER

~~~~~~~

∿\\\\\\∿

THANKS TO THE PROLIFERATION OF SPECIALTY WINE STORES, THE sources for collectible wine are more plentiful than ever. A top wine merchant may carry hundreds of listings that deserve a place in your cellar. And you can make those retail purchases without the worry that you may be unsuccessful in a wine auction in purchasing a specific item. What's more, you'll be able to tap the advice of salespeople who have tasted an enormous amount of wine and can serve as your guides in the collecting process.

Beyond helping you navigate their own inventory, good wine merchants can locate hard-to-find bottles. Qualified retailers cultivate relations with wineries and dealers and may be able to secure limited-production releases not otherwise available through traditional channels. By subscribing to newsletters and e-mail blasts, or just being part of their databases, you can remain informed about new or interesting arrivals. Once you've found a couple of retailers you like (it's best to diversify if possible), it pays to cultivate long-term relationships. As they get to know your palate, they can help you develop and fine-tune your cellar, and will set aside bottles they think might be just right for your collection. For people who have the funds and want an even more personalized touch, private wine consultants can act as your scouts, doing everything from locating esoteric bottles to organizing your entire cellar.

But you don't have to spend a fortune to obtain personalized service from a fine wine merchant. I regularly receive wine-related e-mails from as far afield as London and Los Angeles announcing special offers. The range can be enormous: Domaine Jean-Marc Brocard Chablis 2001, Léoville Las Cases 2000, Chateau Montelena Estate 1997, and Santa Faustina Syrah 2001 from Argentina. I usually cross-reference the retailer's price on Wine-Searcher.com (see page 106, Wine Websites as Research Tools) before placing an order or by seeking out another retail source.

Even just being on a retailer's mailing list can be invaluable. When Zachys, the Scarsdale, New York, wine merchant, bought a heavily discounted shipment of top-quality Puligny-Montrachet, the store immediately e-mailed all its customers who had spent between $30 and $50 on any kind of Chardonnay to see if they would be interested in the offer—with great success. Thanks to highly sophisticated computerized databases, merchants like Zachys are now able to micromanage clients' interests and tastes based on their previous purchases.

49

FINDING A GOOD RETAILER

A store may look attractive, but it's the knowledge of its staff that makes it a worthwhile place to shop. Not long ago, I ventured into a respectable retail outlet in Massachusetts and asked if they carried a Volnay from Comtes Lafon. I was met with a totally blank stare, even though Lafon is one of Burgundy's finest producers. A good retailer will hold regular tastings for its staff to keep their palates up to date. For example, at Sherry-Lehmann in Manhattan, the store's chairman, Michael Aaron, opens fifty to sixty bottles every month for his employees to sample, often in the company of the vineyard owners themselves. "If a salesperson can say, 'I had Château Lafite Rothschild 1998 with owner Baron Eric de Rothschild, or I had this Montrachet with the winemaker and you should consider it for your cellar,' you can trade on that," Aaron says, because it gives the retailer knowledge and credibility customers can trust.

Ultimately, observes Aaron, "If you don't feel that sense of trust with your wine store, then you should move on. Your passion needs to be matched by the store's staff."

Top Questions For Choosing a Retailer

How do you choose your retailer? Here are some questions to ask yourself or your retailer:

1. How do the store's markups compare with those of its competition? *The service or selection may be worth the difference if prices are higher.*

2. How large and sophisticated is the inventory? Does it offer depth as well as breadth? *Collecting for your cellar means having more specific and focused needs than a casual wine buyer, so you'll benefit from a retailer with an extensive inventory that shows vertical and horizontal concentration.*

3. How knowledgeable is the staff? *It's important to be able to trust their advice.*

4. How often are staff tastings conducted? *The greater the number of wines salespeople taste, the better position they're in to make recommendations.*

5. Does the store conduct public tastings? Will you have a chance to meet the winemakers or their representatives? *An interactive relationship with a retailer is a great way to expand your taste bank.*

6. Are the advertised items usually in stock? *Some retailers attempt to lure customers with a loss leader; customers then discover there was only ever a handful of bottles on hand.*

7. Does the retailer travel to wine country or conduct regular in-house tastings of new releases to keep current with the wine market? *The more exposure a retailer has to the product, the better he or she can serve you.*

8. Does the retailer have a climate-controlled storage warehouse? *(If not, move your wines elsewhere.)* What is the per-case charge for storage? Can you store wines there that you purchased elsewhere? *This is a nice perk, but not all retailers extend their storage space to other retailers' wines.*

9. Are the merchant's delivery trucks temperature controlled? *This is desirable, but not essential.*

10. Does the retailer offer a futures program for investing in recent (still-unbottled) vintage of the current vintage of Bordeaux? Can he be relied upon to deliver the goods? *If he doesn't offer a futures program, he may not be that well connected with foreign distributers.*

11. Will the retailer special-order a wine that is not in inventory? Is there a minimum dollar value or quantity per such order? *A retailer with good trade contacts should provide this service. The minimum order is often one twelve-bottle case.*

12. What is the store's return policy for bad wine? *As long as you don't abuse the practice, you should be able to return a wine that is "off."*

Starting Your Collection

If you're unsure of how to begin a collection, introduce yourself to a store's owner or manager and explain that you're interested in starting a cellar. Convey your goals for the cellar and your budget. Together you can come up with a plan. Remember, a retailer can't read your mind, so it's important to be specific about your objectives. Describe the composition of your current wine stash. Say whether you want to continue in the same direction or branch out. If it's the latter, this is your opportunity to defer to the retailer's expertise and to take advantage of the store's extensive inventory. A retailer or salesperson who shares your palate preferences can serve as a helpful guide.

Consider whether you need bottles that are ready to drink or to be laid away for future consumption. Estimate the time frame during which you expect to consume the collection. Nikos Antonakeas, a director of Morrell & Company (who also runs its auction division), believes people in their thirties should feel comfortable buying Château Latour 2000, whereas people in their seventies might hesitate because the wine may outlive them. A well-stocked retail outlet should offer both young wines that need further aging and mature examples that you can consume in the interim.

Branching Out

A savvy retailer can steer you through difficult territory, such as off-vintages, and introduce you to new wines. Not so long ago, creating a wine collection was a fairly simple exercise. Your choices were pretty much limited to Bordeaux, Burgundy, and Champagne, plus a handful of wines from the Rhône, Italy, and California. The past twenty years collectors have witnessed an explosion of potential candidates for your cellar vinified in Australia, Argentina, South America, and Spain, not to mention exciting new labels from more established viticultural regions. The multiplicity of offerings on the market can be dizzying, and trying to formulate personal preferences on a trial-and-error basis can prove time consuming. A good retailer should keep you abreast of the best prospects and send you samples (that you pay for, of course) for consideration.

Jim Knight of the Wine House in Los Angeles recommends that collectors leave room for some great Vouvrays and Anjou Blancs alongside the blue chips. He says that wines such as these are often overlooked because they are not high scorers or made by a well-known producer. "Not everything has to be Château Latour or DRC," he counsels. Personally, I find there's no trick to buying a great Burgundy or premium California wine. It's just a function of the size of your wallet. But choosing inexpensive yet good-quality everyday wine, such as Guigal Côtes du Rhône, Comtes Lafon Mâcon Milly, or Catena Chardonnay (from Argentina), is much more of a challenge. I usually rotate these wines so that I don't tire of them. And I regularly defer to my retailers to see if they can come up with something new that I will enjoy.

Off-vintages present an equal challenge. Just about everyone who has embarked on the collecting circuit is familiar with signature vintages like 1982 and 2000 in Bordeaux or 2001 and 1997 in California. But should a harvest that did not receive a high rating from the wine press be avoided altogether? Not necessarily. Off-vintages usually get overlooked when they are sandwiched next to a stellar vintage. Bordeaux from 2001, 1999, and 1998; Burgundy from 2001, 2000, and 1998; and California from 2000 are all examples of off-vintages worth cherry-picking. I particularly like the 1997 Corton from Chandon de Briailles, even though it hails from a fairly weak vintage. It still boasts a lot of character, and at about $30 per bottle, represents good value. Understand, however, that off-vintages are unlikely to appreciate significantly.

Price is a major consideration. You don't want to pay a premium for a less-than-stellar vintage. Some collectors may simply not have the time required to ferret out the best examples from off-vintages and cross-reference the cost. That's where your retailer comes in. Lance Storer, the Dallas-based wine consultant to Centennial Fine Wine & Spirits, says he has gained his customers' trust in off-vintages because key store representatives go to Europe every year to taste new releases and pick the best wines from each region. He then stimulates interest in off-vintage wines with focused client dinners to showcase the wines he likes.

Special Deliveries

As you develop an idea of what you want, you'll find that a retailer may be able to gain access to hard-to-come-by labels through their reputation and connections in the field. Michael Glasby of Premier Cru in Emeryville, California, says his goal is to ensure that his clients always get what they want. Glasby likens himself to the wine butler in aristocratic nineteenth-century homes who consulted with his employer about what to cellar and when to serve it. He works closely with his clients and lets them know when something special comes on the market. For example, blue-chip labels from the 2003 vintage were hard to get in Burgundy. The entire production of the celebrated label Roumier Musigny amounted to only twenty-five cases. Through his contacts, Glasby secured two cases, then doled them out selectively to his best customers. Chris Adams, Sherry-Lehmann's executive vice president, also acknowledges that his store has special client relationships, and when certain hard-to-find wines come in, he gives the appropriate customer a call. Not just anyone can find you a precious bottle of Henri Jayer Vosne-Romanée Cros Parentoux.

The range of special-order possibilities is enormous. At the high end, a retailer may attempt to track down DRC Romanée-Conti from a top vintage, or the equally rare Château Le Pin. Both wineries produce about 500 cases a year. In contrast, Château Pétrus produces about 3,500 cases and Château Lafite Rothschild averages about 20,000 cases. One of my favorite special-order wines is from a tiny vineyard called Domaine Forey Les Gaudichots—a red Burgundy that was once part of DRC La Tâche. It costs about $50 to $65 per bottle, depending on the vintage. One of the many merchants I frequent, Rosenthal Wines in Manhattan, occasionally manages to secure a bottle or two—not bad considering that Les Gaudichot's total annual production rarely exceeds 50 cases.

Many California cult wines, along with their French equivalents, garage wines, are only available upon release through mailing lists, which are almost always oversubscribed. (The wines do crop up at auction.) A well-connected retailer should be able to secure them for you, although your allocation may be small. In other instances, you may have to commit to a full case before a retailer will order it. Either way, you should submit your wish list to your retailer well in advance of a harvest so your merchant will have your needs in mind.

THE FINE PRINT: SHIPPING

Taking delivery from the nation's best wine stores can be problematic, despite a 2005 Supreme Court ruling that overturned certain bans on shipping wine. While interstate shipping from wineries in states that have passed reciprocal legislation is permissible on a selective basis, wine merchants are not necessarily covered by those same laws. Some retailers work around these restrictions by passing title at the time of sale to the purchaser, who, in turn, becomes responsible for the shipment in the event of breakage or other mishaps.

Buying Futures

Almost every year, in the spring following the harvest, top Bordeaux chateaus (and infrequently, blue-chip wineries in California and in Burgundy) offer a preliminary case-price for delivery once the wines have been bottled, about two years later. The practice is known as a *futures* offering (*en primeur* in French). Buying futures locks in availability at a fixed price that is usually lower than the release price will be. Unlike a wine that has already entered the retail market, however, there is no opportunity to taste it before you buy it, so you have to rely on vintage assessments prepared by the wine press or by retailers and distributors who were invited to taste barrel samples of the vintage.

Futures are usually doled out by the chateau in various offerings (there can be as many as three or more) called *tranches*. In a great vintage when demand is intense, the price of a given *tranche* may increase dramatically in a matter of days. Retailers with considerable clout who secure an allocation from the first *tranche* offer their best clients the opportunity of buying in—a reward, in essence, for being a regular. It's a little like playing the commodities game. If the vintage is not well received once the wine is released, the price may stagnate or even drop. Conversely, prices have been known to double upon release, and a supply can quickly dwindle.

⸙ BUYING DIRECT FROM THE WINERY ⸙

Buying directly from a winery—whether in America or in Europe—is
another recourse for the serious collector. The chief advantage lies not in
current vintages (they tend to be priced in line with retail outlets to avoid
problems with distributors) but, rather, with the opportunity to acquire
vintage classics. Several wineries keep an inventory (often called a "library")
of choice older wines, which they release to the public on a selective basis.
The obvious benefit from library purchases is that it assures perfect
provenance: The wines haven't budged from the place where they were
made since bottling. Collectors buying in Europe should seek the advice
of an expediter before making a commitment to buy.

When buying futures, it is essential that you have a seller you trust,
because not all merchants have firm contracts with the estates that assure
them of an allocation. But that may not prevent them from attempting to
sell futures at prices that seem too good to be true. Remember, all you
have is an invoice, which can prove worthless if the company from which
you bought the futures has filed for bankruptcy. In 2001, some disrep-
utable merchants engaged in outright Ponzi schemes, selling phony futures contracts for the highly acclaimed Bordeaux 2000 vintage in order
to finance other purchases.

A good merchant will not only offer you a first-come, first-served
price on futures, but will also assist you in developing an effective buying
strategy. As a rule, if you want to buy wines that will appreciate the most
in value or are likely to disappear quickly from the marketplace, you are
best off buying first growths and their equivalents. Lesser growths may
not have the investment potential, but they may also be hard to find upon
release, especially if they were produced in small quantities, so they're
worth considering nonetheless.

Becoming a Regular

Once a retailer knows what you like, he can set aside bottles that might be just right for your cellar, or place you on a priority list for one-of-a-kind offerings or futures arrivals.

It doesn't end there. Many retailers organize exclusive wine tastings and dinners at which priceless wines are poured. Getting on the guest list is an opportunity not only to expand your vintage tastebank, but also to network with other collectors whose experiences may prove of great interest. In December 2005, Zachys, the Scarsdale, New York, based fine wine merchant, hosted a gala charity BYOW dinner to benefit the Hemophilia Association of New York. Guests dug deep into their cellars and donated dozens of extraordinary wines such as Jaboulet Hermitage La Chapelle 1978, Cheval-Blanc 1921, and DRC Romanée-Conti 1945. Not your everyday wine dinner.

A special benefit of being a longtime regular has developed in response to a recent phenomenon in the collecting scene. The average age of today's collector is now thirty-five or so; a decade ago, average buyers were about fifty. You would think that older collectors would automatically spend more on wine than younger ones, but this isn't always the case. The reason is that the wealthy newcomers arrive on the auction scene unaware of price structures and ceilings established years ago. Lacking any preconceived notions of the maximum a wine should cost, they are pushing the upper limits of auction sales into the stratosphere. Older collectors, who have seen wine prices change over a longer period of time, are more likely to have certain mental caps on a wine's value. When they see the value of their own wines (which may have been purchased for a far more modest amount) rise beyond this cap, they may become uncomfortable drinking them. For that reason, many stores will accept trades from their regular customers for high-valued wines, either in exchange for cash or for a larger quantity of lesser-priced wines the customer will feel more comfortable

57

drinking (the precise nature of the transaction is determined on a case-by-case basis).

Let's say you purchased Château Pétrus 1982 for the going rate of about $600 per case in 1983 and for some strange reason, never got around to drinking it. Today it has a retail value of anywhere from $25,000 to $36,000 per case—more than some collectors are prepared to stomach. The precise exchange value will be subject to negotiation, reflecting profit margins, interest, and, of course, prior storage conditions. It will further depend on whether you want to exchange the wine for other items in the store's inventory or whether you are seeking cash. A retailer with whom you have established a long-term relationship may further assist in assessing how a middle-aged collector might effectively thin out other elements of his or her cellar.

As Jim Knight succinctly puts it, "A wine collection is a gift from your younger self to your older self," an intriguing concept that, when you think about it, is what collecting wine is all about. The wines you drink today are often ones you bought ten, fifteen, even twenty years ago. If you are lucky enough to find a retailer who shares your taste considerations and is sensitive to your collecting needs, then you may have found a cellar-mate for life, one whose recommendations you may enjoy long after the fact, and whose ongoing advice can prove invaluable.

Over the past decade, a new breed of wine merchant has appeared on the collecting scene, largely because of the legalization of wine auctions, the vast increase in the supply of fine and rare wines, and the army of high net worth individuals of all ages who have descended on the wine market. Technically, a private wine consultant is not a merchant because he usually doesn't own a wine store or carry an inventory. Rather, this figure functions as rarefied agent for wealthy collectors, buying for them at auction and through other channels. Much as with private art dealers, clients depend on the consultant's personal expertise to locate and purchase wines at an optimum price and assist clients in assembling their wine cellars.

For example, there is Connoisseurs' Collection (908-684-4654), owned by Gorky Rahman, which caters to the needs of upscale wine collectors. Rahman has an extensive retail background, having worked for eighteen years at various New York wine merchants, from Park Avenue Liquors to Morrell & Company. He got his start as a consultant when Chuck Dolan, the legendary chairman of Cablevision, asked for his assistance in buying fine wine and organizing his cellar. In addition to Dolan, Rahman lists another ten key clients, for whom he consults on a weekly basis.

Rahman buys at auction, from overseas sources, and from private collectors. One of his clients has given him a $10 million wine budget. The people for whom he works are very knowledgeable; nevertheless, he makes an effort to widen their tastes. As a result, one of them has become a great fan of Penfolds Grange, the highly acclaimed Shiraz from South Australia; another has become so enamored of the famed Phelps Insignia that he serves it as his house wine.

Even though Rahman's clients are high-net-worth individuals, he tries to be as cost effective as possible in his purchasing, avoiding mediocre vintages and overpriced offerings. Rahman charges a fee of $800 a week for his services, which amounts to $40,000 annually. Initially, he may spend twenty to twenty-five hours per week working with a new client on all aspects of his or her collection.

Then there are consultants who can assist with a range of fine collectibles, wine as well as fine art and similar objects. Kevin Swersey and J.

Patrick Cooney founded the Connoisseur's Advisory Group (212-983-4641) to assist big-time collectors with wide-reaching interests. They can help their clients purchase, divest, and vet their collections. Swersey, a fifteen-year veteran of Zachys, is the wine specialist; Cooney, a former director of Christie's client advisory services, is the art expert. Swersey says there is a natural affinity between wine and art collecting, which together they are able to address. Their target is to foster a new generation of collectors who have broad interests. It doesn't always follow that a major art collector owns a great wine cellar, but with the firm's help, many art lovers have become wine lovers, and vice versa.

Swersey notes how surprising it is how many collectors have been exposed to mid-level California Cabernet Sauvignons and Chardonnays but have never tasted a good Bordeaux or white Burgundy. So Swersey tries to expand his clients' knowledge bases as well as their collections.

As a member of the Appraisers Association of America, Swersey says one of the worst mistakes a collector can make is to underinsure his or her wine, or to assume a collection is fully covered by a typical homeowner's plan. (It's not.) "Would you want a priceless bottle of Château Mouton-Rothschild 1945 replaced by a current vintage like 2004?" he asks. "That's often what happens if you don't have proper coverage."

Almost all of Swersey's business comes from referrals. He takes on about fifty clients per year, and his fees are determined on a case-by-case basis.

If the sky's the limit, there is Brian Orcutt (212-737-8834), who also draws a parallel between his work as a private wine consultant and that of a private art curator. In addition to advising on acquisitions and depletions, he plans cellar logistics and redesigns existing cellars to make them more effective, even physically rearranging entire collections. Orcutt is a former director of Christie's New York's wine department, and has about a dozen clients. The largest cellar he oversees consists of a staggering ninety thousand bottles—his work is equivalent to managing the wine inventory of a fair-sized restaurant with branches all over the country. "Sometimes a client has several collections spread out over multiple cellars in multiple locations. He may have lost track of his inventory, or have loaded up on wines he is no longer drinking," Orcutt says. So Brian comes to the rescue with a new cellar plan, or a schedule of wines to divest of in the event that too many of the client's wines are reaching their peak.

RETAILER'S ROSTER

This list of top retailers is not meant to be definitive, nor are the stores necessarily unique. What follows is a listing of highly experienced, well-established merchants that consistently offer good advice to their clients, while cellaring a broad spectrum of collectible wines from which to choose.

ACKER MERRALL & CONDIT

160 West 72nd Street, New York, NY 10023

(212) 787-1700

ackerwines.com

Acker boasts a comprehensive collection of fine and rare wine, plus educational services, tastings, and wine clubs. Its wine workshops, ranging in price from $75 for an *Essentials of Wine* class to $1,295 for an eighteen-vintage vertical examination of Château Mouton-Rothschild, represent excellent learning opportunities.

CENTENNIAL FINE WINE & SPIRITS

10410 Finnell, Dallas, TX 75220

(214) 630-5000

centennialwines.com

Founded in 1936, Centennial now has twenty-seven stores in the Dallas area. Its inventory of six thousand wines provides ample opportunity for the diversification of your collection. The store employs certificate-level sommeliers to assist customers in their collecting queries.

CLARETS

115A West Micheltorena, Santa Barbara, CA 93101

(805) 899-3367

clarets.com

Richard Torin's retail shop specializes in fine wine—primarily rare Bordeaux and Burgundy from the nineteenth century through the present.

61

CRUSH WINE & SPIRITS
153 East 57th Street
New York, NY 10022
(212) 980-9463
crushwineco.com
Created by restaurateur Drew Nieporent, Josh Guberman, and Robert
Schagrin, this architecturally stunning store (all bottles are racked on their side
from floor to ceiling) specializes in hard-to-come-by and boutique bottlings.

LE DÛ'S WINES
600 Washington Street
New York, NY 10014
(212) 924-6999
leduwines.com
A boutique wine store opened in 2005 by Jean-Luc Le Dû, former wine
director of Manhattan's four-star restaurant Daniel, with an eclectic
inventory specializing in hard-to-come by offerings at all price points.

MacARTHUR BEVERAGES
4877 MacArthur Boulevard, N.W.
Washington, DC 20007
(202) 338-1433
bassins.com
Founded in 1957 by Addy Bassin, MacArthur Beverages has become a D.C.
fixture for fine wines and collectibles. They stock an extensive selection of
classified Bordeaux and premium California labels. Prices are very competitive.

MORRELL & COMPANY
One Rockefeller Plaza, New York, NY 10020
(212) 688-9370
morrellwine.com
For more than fifty years, Morrell & Company has specialized in fine wine
from leading producers. A family-run business, the Morrells were among the

first East Coast merchants to champion California wine. They have also been active in wine education. You can contact store experts on premise or online.

PREMIER CRU
5890 Christie Avenue, Emeryville, CA 94608
(510) 655-6691
premiercru.net

Premier Cru is renowned for well-priced, cellar-worthy wines from the world's major wine-producing regions. Rare Burgundies are among its strong points, as are scarce California labels and older vintages of Bordeaux. The store is a favorite among collectors who are seeking hard-to-come-by labels.

ROSENTHAL WINE MERCHANT
318 East 84th Street, New York, NY 10028
(212) 249-6650
madrose.com

A distinctive outpost for hard-to-come-by labels personally selected by owner Neal Rosenthal. He seeks out premium wines made by growers committed to producing limited-quantity, top-quality varietals. Rosenthal also distributes wines in approximately thirty-five states.

SAM'S WINES & SPIRITS
1720 North Marcey Street
Chicago, IL 60614
(312) 664-4394
samswine.com

A family business established by Fred Rosen in 1942, Sam's prides itself on a high level of service accomplished by extensive staff training. The store boasts good breadth and depth of selections from major wine producing regions. Prices are competitive. In addition to the flagship store on North Marcey Street, Sam's has two other locations in the Chicago area.

SHERRY-LEHMANN

679 Madison Avenue, New York, NY 10021

(212) 838-7500

sherry-lehmann.com

A Manhattan institution since 1934, Sherry-Lehmann was one of the first retail merchants in the country to champion the joys of fine wine in the immediate post-Prohibition era. It began its first Bordeaux futures campaign in 1959. It remains a full-service operation, with a massive inventory and storage facilities and an ongoing focus on fine wine. Sherry-Lehmann conducts frequent public winemaker tastings and wine classes.

WINE HOUSE

2311 Cotner Avenue, Los Angeles, CA 90064

(310) 479-3731

WineAccess.com

The Wine House stocks a good range of fine and rare wines from France, Italy, and California. It hosts wine classes as well as regular Friday night wine tastings for $5 to $40 per person, depending on the wines to be sampled.

ZACHYS

16 East Parkway, Scarsdale, NY 10583

(914) 723-0241

zachys.com

A family business founded in 1944, this store is now one of the largest wine retailers in the country. Zachys features an extensive portfolio of fine and rare wines, with an accent on customer service. It organizes an eclectic range of tastings and events, as well as major wine dinners, often to benefit charitable causes. Its website provides information from its staff of experts. Zachys also offers a futures program for its clients.

︿〰〰〰〰︿

There aren't many women in the wine collecting world—less than 10 percent of collectors by most assessments. Kim Vernon, an intense, intelligent, and confident wine enthusiast, is a refreshing exception to that rule. She did not grow up in a wine-drinking family, but became inspired by estate bottlings she tried during travel to Italy and France. To further her wine knowledge, she enrolled in Kevin Zraly's famed "Windows on the World Wine Course" in Manhattan in 1994. "I learned to drink and think and pay attention to everything that was going on in the glass," she recalls.

Vernon, a past vice president at Calvin Klein, boasts an eclectic cellar of more than three thousand bottles. She credits Mike Densen, an ex-boyfriend who was a partner in D. Sokolin Co., the Bridgehampton, New York, based rare wine dealer, with fine-tuning her palate and instilling a deep-seated passion for fine wine. "Every weekend was a wine tasting. It was like a crash course in great labels. We'd go to wine destination restaurants like Manhattan's Veritas and talk about what we drank and consumed for days afterwards. It was fun, social, and educational all at once. I can no longer go through an evening drinking mediocre wine!"

CREATING HER CELLAR: In 1999, Vernon moved into a new apartment and installed a 144-bottle wine storage unit in the kitchen. "I just had to fill it right away." She concentrated on wines she had discovered—and loved—during tastings and wine dinners. Initially it was a small and very personal collection, focusing on high-end labels like Kistler Chardonnay Sonoma County Cuvée Cathleen, some 1985 Burgundies from Armand Rousseau (a classic producer in a classic vintage), and Caymus Cabernet Sauvignon Napa Valley Special Selection.

She also assembled a vertical selection of Phelps Insignia Napa Valley, a red wine she first discovered in a restaurant. True to her didactic nature, Vernon also put together various horizontal selections from the mid-1980s to the mid-1990s. "Even though my present collection includes Châteaux Lafite

Rothschild and Mouton-Rothschild, you don't have to be a genius to buy first growths," she notes. "I like to focus instead on second and third growths and I thoroughly enjoy Super Tuscans. Having a large wine cellar enables you to watch your wines mature under optimum conditions."

BEST BUYS: When she entertains over dinner, Vernon likes to mix and match the wine list. That might mean serving a top-quality Châteauneuf du Pape from Domaine du Pégaü along with California labels like Talley or Silver Oak. She's equally conscious about matching her selections to the guest list. She won't serve the same wines to a group of connoisseurs that she would offer to friends who are neophytes. She also likes to have a selection of half-bottles on hand to avoid opening a 750-ml. bottle for someone who just wants another glass.

BEST BOTTLES: Vernon doesn't buy at wine auctions. Instead, she works almost exclusively with Dave Sokolin, president of D. Sokolin Co. "He's like my personal shopper—a great friend and a reliable counsel," she says. "His firm has lots of clout and can access special, hard-to-come-by offerings. I'm on their VIP e-mail list, so when I see an offer for Château Rayas," another favorite Châteauneuf du Pape that ranges in price from $115 to $600 a bottle, depending on the vintage, "I'll go for it. In contrast, Sokolin will actually dissuade me from purchases he doesn't think represent good value."

COLLECTING WISDOM: Vernon emphatically steers clear from wines she feels are overpriced, especially California cult wines. "I'm not interested in paying a huge price for a young wine you can't drink for years. I don't buy $1,000 bottles, even when they are mature. I may be a committed collector, but what that really means is I am a sensible buyer and drinker. I buy to drink, not to flip. There is a cap on what I'll spend. Wine is life's joy, not something that a financial planner should recommend. It may be extravagant, but it's a great extravagance."

Vernon isn't surprised that so few women have joined the collector's circuit. She feels it's more of a male culture to learn about and lavishly spend money on wine, partly because men are bigger wage earners. "For most women, wine is a luxury, not a priority. Those women who receive large salaries tend to spend their money on clothes and jewelry. I love people who love good wine. Usually it means that they are fond of life. I just hope that whomever I'm dating shares my interest and doesn't think I'm frivolous!"

VOSNE-ROMANEE 1ER CRU
1999
RED BURGUNDY WINE
PRODUCE OF FRANCE
H 03176 2935
RICHEBOURG
1999
RED BURGUNDY WINE
PRODUCE OF FRANCE
H 01607 1527
ROMANEE-ST-VIVANT
1999
RED BURGUNDY WINE
PRODUCE OF FRANCE
H 01917 1837
LA TACHE
1999
RED BURGUNDY WINE
PRODUCE OF FRANCE

BUYING AND SELLING
AT AUCTION

〰〰〰〰〰

~~~~~~

ANYONE SERIOUS ABOUT WINE COLLECTING LEARNS TO TAKE WINE
auctions seriously because they are one of the most efficient and reasonable means of acquiring fine and rare wine. Before the legalization of wine
auctions in New York State in 1994, less than $15 million worth of col-
lectible wine was sold at auction in America. By 2005, U.S. wine auctions
passed the $166 million mark, with New York accounting for $79 million
of the total. Over the past decade, auctions have changed the way collectors purchase cellar-worthy bottlings, because more fine and rare wine has
been finding its way into the auction circuit than was ever before possible
by other means. Auctions offer top-quality vintages (primarily mature examples that are not readily available through traditional distribution channels) at the going market rate—which normally falls 25 to 35 percent
below retail markups.

Whether starting a collection from scratch or simply filling in gaps
in an existing cellar, auctions have become one-stop shopping outlets for
many wine collectors. With anywhere from a few hundred to several thousand lots valued from less than $50 to more than $5,000 per bottle, the
range of possibilities at a given sale can be enormous. You could theoretically acquire a complete cellar of considerable breadth and depth at a single auction, provided you had the discretionary funds and knowledge. You
can also sit through an entire sale hoping to snare a bargain or a scarce
vintage only to watch it fall into someone else's hands.

Auctioneers sell a desirable object to the highest bidder. Because they
depend on the attendees' knowledge of the wines and their value (which in

turn draws heavily on published ratings and tasting notes), auctions tend to be a venue for wines with established track records rather than for new labels with an unproven shelf life. Increasingly, however, rising stars that have garnered favorable press are also finding their ways into the auction arena.

Notwithstanding occasional aberrations, specific categories of wine routinely command the highest bids, defining the composition of a typical sale. Classified red Bordeaux constitute the lion's share of wine offered at commercial auctions, followed by Burgundy and, increasingly, premium and cult California wines. Italian and Australian estate bottlings, vintage Port, and premium Spanish wines round out the mix. Auctions are often the exclusive venue for hard-to-come-by labels and large-format bottles consigned directly by their producers as well.

Auction houses do not own the wines they sell: Instead, they function as agents, and are therefore not subject to the same margins (i.e., long-term interest, storage costs, and insurance fees) incurred by retailers and restaurants. So theoretically, they can offer wines at a relative discount to the retail trade. Savvy collectors meticulously cross-reference retail prices and auction estimates, for there is clearly no point in bidding more than a retail outlet is charging for the same product.

Whether you are planning to attend a live wine auction or bid online, virtually the same strategies apply. To maximize your chances of securing specific wines at a reasonable price, formulate a game plan before you raise your paddle or click your mouse. Otherwise, the odds of getting carried away or ending up empty handed are stacked against you.

Learning the ropes is a fairly straightforward process, but requires a bit of practice—and patience. Most buyers are initially more comfortable in a retail environment where they feel in total control of the transaction. John Kapon, director of the auction division of Manhattan retailers Acker Merrall & Condit, admits that auctions can be intimidating. "There's no guarantee you'll get what you want," he notes, "and some individuals don't want to spend a good portion of the day attending a sale. They would rather procure the wine in a store on the spot." Kapon recommends that beginners start with Internet auctions because they can buy in smaller quantities than at live sales, where wines are typically offered by the case. (See the following chapter, "Wine on the Web," for more on this.)

The best way for a first-time auction-goer to get the hang of the live auction process is to attend one without any intention of bidding. Don't even register. Just sit in the back, take in the entire room, and get some perspective on what's going on. Watch the bidders, learn the bid-steps, follow the auctioneer's movements, and get the overall rhythm of the sales. You'll soon ascertain what is—and is not—in demand. Unlike an art or furniture auction, there's not much to see at a wine auction, so be fore-warned. You'll settle in for a long stretch as the auctioneer rattles off a litany of lot numbers and label descriptions.

72

A Day at the Auction

American wine auctions have changed dramatically since their inception in the mid-1990s. Back then, houses favored a classic lecture-hall set-up. Dress was fairly formal, and the overall atmosphere was rather stiff. Zachys, the retailer and auction house based in Scarsdale, New York, was the first auction house to abandon this schoolroom environment in favor of a more relaxed atmosphere. The firm began to hold its sales at the sumptuous four-star restaurant Daniel in Manhattan; collectors assembled around tables and enjoyed a buffet lunch while ordering from an extensive wine list. Attire was casual.

Other auction houses soon followed suit. Acker Merrall & Condit created a similar ambiance at Cru, a Manhattan restaurant known for its focus on wine. Aulden Cellars-Sotheby's provided registered bidders with a complimentary lunch prepared by the firm's boardroom chef and encour-

An auction held by Zachys at Restaurant Daniel in New York City in the fall of 2005. The atmosphere is casual, but bidding is serious. Auctioneer Fritz Hatton, gavel in hand, presides over the podium. Electronic monitors keep track of the previous two winning bids.

aged participants to bring their own wine. NYWinesChristie's launched a celebrity chef program (the first guest chef was Thomas Keller of restaurants Per Se in New York and the French Laundry in Napa) with attendees bringing their own wine.

The biggest surprise for newcomers is usually how quickly an auction moves—often covering as many as two hundred lots per hour. Sometimes the contest over a particular lot is over in a matter of a few seconds. Rarely does it ever go much beyond a minute. "Neophytes discover early on that they should make most of their decisions and devise a buying strategy before arriving in the salesroom," says Jeff Zacharia, auction director for Zachys. "The pace is often too quick to make decisions on the fly. Auctions are a great way to snare terrific values, but it is a matter of timing. The more effort you put into studying the catalog, the more you will get out of a sale."

Richard Brierley, Christie's North American auction director, concurs. "Reading the catalog during the auction leads to missed opportunities and snap decisions," he advises. Brierly suggests that you listen carefully to the auctioneer, as he or she may drop hints about whether there is a lot of interest in an item, or whether a wine can be purchased at a good price (see page 76 for further discussion).

THE BEST PART OF THE AUCTIONS: PRE-SALE TASTINGS

∧∖∖∖∖∖∖∨

The most satisfying (and informative) aspect of a wine auction is the presale tasting, which usually occurs either the morning of or the evening before the sale. For around $50 to $100, attendees can taste dozens of fine wines slated to be sold. No matter how valuable professional wine ratings may be, there is no substitute for tasting a wine yourself to determine whether it's bid-worthy.

Christie's auction director Brierley encourages beginners and seasoned collectors alike to attend as many presale tastings as possible. "By exploring wines from different wine regions, first-timers will start to understand their own palates and develop preferences," he counsels. "Collectors should look for opportunities to broaden their horizons." Brierley adds that theme sales focusing on a specific wine region or country, such as Spain, Australia, or Italy, provide the chance to acquire fine wines that the average collector might not necessarily buy on a regular basis.

The wines poured at pre-sale tastings may range from solid, everyday Bordeaux and Burgundy to spectacular, hard-to-come-by labels. Once, prior to an important Burgundy and Côtes du Rhône auction, Aulden Cellars-Sotheby's presented an impressive tasting lineup that included DRC Echézeaux 1998, DRC La Tâche 1997, and Guigal Côte Rôtie La Mouline 1996. Morrell & Company once hosted a horizontal examination of select 1985 Bordeaux. Acker Merrall & Condit routinely offers tastings of rare French, California, and Italian bottlings. At a preview of a single-owner private cellar in Los Angeles, NYWinesChristie's uncorked Château Langoa Barton 1961, Château Léoville-las-Cases 1966, and DRC Montrachet 1970.

Tastings can also be a way to discover relatively unknown wines that are up for bidding. In 2004, at an Aulden Cellars-Sotheby's tasting, I came across a totally unfamiliar St. Emilion *Grand Cru* called Château Patris, which displayed surprising finesse and smoothness. A tiny property of less than 13 hectares, it belongs to Michel Querre from Pomerol. The day of the sale, I was one of the few bidders who knew about Patris because only a small quotient of the audience had attended the pre-sale tasting, and even fewer had bothered to taste the wine. (This one took place several days in advance of the auction.) Since there was next to no competition for the lot, I was able to snap it up toward the low estimate of $400. I only wish there had been more than one case on offer.

Thanks to pre-sale tastings and the more relaxed nature of auctions, it is now increasingly possible for collectors to interact with one another. Auctions are becoming venues for collectors to meet and forge relationships that can lead to creating tasting groups where they can share experiences—and expenses. While it can be prohibitively costly for one person to organize a tasting of cult California wines, First Growth Bordeaux, or premium Burgundies, dividing the tab by twelve or fourteen participants (the maximum number of tasters a bottle will accommodate) makes a tasting more affordable, and more fun. It also allows for lively debate and discussion.

What's It Worth to You?
Determining How Much to Spend

∿∿∿∿

Before participating in an auction, familiarize yourself with retail price lists, back issues of auction catalogs (which are available from auction houses), and realized prices of past sales (which are often available online or printed in the catalog following the previous sale) to get a feel for current demand. It's easy to lose track of an auction house's sale dates, tastings, and special events unless you become a subscriber to their regular catalogs. By subscribing to as many catalogs as possible, you will keep current with the overall wine auction scene and become familiar with the range of wines on offer, and estimated prices as well. Annual subscription rates range between $150 and $200.

A good source for retail prices of fine and rare wine both in America and abroad is WineSearcher.com—see page 107. The *Wine Spectator* Auction Index is a tremendously important tool for analyzing recent auction results. Appearing biannually in *Wine Spectator*, it records high, low, and average prices for more than 150 frequently traded labels. The expanded online version (excerpted on pages 210 and 236) covers more than sixteen thousand listings. By looking at the percentage change information, along with the price spreads, it's possible to see which wines are hot and which are not. Moreover, the averages serve as a barometer of the going rates at auctions.

Once you've obtained an idea of the average prices of the wines that interest you, take a good look at the catalog for the auction you plan to attend. As you formulate your bidding strategy, there are two price points to consider—one that's printed and one that's left to speculation.

1. Estimates

The first consideration is the *estimate*—a high and low valuation representing the auction house's projected selling range for every lot. Auction estimates reflect current realized prices of the same wine, taking into account recent highs and lows achieved in the saleroom, and they are printed in the catalog for each lot on offer. While helpful, these should be used as a guideline, not a guarantee. Hotly contested items sometimes sell for double or triple the high estimate, whereas sometimes auctioneers can barely manage to find a buyer for lots that do not garner much interest. It is not in the auction house's interest to inflate its estimates in the hopes of securing higher prices, because customer resistance will set in. Similarly, estimates that are intentionally too low may come off as a ruse to attract gullible buyers. Therefore, it's wise to cross-reference the estimates against online databases, and other sources of recent sales figures.

77

2. Reserves

Almost all lots offered at an auction (whether wine, art, antiques, or stamps) are subject to a *reserve*—a privately agreed upon sum (not stated in the catalog) between the consignor and the auction house below which the item cannot be sold. For wine, the reserve is usually set somewhere between 80 and 100 percent of the low estimate, but never rises above it. So don't expect to snare a case for much below the low estimate. (Infrequently, in the event of a liquidation sale, wines are offered without a reserve, but the winning bid usually rises to the going market rate.) It's worth noting that, because consignors set reserves individually, identical case-lots may not necessarily have the same reserve, which means there can be a disparity in price to take advantage of, provided you've scoured the catalog carefully.

When considering prices, remember to factor the supplementary charges that will be added to the final cost of your bid. A successful $350 bid placed at auction in New York can cost approximately $465 by the time the wine has been delivered locally. How is this possible? Most auction houses levy a buyer's premium ranging from 10 to 18.5 percent of the purchase price (though some online transactions are free). Sales tax, shipping, and insurance charges can add another 15 percent to your bill. (Since some states ban interstate wine shipments, check on the legality of a potential shipment before you buy.)

Once you've done the math, set a ceiling for your maximum bid for each lot you want and stick to it. Don't fall prey to auction fever. Unlike artwork, few collectible wines qualify as unique or one-of-a-kind items that justify frenzied bidding. For the most part, the wines you are after will come around again.

Rather than attending a live auction in person, many seasoned collectors prefer to place absentee bids by fax or e-mail, not only for convenience but also to prevent their emotions from getting the better of them on the salesroom floor (see "Absentee Bidding," page 89). However, by attending a sale in person, you maximize the possibility of noticing and snaring something special that might not have initially caught your eye.

Not every consignment goes to auction. It's a well-kept secret that some private sales are conducted by the auction houses themselves. If you are seeking a particular wine or vintage that you don't see in the catalog, let the auction house know. The house will inform you if and when the wine has been consigned, and at what future sale it will appear.

THE PRICE OF PROVENANCE

∧∧∧∧∧∧

The most desirable lots at any given sale are those that have been consigned directly by a winery or chateau, followed by single-owner wines
that were acquired upon release and stored in a single climate-controlled
facility. Because these wines haven't budged since they were first cellared,
their condition should be impeccable and the chance of spoilage minimal.
Pristine provenance may significantly increase the hammer price, but
many collectors feel the inherent benefits are worth it. Wines kept in a
professional storage facility or in a temperature- and humidity-controlled
home cellar are far preferable to ones housed in natural or passive underground cellars.

Climate controlled wine cellars are largely the product of the post-
war period, although choice old collections, such as the Doris Duke cellar,
were refrigerated as early as the 1930s. This means that the very old wines
that occasionally surface at auction will have spent some period of their
lives in natural cellars. However, many of the famed nineteenth-century
British wine collections, like the Glamis Castle cellar, were housed in naturally cool (48° F), damp environments—conditions fairly equivalent to
those of modern storage units.

Since few Americans collected wine from the enactment of Prohibition through the end of World War II (whereupon regular wine shipments
from Europe resumed), prior storage is not likely to be a major issue for
wines purchased from American collections so long as they have been
properly stored since the post-war era. Most of America's top cellars were
forged after 1966, when Christie's reopened its wine department, by

which time temperature- and humidity-controlled storage facilities were in wide usage.

Where applicable, the salient details of a wine's provenance are printed in the catalog alongside a lot's description (or in the case of a large collection, as a preamble to the consignment). When a cellar from an important collector goes on the block, auctioneers usually promote the fact on the spot. Apart from a full description of prior storage conditions, look for comments indicating if a wine has been shipped directly by a winery or chateau or is part of a single-owner sale. If there are no comments about a wine's provenance in the catalog, refer any questions about storage, etc. to the auction house's wine department. The foremost question to ask is whether the wines have been stored in a temperature- and humidity-controlled unit.

Michael Davis, president of Hart Davis Hart Wine Company in Chicago, is a seasoned auctioneer who started his career with Christie's in early 1982. He recalls several instances when an auctioneer's insight into a wine's provenance produced unexpected results. "While many collectors would be reluctant to spring for a thirty-year-old white Burgundy, it's another story when you know it comes from exceptional long-term storage," he says. In the course of auctioning an unusual or atypical lot, Davis and several of his counterparts will often let the audience in on its background, or refer to a tasting note.

Davis adds that wine from a lesser vintage but with special provenance can prove an unexpected treasure. His favorite example is a large cache of Château Lynch-Bages 1973. The wine was poorly rated, but it had been acquired on initial release by the owner and kept undisturbed in a very cold cellar. Having bought two cases myself, I can tell you that it was very good drinking.

The auction market has been particularly hot since the end of 2003, and much of that is due to dramatic offerings of impeccable provenance. Five- and, occasionally, six-digit hammer prices are not uncommon. In 2003, Christie's auctioned several major ex-chateau offerings of the celebrated Château Latour (Christie's owner, François Pinault, is also the chateau's owner), which were arguably the finest single consignment of estate-sourced Latour ever to appear at auction.

Those seventy-seven lots of vintage Latour brought $439,450, exceeding the presale high estimate by 65 percent. A case of the classic Latour 1961 sold for $54,950—252 percent above the *Wine Spectator* Auction Index average.

The pristine provenance of the cellar of famed heiress Doris Duke (the wines had never been moved from Duke's cellar in Somerville, New Jersey, since their purchase in 1937 and 1938) propelled an army of collectors into bidding wars not seen since the first days of New York wine auctions. Buyers packed into Christie's salesroom. The sale's highlight was a case of DRC Romanée-Conti 1934 that sold for $111,625 (126 percent above the first quarter 2004 *Wine Spectator* Auction Index).

A spectacular consignment direct from Domaine Clarence Dillon (owners of Château Haut-Brion and La Mission Haut-Brion) sent prices soaring above the estimates at Aulden Cellars-Sotheby's in December 2004. World records were established for cases of the 1945, 1959, and 1961 vintages of Château Haut-Brion, which sold for $30,550, $35,250, and $41,125, respectively.

And at Zachys in April 2005, a single bottle of Giacomo Conterno Barolo Monfortino Riserva Speciale 1937, estimated at $700 to $1,200, brought in $3,290, making it the priciest bottle of Italian wine ever sold at auction. The previous October, Zachys had sold a bottle of Château d'Yquem 1847 for a staggering $71,675: the most expensive bottle of wine ever auctioned in the United States, and the highest price ever realized for a bottle of white wine worldwide. In both instances, pristine provenance was a primary factor.

In late January 2006, Acker Merrall & Condit broke new ground with a record $10.64 million auction—the highest sum generated by a single-owner cellar belonging to an American and the third-highest sale total ever. Bidding on such rarified lots as six magnums of DRC Romanée-Conti 1971 that sold for a record $136,275 was very aggressive. A case of

Château Latour-à-Pomerol 1961 sold for $118,500 (up 17 percent) and a dozen bottles of Armand Rousseau Chambertin 1962 sold for a staggering $71,100 (up 236 percent).

In March 2006, NYWinesChristie's held an evening sale that focused exclusively on the finest and rarest wines. The average price per lot was $22,000—about ten times the average hammer price at a typical sale. Five lots surpassed the $100,000 mark, notably six magnums of DRC Romanée-Conti 1985, which commanded $170,375—the highest price ever paid for a case of wine at a commercial wine auction. A jeroboam of Château Latour 1961 fetched $135,125 (up 201 percent) and a jeroboam of Château Pétrus brought $123,375 (up 119 percent).

Such lots are so highly prized because their origins can be carefully ascertained. If you are considering the purchase of an extremely valuable lot of wine, learn everything possible about its provenance. You'll want to know the storage conditions provided by the present owner, and, when applicable, its previous owner (or owners). Trace its lineage back as far as possible, including the original retailer. You have to be able to trust the source putting the wines on the block. Thanks to the meteoric appreciation that great wines from classic vintages have undergone, there has been an escalation of fakes on the market, especially in large-format bottlings.

Many of them are said to hail from Singapore, and unfortunate buyers may have no idea that they have bought fakes until they taste them, sometimes years later. Anyone contemplating the purchase of a very large-format bottle from a classic historic vintage should perform as much due diligence as possible (even contacting the chateau to see how many were made) before placing a bid.

Much as American auctions have eclipsed their English counterparts in terms of overall sales volume, that's not to suggest that UK sales should be ignored. While it does not make much sense to buy wines that are generally available in America at the same price (why incur unnecessary shipping hassles and customs duties?), UK sales are often home to pristine consignments from great private cellars that do not necessarily crop up in the American marketplace. That might mean a scarce bottle of Château d'Yquem 1925 such as the one that sold at Sotheby's in November 2005 for $755 or a bottle of Armagnac Castarède 1900 that fetched $595, which you could easily slip into a carry-on bag.

Needless to say, when ultra-rare offerings such as a full case of Château Cheval-Blanc 1947 or Château Mouton-Rothschild 1945 go on the block in London, collectors and dealers from all over the world join the bidding fray. (American bidders at UK auctions can participate via phone, fax, or e-mail, so that they are on an even playing field with their English counterparts.) Many veteran collectors believe that older vintages offered for sale in London tend to be in better shape than similar American consignments because of superior storage conditions. This is especially true of nineteenth century classics housed in naturally cool and humid underground cellars in English or Scottish country houses. As a rule, Christie's and Sotheby's will assist successful American bidders who wish to ship their purchases to the States. There's a lot of paperwork involved, however, and charges will vary depending upon the destination.

It costs about $170 to ship a single case of wine from London to the United States. However, the price drops dramatically as volume increases. Shipments to America of twenty cases or more will run about $50 per case. For information about international shipping agencies and rates, contact Wine Cellars Ltd., winecellarsltd.com, (914) 762-6540; World Wide Cargo, worldwidecargo.com, (516) 371-2300; or Adventures in Wine, adventuresinwine.com, (415) 467-0130.

There's More
to a Wine than Its Label

∧⟋⟍⟋⟍⟋⟍⟋

Each auction house has its own conditions of sale, and it's wise to familiarize yourself with the specific terms before you place a bid. Examine the catalog's notes regarding condition, warranties, liabilities, etc. Unlike at a restaurant, where you can send back a wine that has gone bad, at auction, you are buying as is. All major auction houses carefully inspect the wines they sell. You are dependent on the accuracy and integrity of a firm's published reports, and unless there was something patently wrong in the description, you have little recourse. Before you bid, be sure you know what you are dealing with. Don't hesitate to contact the auction specialist if you are unsure of any aspect of a lot on offer.

You also want to pay attention to the level of the wine in the bottle, known as *ullage*. This is the barometer of a bottle's condition and should be listed in the catalog. Levels may vary according to a wine's age and the manner in which it was stored. Top- or upper-shoulder levels are not uncommon for thirty-year-old wines, but are unusual for a ten- or twenty-year-old vintage, whose levels should still be into or close to the bottle's neck. Simply put, you run a high risk with lower-than-average levels. That's why prices for classics from the 1960s and earlier fluctuate enormously. There is usually a diagram (like the one included here) in the auction catalog depicting different degrees of ullage to facilitate your understanding of fill levels. In the event there is no reference made to the wine's ullage be sure to inquire about that as well. (Some houses do not list the ullage of wines post-1990, which are still packed in their original wooden cases.)

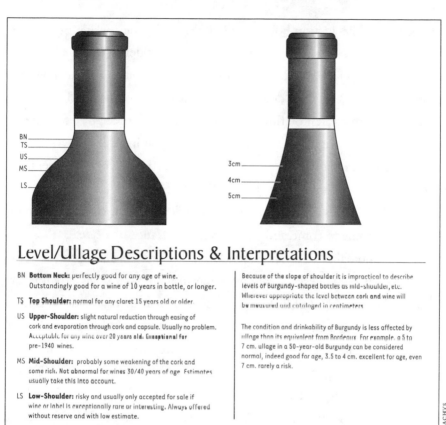

Level/Ullage Descriptions & Interpretations

BN **Bottom Neck:** perfectly good for any age of wine. Outstandingly good for a wine of 10 years in bottle, or longer.

TS **Top Shoulder:** normal for any claret 15 years old or older.

US **Upper-Shoulder:** slight natural reduction through easing of cork and evaporation through cork and capsule. Usually no problem. Acceptable for any wine over 20 years old. Exceptional for pre-1940 wines.

MS **Mid-Shoulder:** probably some weakening of the cork and some risk. Not abnormal for wines 30/40 years of age. Estimates usually take this into account.

LS **Low-Shoulder:** risky and usually only accepted for sale if wine or label is exceptionally rare or interesting. Always offered without reserve and with low estimate.

Because of the slope of shoulder it is impractical to describe levels of Burgundy-shaped bottles as mid-shoulder, etc. Wherever appropriate the level between cork and wine will be measured and catalogued in centimeters.

The condition and drinkability of Burgundy is less affected by ullage than its equivalent from Bordeaux. For example, a 5 to 7 cm. ullage in a 50-year-old Burgundy can be considered normal, indeed good for age, 3.5 to 4 cm. excellent for age, even 7 cm. rarely a risk.

85

This chart shows the fill levels (otherwise known as "ullage") that may be present in a bottle of wine, depending on its age and condition. The left image depicts a Bordeaux bottle; at right is a Burgundy bottle. Generally speaking, the lower the fill level, the more likely the wine may be at risk. These levels apply equally to other wines bottled in Bordeaux- or Burgundy-style containers, such as Rioja, Barolo, and Champagne.

If the catalog description contains the phrase "signs of seepage," that should raise a red flag for standard, 750-ml bottles because it is quite unusual for the contents of a standard-issue bottle to leak unless there has been a storage problem. Seepage is less of an issue in larger-format bottles: a cork may not immediately conform to an oversize bottle, and so seepage is more likely to occur even under the best conditions. A wine's capsule can reveal other potential problems. A shrunken cork is an indication of dry cellar conditions. If the cork is protruding, the wine may have experienced extremes in temperature. The auction house generally removes the capsule in order to examine the cork if it suspects there has been an incident. (Capsules are also routinely cut to reveal the date stamped on the cork when the label has deteriorated, but this practice does not affect the value of the wine.)

If you are contemplating a major purchase—especially of a fine or rare older bottle—most auction houses will let you inspect the wine yourself at their warehouses. "We don't make a practice of inviting clients to come and kick the tires," says Jamie Ritchie, Sotheby's senior vice president and head of its North American wine department, "but serious bidders are welcome to come and take a look in advance of a sale."

Two anomalies of today's auction market present an opportunity for the private buyer. Unless you are planning to resell your wine, a scuffed or stained label should be of little consequence. However, trade buyers generally avoid damaged labels because they must offer a pristine product, so a watermark or a tear can eliminate trade buyers from the ranks and minimize competitive bidding. Similarly, wine in its original wooden case (OWC) tends to be more expensive than wine repacked in cardboard (the difference can be as much as several hundred dollars per case) because OWC is preferable to trade buyers. Trade buyers have to resell their wines; the average consumer does not. That gives private bidders a built-in edge. They can go the extra bid-step without worrying about eating into profit margins.

THE BIDDING PROCESS

∿∿∿∿

Auctions are conducted in a systematic fashion, although the precise procedure varies from firm to firm. To save time, some auctioneers open the
bidding at the reserve; if there is no interest in the lot, it is *passed* or *bought
in*. (If a wine doesn't sell, the auctioneer is bound by law to say so. Some
auction houses will re-offer unsold lots to private clients at more attractive
rates after the sale—another reason to subscribe to auction catalogs.)

At several houses, the bidding intentionally starts below the reserve.
Auctioneers are legally allowed to take nonexistent bids (often called *bidding off the chandelier*) to gain some momentum until they arrive at one bid-
step below the reserve. If there is no further activity, the wine is passed. In
contrast, if there are a number of aggressive absentee offers, an auctioneer
may actually open the bidding close to or above the high presale estimate.

87

Bid-steps are the standard price increments by which a lot will increase during bidding. They are listed in the auction
catalog. Acquaint yourself with the inter-
vals, because at select stages (which may
differ from house to house), the bid-steps
may jump in increments of $50 instead of
$25, or $100 instead of $50. On extremely
expensive items in excess of $10,000, there
is usually some flexibility, and auctioneers
may accept a half bid-step.

BID-STEPS	
current bid	*bid increment*
up to $500	in 25s
$500–$1,000	in 50s
$1,000–$3,000	in 100s
$3,000–$10,000	in 250s
$10,000+	in 500s

*Each auction house has its own set of
bid-steps, or the increments a lot increases
during bidding. This listing comes from
Aulden Cellars-Sotheby's and is fairly
representative of competing houses.*

Bidding Tactics

All seasoned auction-goers have their own bidding techniques. Some simply hold their paddles up until they have either snared an item or exceeded their spending limits. One particularly effective tactic for high-priced items is to enter the fray at the very last minute when the high bidder thinks the lot is won. This tends to demoralize an opponent, but can backfire if the underbidder has very deep pockets, or if your timing is off and the auctioneer brings down the gavel before spotting your raised paddle.

Look for price disparities that arise when *parcels,* or multiple case-lots of the same wine, go on the block. This often happens when there are several lots of an identical wine—say, ten lots of Opus One 2001—on offer. In the event that they are not all snapped up by a single buyer (the winning bidder would have the right to exercise this option and buy all remaining lots), prices tend to drop as the auctioneer proceeds to the end of the ten-lot offering: it's a simple case of supply and demand. However, if you desperately want to own the item, you should get in at the beginning, even at the risk of paying a premium, because you never know if the winning bidder will take the entire parcel.

Auction regulars contend that prices often falter later in the day, on the theory that some bidders exhaust their capital in the morning session. At particularly large sales, there are often quiet moments when some lots sell at low-ball levels. Prices sometimes soften after a very expensive lot has been sold. Committed bargain hunters always attend a sale in person in anticipation of such events.

Understand that today's auction-goers are quite sophisticated, so be realistic about your prospects. If you spot a lot that appears to be an outright steal, you are probably not alone. However, the more obscure the label, the greater the possibility that only a handful of bidders will go after it.

♒ Sharks Stick to Deep Waters ♒

While auctions may seem like an inherently unequal playing field for novices, the auction market has polarized over the past several years. Veterans are more likely to go after esoteric or high-end items of little interest to the newcomer. While the bidding frenzy over these extremely rare items may be fierce, at the lower end of the price spectrum, bidding generally remains relatively calm—which is a good thing for anyone not targeting trophy wines.

Absentee Bidding

If you cannot attend a sale in person, you can always submit an absentee bid. A printed form is normally contained in the back of the catalog, and many firms now enable registered bidders to place an absentee bid online as well. Decide on the maximum amount you are prepared to pay for a lot (exclusive of the buyer's premium, taxes, etc.) and enter it in the appropriate column. If yours proves to be the winning bid, you will pay no more than one bid-step above a competing bid from the floor or the *order bid*—the book that contains all the other absentee bids. In the event of a tie bid, the lot goes to the bid submitted earliest.

For example, if you submit a $1,000 absentee bid on a case of wine and the underbid was $700, you would pay only $750—not your $1,000 maximum. As a rule, established auction houses do not accept *buy bids*—when the auctioneer bids on behalf of the seller until he wins the lot—because it can prove disastrous for all parties if there is an equally determined buyer in the room, and the bidding rages out of control.

Some collectors prefer to bid by telephone. It assures anonymity (which is very important for high-powered CEOs who prefer their employees and shareholders not know about such discretionary purchases), yet provides complete control over the bidding process. The mechanics are simple enough. Provided you are bidding on an item that is worth roughly

$2,000 (the minimum sum will vary from house to house) you can pre-arrange a telephone hook-up with the auction house. A representative will call a few minutes before your targeted lot goes on the block, and possibly give some indication of the flavor of the sale. When the lot comes up, he or she will repeat the current bid and ask whether you wish to up the ante or to stop. It's much like being there in person, except that you are placing a bid through the intermediary of the auction house's agent.

Anyone unfamiliar with a live auction should attend the sale in person in order to better understand whom you are bidding against and where the bidding falls relative to the estimate. But even seasoned hands often prefer to attend in person in order to spot and grab what may become an unforeseen bargain when the bidding doesn't go as high as was expected. Attending in person means you're more likely to come away with wines you didn't expect to buy.

It also means you'll be able to take advantage of hints from the auctioneer. For example, Christie's North American wine director, Richard Brierley, may ask an underbidder on the floor whether he wants to go "one more." It's almost always a clue that the absentee bidder's maximum has been reached, and that the buyer on the floor will win the lot by going an additional bid-step. Similarly, when the auctioneer says, "He's getting the parcel," it means that unless the underbidder bids more aggressively, he or she won't get any of the lots on offer: they'll all go to the absentee bidder instead.

Best Buys

Brierley suggests that new buyers, or those with a modest budget, focus on six-bottle mixed lots at first, both to broaden their experience and to keep a lid on costs. Mixed lots containing *vertical* offerings (different vintages of the same wine), *horizontal* offerings (different wines of the same vintage), or an assortment of diverse wines often represent exceedingly good bets, apart from serving as an excellent means of sampling a wide selection of wines and learning their characteristics. Sometimes the lot's estimate—

There is no trick to buying Domaine de la Romanée-Conti, Château Le Pin, or Screaming Eagle. It just requires a bit of resolve and a lot of cash. In contrast, auction regulars look for anomalies in the process to detect buying opportunities.

To take advantage of a potential disparity in hammer prices, it's advisable to attend a sale in person with your paddle at the ready. Prices for classified red Bordeaux from highly acclaimed 1989 and 1990 vintages can be volatile, especially for the mercurial first growths. Château Latour 1990 recently ranged from a high of $612 per bottle at Aulden Cellars-Sotheby's to a low of $351 at Acker Merrall & Condit in New York.

Clarets from the 1988 vintage remain the sleeper of the decade, despite very favorable ratings. Many classified growths of Bordeaux still sell for under $50 per bottle. Anyone in search of an affordable mature wine should consider the undervalued 1988s.

Auction prices for so-called off-vintages (claret from 1994, 1999, and 2001, and red Burgundies from 1997 and 1998) are fairly soft. They represent a good bet for anyone seeking everyday drinking wines from quality producers. Provided the condition reports are good, older vintages of Bordeaux, such as 1981 and 1979, also qualify for consideration.

Lesser known labels can also constitute a good buy, because many bidders are reluctant to venture into the zone of unfamiliar bottlings. I've encountered several unfamiliar wines at pre-sale tastings that formed part of a large consignment (and would probably not have been included in the sale otherwise), which I confidently snapped up below estimate, having sampled them the day before.

If you haven't already stocked up on 1995 and 1996 red Bordeaux, there is still time to acquire them before prices rise much further. The ultraexpensive 2000 vintage of Bordeaux, along with the 2003 and the 2005, is likely to put upward pressure on relatively mature vintages, which are selling for much less. Although the euro remains somewhat volatile, replacement costs at the retail level for French wines have risen substantially, placing upward pressure on wines already in the auction pipeline.

California cult wines continue to increase in price, with new records seemingly set at every sale. Hammer prices tend to vary according to the number of six-packs or three-packs on offer, so if your heart is still set on Harlan, scrutinize the catalog index carefully. You'll have a better chance when there is a large quantity up for grabs.

Older vintages of premium California wine often sell at an attractive discount relative to the cost of recent releases. A case of Diamond Creek Volcanic Hill Cabernet Sauvignon 1986 fetched $863 at a recent Zachys-Christie's sale in New York, about half the price the 1997 vintage commands at retail. The highly rated 2001 and 2002 vintages of premium California wine are placing increased pressure on prime older examples.

New-wave wines from Italy and Spain are generally in strong demand and short supply. The increasing number of theme sales that focus on a specific wine-producing region provide the best venue for making an acquisition, because prices tend to reflect the quantity on hand.

and hammer price—falls below the combined value of the individual wines contained in the lot because not all bidders take the time to calculate the value of the lot item by item.

Curiously, three- and four-bottle lots of premium wine often command proportionately less than lots of a full dozen, yet single bottles may be pricier. Large case-lots containing two to three dozen bottles may also sell at a discount.

ASK YOUR AUCTIONEER

~~~~~~~

One of the most valuable resources an auction house has to offer is its in-house expertise. Unlike retail wine shops, whose offerings span a broad spectrum of the world's winemaking regions, auction houses specialize exclusively in fine and rare wine. By interacting with consignors, sampling a vast array of bottles from private collections, and hosting pre-sale tastings, auction reps are in a good position to advise neophytes and seasoned buyers alike on the fine points of creating a wine cellar. Their opinions can serve as an additional yardstick alongside tasting scores and evaluations prepared by conventional critics.

It's worth cultivating a relationship with at least one member of an auction department's team to gain an inside edge on current and upcoming consignments. While by law auctioneers cannot reveal the identity of a specific vendor, they can provide additional information about a wine's provenance and condition that may facilitate your decision-making process.

Serena Sutcliffe of Sotheby's says that having fixed ideas about what to buy is a typical rookie mistake. "Sometimes clients have only heard of a few labels and are reluctant to take advantage of the full spectrum of fine wine. Instead, they want to stick to known commodities." Sutcliffe feels that position is limiting—and boring—and this is where a professional auctioneer can be of real help. "We try to eliminate these fixed ideas. Someone might pay a fortune for something just because they have heard of it, whereas something much better will go for nothing right beside it. It makes you cry," she adds.

Sutcliffe has convinced experienced Bordeaux drinkers with very large cellars to take the plunge into Burgundy. "I started talking to them about

Burgundy and its sheer value on the secondary market, and they have been enthralled by what they have bought and drunk from really good domaines, which they had hitherto found a minefield," she notes with pride.

Talking with an auctioneer can also help prevent newcomers from succumbing to "vintage mania." Sometimes they don't understand that a vintage that was a not a great success in Bordeaux, such as 2002, was actually very good in Burgundy or in California. The same is true of 1993 Burgundy, which was a fairly mediocre year in Bordeaux. Other collectors altogether avoid vintages that don't garner top ratings in the wine press, without realizing that many of them represent excellent value and constitute attractive everyday wines. Buying opportunities present themselves when you are aware of vintage anomalies. Every auctioneer should be able to give a beginner a crash course in vintage ratings and clear up any uncertainties. Not during a sale, of course, but either during a tasting or by appointment.

Hart Davis Hart's Michael Davis says that spending two decades as an auction professional taught him that there is no stock solution for helping wine drinkers cultivate their collections: clients have to be approached on an individual basis. "First-time buyers are initially a bit guarded about their budgets. Many are too modest to admit how much they have to spend, or embarrassed to confess how little." Once a client's bidding habit—and tactics—become clearer, Hart says, he is in a better position to offer advice or assistance. "After the first auction, we can better judge their limits and priorities and come up with a plan for future sales," he says.

Veteran collectors give him more leeway. "I've dealt with numerous clients for many years and that has created a great deal of comfort and trust," Davis says. His advice for long-term collectors can take the form of sharing a recent tasting experience (a specific vintage showing particularly well, for example), suggesting a varietal or blend that is consistent with the collector's preference, or recommending something on the basis of its provenance.

How to Sell Your Cellar at Auction

∿∿∿∿∿

Although the conventional causes for selling anything at auction are the "Three Ds"—death, divorce, and debt—with wine, many other factors may intervene. Tastes change. Some collectors want to thin out their inventory to accommodate new purchases. Others find the notion of uncorking a bottle that has doubled or tripled in value excessive, regardless of the initial cost price. Still others realize they have accumulated more wine than they could ever possibly consume. Either way, there is no point tying up funds and space in bottles that no longer interest you.

A simple analysis of auction catalogs and online listings will determine whether the wine you wish to sell corresponds with the kind of lots commonly on offer. Most auction houses feature fine and rare wines exclusively, with an accent on classified Bordeaux, premium Burgundies, and blue-chip or cult California wines. As a rule, simple table wines don't qualify for inclusion.

Brick-and-mortar houses tend to set a minimum value of $2,000 to $5,000 for consignments, although they may make exceptions for unusual bottles. Many online sites, like eBay, where you function as your own agent, do not set any minimums whatsoever.

Deciding on the best route for you may boil down to the fees a firm charges sellers. They now vary from zero to more than 10 percent of the sale price based on a sliding scale. For collectors with pristine collections, auction houses may compete so intensely that a portion of the house's buyer's fee may actually be offered to the consignor as an added inducement! In other words, anyone with a major collection is in an excellent position to negotiate aggressively.

95

The major auction houses (see page 200) rarely buy collections outright. However, if they have a vested interest in a lot, or if they have offered the seller a guarantee, an icon indicating as much will appear in the catalog. (Guarantees are sometimes offered on exceedingly valuable collections to entice a consignor, who then receives a specified sum regardless of whether all the lots sell.) Instead, they take them on consignment and render payment (usually thirty-five days after the sale) after they have been paid by the buyers. If for some reason a buyer fails to pay the bill, an auction house is not required to remit payment to the seller, although it will do its utmost to secure payment. Some Internet sales last only a few days, and successful buyers are required to submit payment within seventy-two hours, which speeds up the collection process substantially.

If you want to sell your wine at auction, prepare an inventory supplying as much information as possible about your wines' provenance: indicate how long you have owned the wines, and if possible, where and when you acquired them. Specify the nature of your storage conditions. (Don't be overly optimistic about "treasures" you have discovered in grandmother's attic.) The major auction houses will eventually inspect your wines in person. However, you may be requested to supply a tentative condition report, indicating the extent of your wines' ullage levels (see page 84 for a discussion). On auction websites that simply host a seller's collection, it's paramount to supply detailed information about wine levels, provenance, and storage in order to inspire confidence and encourage serious bids.

Final estimates are a reflection of recently realized prices and the specific attributes of your consignment. As a protection, you set a reserve (see page 77), which usually falls somewhere between 80 and 100 percent of the low estimate. On some websites, the final valuation is left up to you. Historically, aggressive reserves and estimates result in unsold lots, so if you are serious about selling, be realistic about your collection's worth. Don't tie the auctioneer's hands.

Charity Auctions

Other than the fact that they sell wine, charity wine auctions share little in common with their commercial counterparts. They are fundraisers whose auctioneers try and coax the highest possible bid for a specific item, sometimes cajoling or bantering with the audience in the hope of squeezing another bid increment (actions that would be frowned upon in a commercial auction). Estimates may be aggressive, yet it's done in good faith and, primarily, for a good cause. Value-wise, at the end of the day, you may get a good tax deduction and even some good wine.

The quality of wine that goes on offer at a charity event can vary dramatically. Some organizations will accept virtually every donation they receive, regardless of condition and provenance. Others may actually have a vetting committee that inspects the consignments. Catalogs may not necessarily bear detailed descriptions of the wines on offer, yet others may contain superb lots that have been donated directly from a celebrated winery, thereby guaranteeing pristine provenance.

Much as they can be raucous, charity auctions aren't frivolous affairs. In 2005, the top ten-grossing charity wine auctions in America brought in $29 million, led by the Naples Winter Wine Festival that raised $11 million and the Napa Valley Wine Auction that brought $10.5 million. The latter event (which raises funds for various health care, youth, housing, and educational organizations throughout Napa County) is a scene to spectacular donations and bids. A Hong Kong collector recently snared three scarce 3-liter bottles of Screaming Eagle from the 1995, 1996, and 1997 vintages for a whopping $220,000.

Traditional bidding strategies don't necessarily apply to charity events, where estimates and winning bids may have no semblance of a relationship. If you have your sights set on something relatively inexpensive (say a case of wine estimated under $500), there's no harm in throwing caution to the wind and joining the bidding fray with abandon. However, if it's a single *bottle* estimated at $500 or more, then it's prudent to contact the event organizer and ask what he or she knows about the donation. There's nothing wrong with requesting to inspect a bottle yourself, if practical. Sadly, some wines that would never be accepted by a commercial auction house have a way of insinuating themselves into charity sales.

As for the deductibility of your purchase, check with your accountant. Although some bidders deduct the full amount of their purchases, others deduct only the spread between the lot's estimate and the actual hammer price.

IMPECCABLE PROVENANCE:
CHARLES KLATSKIN'S CELLAR

⁀⋀⋀⋀⋀‿

Charles Klatskin, a real estate developer from New Jersey, has assembled an extraordinary wine collection of more than ten thousand bottles consisting primarily of rare red Bordeaux and top-notch Burgundy. Throughout his collecting career, Klatskin has been guided by an almost feverish preoccupation with provenance, along with a quest for large-format bottles.

CREATING HIS CELLAR: "When I examine an auction catalog, provenance is the most important thing I look for," Klatskin told me. "When it comes to choosing a fine wine to serve for a dinner party, I would rather pay 20, even 100 percent more for a bottle with good provenance than snare a bargain whose origins I'm unsure of." He feels that serious collectors of all ages who are keen on cellaring vintage classics should be prepared to go the extra mile for pristine provenance.

He once spent $1,300 for a single bottle of Latour 1934, originally estimated at $300 to $500, because it came directly from the chateau. Klatskin recalls that magnums of Château Gruaud-Larose 1982 purchased at Christie's from the single-cellar sale of veteran collector Tawfiq Khoury were a revelation because they were so well stored. The same was true of a case of Château Palmer 1961 consigned to Zachys by the celebrated Bordeaux shipper Mahler-Besse.

BEST BOTTLES: Klatskin owns all the highly-rated classified clarets from 1982, along with rarities such as Château Ducru-Beaucaillou 1953 in magnum and imperials of Château Mouton-Rothschild 1961. In fact, big bottles are a favorite of his, and he has been collecting them for more than thirty years. At its peak, his cellar numbered sixteen imperials, thirty jeroboams, and approximately two hundred cases of magnums, 85 percent of which were from Bordeaux. Magnums are Klatskin's format of preference, primarily because they have a longer shelf life (sometimes ten to twenty years) than the standard 750-ml bottle. In his estimation, magnums from the same vintage taste richer and come across as younger than their smaller counterparts. He believes they're perfect when entertaining another couple at dinner. And "they look better on the table," he adds.

Klatskin reserves double magnums (equal to four regular bottles), jeroboams (equal to four to six regular bottles), and imperials (equal to eight regular bottles) for big parties. "To avoid leftovers, a big risk with big bottles, any time I open an imperial of rare wine, I do it in the company of true wine aficionados, rather than social drinkers. As a rule, I allow one-third to one-half bottle of wine per person, so an imperial will generously serve sixteen people," he explains. His rule of thumb for decanting pre-1982 imperials is to let the bottle breathe for one half hour for every year of its age.

BEST BUYS (AND SELLS): The realization that many of his bottles were approaching maturity faster than he could drink them prompted Klatskin, who is in his late sixties, to consign fifty cases to Christie's and another 117-lot offering to Aulden Cellars-Sotheby's. At the latter sale, a world record price of $44,650 was established for six magnums of Château Mouton-Rothschild 1959, in part because of his own cellar's pristine conditions. "I am getting older and so are many of my wines," he said at the time, "and there's no point in hanging on to things I don't foresee drinking in the near future."

That's not to suggest that Klatskin has laid down his paddle for good. True to form, he recently snapped up four cases of magnums of Château Cheval-Blanc 2002, a sleeper that is approaching drinkability. His current house wine is Avvoltore 2001, a Tuscan bottling from Morris Farms that retails for about $40. Klatskin is also enjoying Château d'Issan 1999, a third growth from Margaux that retails for about $40.

COLLECTING WISDOM: Because of the dizzying selection of labels now available at any major wine store, Klatskin suggests that younger enthusiasts who are just starting a wine collection should join a wine club—either the kind that conducts organized tastings or the subscription-based variety that sends its members a bottle or two of something different every month.

After collecting for almost thirty years, Klatskin likes to say that there's something inherently compulsive about every wine collector. "There is always a bottle you just can't pass up, whether it's a Château Latour 1900 for $11,000 or a Château Léoville Las Cases 1986 for $200. I know, because I am one of these collectors. So if you have your heart set on something special, go for it," he advises. "You only go around the track once."

WINE ON THE WEB

~m~

~\\\\\\\~

WITH THOUSANDS OF CYBERSTORES SELLING WINE ONLINE, there's clearly an Internet address for every palate and pocketbook. Whether you want to join the bidding fray on a $6,000 mixed case of Domaine de la Romanée-Conti 2000 on WineBid.com, hunt down the best price for a bottle of vintage Côtes du Rhône on Wine-Searcher.com, or research recommendations for great table wines under $15 on Wine.com, there's a website to satisfy every possible drinking need and desire.

Notwithstanding the complexities of shipping, there are many good reasons for buying online. It's certainly convenient. You can place orders 24/7 without leaving your home or office. It's very often faster than visiting a store in person to make a purchase because of the efficient nature of online shopping carts. You are somewhat less likely to fall prey to impulse buys online, as you are not physically in contact with artfully merchandised displays. Some wine lovers simply enjoy the anonymity factor: there's no need to interact with a potentially pushy or intimidating salesperson.

Don't be swayed by elaborate, flashy animations, streaming videos, or virtual wine tours unless they come bundled with old-fashioned concepts like personalized service, professional storage, inventory management, and competitive pricing. It's no surprise that some of the best wine websites belong to traditional brick-and-mortar retailers that have combined decades' worth of experience with user-friendly web technology.

Purely "virtual" wine shops may not even own the wine they offer, acting instead as brokers for private collections or for wineries with which they have exclusive arrangements. Yet many online ventures have invested in elaborate wine warehouses. If it's not made explicit, send an e-mail to ascertain the exact nature of the storage conditions. If you are contemplating the purchase of classic older vintages, ask about the fill levels of individual bottles. And always cross-reference the asking price against retail or online price lists.

Websites belonging to brick-and-mortar wine stores may offer fewer bells and whistles than their Internet-only cousins, but the best of them boast substantial inventories of awesome breadth and depth, often with thousands of different labels. Their wine descriptions tend to be more authoritative and, most importantly, the wines themselves are almost always housed in temperature- and humidity-controlled storage facilities. Just about every major wine store now has an online outpost. And many top-ranking retailers have websites as elaborate as any store that exists only in cyberspace.

THE FINE PRINT

Unlike buying a digital camera or an iPod online, wine purchases come fraught with legal restrictions. For starters, you must be twenty-one years of age, and be able to prove it, to buy alcoholic beverages. Many e-tailers require that you fax them a copy of your driver's license as proof. What's more, interstate shipping of wine by merchants is illegal in many parts of the country, even though over half the states permit the shipment of wines by wineries. Most websites stipulate whether they are able to deliver to your home state. Others transfer the title and responsibility for wine shipments directly to the buyer. Some have free intra-state shipping but require a minimum purchase. Read the details carefully before you order.

Wine Websites as Research Tools

∧∧∧∪∪∪

What I like most about wine websites is being able to use their sophisticated search engines to explore extensive databases. These online search tools have all but eliminated the endless thumbing through catalogs or newspapers that once formed a time-consuming element of seeking out specific wines.

One of the most important tools online wine databases provide is the ability to cross-reference a wine's retail price and availability at different outlets nationwide. This lets you efficiently compare varying retail prices along with auction estimates to pinpoint the best deal for a specific wine. Why pay more than the going rate?

It can be surprising to see how widely a wine's price can range. A search on WineSpectator.com for Château Léoville-Barton 1995 revealed an average auction price of $54 per bottle. Searching for the same wine at Wine-Searcher.com, I discovered that McArthur Beverages (see page 62) offered it for $49.99 per bottle, whereas at Winfield-Flynn Ltd., a New York-based wine merchant, it had a $99.99 sticker price. Quite a spread. Varying markups and overhead considerations can result in huge price disparities, so spend the time checking out the competition before you click.

Anyone planning to buy a given wine at auction should use retail price data only to establish a maximum ceiling. Your bid should fall below the lowest quote you find to accommodate the buyer's premium and other charges; otherwise, you'll end up overpaying.

Almost every wine website now includes tasting notes and serving tips. Some of this material is invaluable; other information can be self-serving. The same is true of many wineries' websites. For a more impartial view, there are several detailed sources of information that include reviews of specific wines, scores from tasting panels or individual critics, and information about best buys and new releases. Most of them are accessible only on a subscription basis, but it's well worth the $50 to $100 annual charge given what you'll eventually save. More often than not, the cost of subscribing to an online database pays for itself in a single click with insightful tasting notes or tips on where to find the best buys.

Best of the Web: Research Sites

An excellent site for combing through retail prices and finding hard-to-come-by labels is Wine-Searcher.com. Entering the name of a wine or vintage will display a list of retailers across the country (and, optionally, in Europe) at which the wine is available. You can use this site to cross-reference wine prices, as well as to order directly from any of the linked store's websites. For full access to the database of 1.5 million listings culled from more than seven thousand wine merchants, there is an annual fee of $29.95. Nonsubscribers can access a limited roster of retailers.

WineAlert.com is similar to Wine-Searcher.com in concept, but its pool of listings is smaller. This website includes a handy pronunciation guide to wine labels. It costs $29.95 per year to access WineAlert's "gold package"; the more limited "silver package" is free.

Winespectator.com is a highly reliable reference source for comprehensive tasting notes and auction pricing information, accessible by subscription for $49.95 per year. The *Wine Spectator* Auction Index lists prices for approximately sixteen thousand wines frequently traded at auction, along with high/low comparisons, and percentage price changes from previous quarters (see excerpted Auction Index, page 210). The database of wine reviews and scores compiled by the *Wine Spectator* magazine's tasting panel includes more than 160,000 listings. Other useful tools are its detailed vintage charts, harvest reports, and dining and travel guide, along with daily wine news. An articles archive contains features that appeared in the *Wine Spectator* print version dating back to 1994.

Decanter Magazine's Fine Wine Tracker traces the price (in pounds sterling) of select wines at auction from January 1978 to the present (decanter.com). *Wine Enthusiast* magazine (winemag.com) also offers an extensive buying guide.

Robert Parker's website, erobertparker.com, is an easy-to-use search engine that enables users to browse Parker's (and associate Pierre-Antoine Rovani's) copious tasting notes. An advanced search engine allows subscribers to search a wine by its salient characteristics such as color, smell, or taste. Where applicable, reviews are linked to websites of retail outlets across the country. An articles archive provides links to select features that have appeared in *The Wine Advocate*. The cost of an annual subscription is $99.

WineAccess.com (a wine-related Internet portal) hosts wine critic Stephen Tanzer's bimonthly newsletter, *International Wine Cellar*, founded in 1985. Tanzer, a respected voice in the wine community, provides comprehensive coverage of the world's key wine-producing areas. Each issue contains between five hundred and eight hundred tasting notes, along with articles and interviews. A one-year subscription costs $90.

Wine writer Jancis Robinson has launched a by-subscription ($129 a year) website, www.jancisrobinson.com, for wine enthusiasts. Her independent tasting notes and wine ratings are the primary draw, along with food and wine matching suggestions, profiles of major grape varieties, and a fine wine reference that covers frequently asked questions.

Burghound.com is a well-regarded source for buying recommendations and in-depth reviews of fine and rare Burgundies. Compiled by wine authority Alan Meadows, a subscription to the quarterly newsletter and full access to the database of forty-five hundred listings costs $110.

Wine blogs come and go almost faster than you can decant a good bottle of wine. Three sites where you can seek them out include foodandwine.com/articles/seven-best-wine-blogs, www.technorati.com, and Eric Asimov's The Pour in the *New York Times*: thepour.blogs. nytimes.com.

SHOPPING FOR WINE ONLINE

∧∖∖∖∖∖∖∨

If you are relatively new to the fine wine experience and need some coun-
seling about how to start a collection, visit Wine.com. It allows searches by
price range—$15 to $50, for example—or according to tasting scores
handed down by the wine press. Another dialog box labeled *Wine Collections* organizes wines by region or by varietal. There's also a wine club,
which sells preselected premium red wines.

Geerlings & Wade (geerwade.com) offers similar features, and includes a wine course and tasting tours for club members. Both are well
suited to the neophyte and offer good value on some of their selections.

So many established retailers of potential interest to collectors are
now online that it is impossible to enumerate them all. Sherry-
Lehmann (sherrry-lehman.com), Zachys (zachyswines.com), and Pops
(popswines.com) all boast substantial inventories of fine wine. Morrell &
Company (morrellwine.com), the Wine House (winehouse.com), K&L
Wine Merchants (klwines.com), and Wally's (wallywine.com) in California, along with MacArthur Beverages (bassins.com) in Washington, D.C.
and Spec's (specsonline.com) in Houston all have extensive websites that
are easy to navigate and full of collectibles.

In addition to mainstream retailers, there are numerous online
sources that target serious collectors of fine and rare wine exclusively. The
Wine Broker Inc. (thewinebroker.com) is a licensed fine wine merchant
based in Dallas specializing in old, fine, and rare wines. It offers sophisticated monthly wine clubs and a selection of everyday wines as well. Since
it acts as a broker for some of the wines it sells, their provenance should be
determined on a case-by-case basis.

Sites by the Massachusetts-based store Table & Vine (tableand
vine.com) and California-based stores Premier Cru (premiercru.net) and
the Marin Wine Cellar (marinwinecellar.com) all tout massive inventories
rife with nineteenth-century treasures like Château Lafite Rothschild
1874 at $3,000 per bottle and twentieth-century classics like Heitz Cellars
Martha's Vineyard Cabernet Sauvignon 1974 for $895. Sites like these
tend to assume a high degree of connoisseurship. They are often devoid of
detailed descriptions, reading instead like laundry lists of expensive rare
wines. The best way to tackle them is to cross-reference their prices
against the auction databases at Wine-Searcher.com or winespectator.com.
Then, for tasting feedback, check out winespectator.com or the wine ratings on Robert Parker's website (erobertparker.com). Finally, e-mail the
store to ascertain specific details on provenance, condition, and storage.

ONLINE WINE AUCTIONS

∿∿∿∿∿

Less expensive commissions and smaller lots (sometimes as few as one to three bottles) are the fundamental draw of online wine auctions. Unlike live auctions, online auction sites usually allow you to buy partial cases: perfect for the collector who wants Beringer by the bottle.

From a technical standpoint, the ability to receive instant notification (either on screen or by e-mail) when you have been outbid is a major improvement over the conventional absentee bidding model, which does not disclose whether your bid was ever in the running until after an auction's conclusion. Unlike traditional auctions, most online sales post a minimum bid, which is usually equal to the lot's reserve price, giving the collector additional bidding ammunition. For the auction junkie, online sales harbor yet another appeal: they run nonstop, and many firms hold a new sale every week or two.

Wherever you bid online, scrutinize the site for the firm's back ground information. Look for a description of the firm's inspection system: does someone physically examine every bottle of wine on offer? Equally important is information about the wine storage facilities. Are they temperature-controlled? Some websites do not display this data, but instead provide an e-mail link through which you can question the actual consignor. Don't even consider bidding on a wine that lacks a proper description. If an estimate sounds too good to be true, it probably is.

Bidding Tactics

Much as with a silent auction, savvy players suggest waiting until the very last moment to place your final bid in order to discourage counterbids that will jack up the price. However, to counteract such practices, most websites now employ sophisticated software that delays a sale's conclusion until fif-

111

teen minutes have transpired without active bidding. Nevertheless, most seasoned bidders wait until a sale is nearly over before posting their bids.

One online feature, called *autobidding*, is essentially the electronic equivalent of absentee bidding. It automatically increases your bid up to a predetermined maximum in response to bids placed by competitors.

Best of the Web: Top Auction Sites

With over 38,000 registered bidders, WineBid.com, the leading online wine auctioneer, claims more subscribers than Sotheby's and Christie's combined. It posts annual sales in excess of $20 million and conducts a new auction every week. Even more revealing is the new breed of buyer WineBid.com is attracting: Two-thirds of its clients have never bought or sold wine at conventional auction houses. One reason is that their business model facilitates one- and two-bottle sales. Enthusiasts who may not need a full case of Château Léoville-Barton 2000 can still pick up a couple of bottles for a tasting or a dinner party. Every single lot on offer is inspected by the firm.

Here's an example of a WineBid.com auction in which I participated. The sale contained over four thousand lots worth just under $1 million. The wine descriptions came complete with provenance and condition reports and included ratings from *Wine Spectator*. I placed an autobid on several items. Having researched the average auction price for a bottle of Abreu Madrona Ranch Cabernet Sauvignon 1999, I bid a maximum of $190 on the item. My winning price was $180. I placed a $200 maximum bid on a magnum of Robert Foley Vineyards Claret 1999 and received an e-mail notifying me that I had been outbid. I upped the ante to $210 (which went uncontested) and snared the magnum.

MagnumWines.com specializes in rare, large-format bottlings, such as 6-liter bottles of Pride Mountain Vineyards Cabernet Sauvignon 2001 and magnums of Château Palmer 1982. (It also auctions hard-to-come-by 750-ml bottles, such as Heitz Martha's Vineyard Cabernet Sauvignon 1974 or Tenuta San Guido Sassicaia 1985.) Its AuctionWatch feature enables a participant to follow multiple bids at the click of a mouse.

The Brentwood Wine Company differs from its competition in that it purchases its inventory outright rather than on a consignment basis. Launched in 1998, this Oregon-based auctioneer (BrentwoodWine.com) is an old-timer by Internet stands. While Brentwood practices rigorous standards of control, estimates can be higher than conventional online firms, so final bids tend to escalate as well. However, an extensive inventory compensates.

In contrast, WineCommune.com largely operates like eBay: Sellers and bidders interact directly, with minimal interaction from the parent company unless you consign your wine directly. As a result, finding a reasonably priced bottle can be more challenging, because the estimates and reserves—determined primarily by the consignors—tend to be on the high side. As a security measure, the site rates and posts the past performance and reliability of participants. Buyers can inquire about provenance and condition via e mail. Because these facts are not checked by the site itself, it's essential to ask how the wine on offer has been stored. Clearly a situation in which the dictum "caveat emptor" prevails, WineCommune.com is perfect for the bidder who seeks instant gratification, as dozens of new wines go on sale every day (other sites tend to run in two-week cycles).

There are many similarly structured auction sites on the web. CellarExchange.com, for example, functions on a similar basis as WineCommune.com. However, like an inexpensive table wine, many of these sites don't have much shelf life—especially those created by techies who have little or no wine experience. It's fun to explore the possibilities, but wiser still to make use of only those auction sites that have a seasoned track record.

Additionally, to varying degrees, all the major commercial auction houses now have a presence on the web:

ACKER MERRALL & CONDIT (ackerwines.com), the Manhattan wine merchant and auctioneer, conducts separate, Internet-only auctions on a regular basis throughout the year. Collectors can also place absentee bids on the house's live sales via the website.

BONHAMS & BUTTERFIELDS (butterfields.com) reproduces its catalogs online as downloadable PDFs (i.e., in portable document format).

CHRISTIE's (christies.com) also posts its catalog online and allows registered users to place absentee bids electronically. A feature called *LotFinder* seeks out a bidder's specific wines in advance of an auction, and notifies the potential buyer when they crop up.

EDWARD ROBERTS INTERNATIONAL (eriwine.com), a Chicago-based boutique auction house, enables bidders to both place absentee bids and bid in real time.

HART DAVIS HART (hdhwine.com), the Chicago-based fine wine retailer and auction house, reproduces its catalog online and accepts electronic absentee bids.

MORRELL & COMPANY (morrellwineauctions.com) hosts live auctions that bidders can attend in person or participate in over the Internet in real time. Registered buyers can also place absentee bids until the day before the auction.

SOTHEBY's (sothebys.com) has a comprehensive website, although its absentee bid form must be faxed or mailed to its New York headquarters.

ZACHYS (zachys.com) posts its catalogs and auction results online.

Although the Internet has made wine auctions more efficient by enabling the potential buyer to search, browse, and bid, it is unlikely that web-based wine sales will replace the brick-and-mortar variety altogether. The camaraderie that joins like-minded auction goers is unlikely to ever be superseded by a monitor and a mouse.

A Refined Palate:
Nicholas Silvers's Cellar

Nick Silvers, a custom homebuilder in Houston, became smitten with fine wine at the young and freshly legal age of twenty-one, when he sampled a bottle of Mouton-Rothschild 1993 at a dinner party in 1998. "In retrospect, it was an unexceptional vintage, but at the time, I was so impressed that I immediately started to experiment with other fine wines," he says. He also began reading about them, which further stirred his curiosity; he credits *Wine Spectator* reviews as a strong influence. Then a local Houston retailer was generous enough to bring him into his tasting group. "Before I knew it, I had a stand-up, one-hundred-bottle wine fridge, and shortly after that, I was building a proper cellar in my home." Silvers now counts about 1,800 bottles in his collection.

CREATING HIS CELLAR: Over the past eight years, Silvers discovered what many other collectors have learned—that experience with good wines leads to a thirst for even better ones. As he began exploring the wide world of wine, his tastes evolved in a somewhat predictable fashion. He began his collection with California Cabernet Sauvignons and then proceeded to more refined classified Bordeaux. The more he experimented, the more his preferences widened. He developed a taste for the Rhône and Burgundy, as well as German Rieslings. Silvers has since sold most of his California wines. "What's the point of holding on to bottles that you have no intention of drinking?" he asks.

Once he became committed to forming a collection, Silvers started forging strong relationships with retailers around the country. "I slowly began buying at auction, primarily at Acker Merrall & Condit, and started using the Internet to find smaller retailers and brokers who received allocations of hard-to-come-by wines yet were willing to sell at reasonable prices." Silver's sources range from the Wine Club in San Francisco to the Chelsea Wine Vault in New York to Richard's in Houston. He now receives regular e-mails whenever merchants receive a shipment they think might interest him. "The most fun aspect of collecting is the treasure hunt when I am in other cities: finding that obscure shop that has one true gem and doesn't realize it," he says.

BEST BOTTLES: Like a lot of collectors, he buys more wines than he needs, sells off the overage at a profit, and invests the proceeds in more wine. As a result, he takes a draconian view of his inventory, and doesn't hesitate to dispose of wines that no longer make sense in the context of his collection. "I bought a lot of 2000 Bordeaux, including Château Lafleur (now worth at least $1,500 per bottle retail) that I have subsequently sold. The 2000s are more expensive than the famed 1982s and won't be ready for years, whereas the 1982s are approachable now."

BEST BUYS: Silvers regrets that Rhône reds, especially the reserve bottlings, are less of a value than they used to be. His new favorite wine, Domaine des Comtes Lafon Volnay Santenots, is a red Burgundy that ranges from $65 to $100 per bottle, depending on the vintage. He's still very fond of Arietta, and Pride Reserve, two sought-after, limited-edition Napa labels. And for $25 a bottle, he says German Riesling Kabinetts represent wonderful value. "Let's face it," he notes, "every wine doesn't have to be an event."

COLLECTING WISDOM: Silvers says that on the surface, wine collecting seems nothing more than a hobby. The difference is the variety and diversity inherent in collecting and enjoying wines. "It is a bit like collecting art or antiques—one must really study the subject matter to understand and fully appreciate it. It is not possible to ever fully 'understand' wine to the point where you know every wine in every vintage," he observes. "There's continual change among unchanging labels."

117

Storing and Enjoying Your Wine

/\/\/\/\/\/\

~~~~~~~

SO YOU'VE PUT A LOT OF THOUGHT AND EFFORT INTO ACQUIRING your wine. You've perused auction catalogs and websites, picked up some unusual vintages recommended by a reliable retailer, and perhaps bid on your first lot or broadened your repertoire to include a new region. Now that you've got your wine, storing it correctly will ensure that younger vintages age perfectly into maturity, and delicate, older bottles remain in good condition until you're ready to remove their corks.

After that comes the fun part—drinking your selections! For a collector, tasting is practical as well as pleasurable: you want to be able to detect which young wines are most suitable for aging. Therefore, I've included some of the basic elements for assessing a wine's faults and virtues, as well as evaluating potential age-worthiness in wines both young and old.

While one fine bottle is sufficient to provide a moment of pure enjoyment, having a wine collection allows you to experience two of the best aspects of wine appreciation, horizontal and vertical tastings, which reveal the subtleties among regions and across vintages. And because a balanced wine collection means always having the right wine for any meal, I've included some essential information on pairing wine with food.

THE RIGHT STORAGE SYSTEM FOR YOU

∧\\\\∿

Whether your cellar is large or small, there is no point in holding on to any wine without having the proper storage facilities. Under the wrong conditions, wine will deteriorate prematurely and lose its long-term aging potential, not to mention its resale value. By overseeing your wine's aging process yourself, you guarantee that its provenance and storage conditions meet optimum standards. If you have a wine collection worth $25,000 or more, it's well worth spending $3,000 to $5,000 on a temperature- and humidity-controlled storage unit that will protect your investment. Even if you have a modest starter collection, you'll want to get a small unit like the Haier (whose ninety-three-bottle facility sells for about $1,000) to house your "Better" and "Best" bottles.

Most wine collectors and industry professionals agree on ideal cellar conditions: a constant temperature of 55° F and a humidity level of roughly 70 percent. This environment approximates the pristine underground cellars found in the caves of Bordeaux. Higher temperatures accelerate the aging process, shortening wine's lifespan and making optimum drinking times unpredictable. Higher humidity causes mold to form on the bottles and cellar walls. Lower humidity levels may cause the wine to slowly evaporate from the bottle.

A closet or a basement space where the temperature may fluctuate significantly as the outside temperature changes during the year poses a substantial risk to collectible wine. In fact, bottles stored at 75° F will age twice as quickly as wine kept at the 55° F standard. You can't convert a kitchen refrigerator into a proper wine storage unit because its relative humidity is too low. An air conditioner won't work either, because it cannot cool a room down to 55° F. An AC also removes humidity from the air.

The only viable natural alternative is a habitually cool and damp underground area that is isolated from sources of heat, light, and vibration. This is known as a *passive* cellar. Not only are such spaces difficult to come by, but, at auction, collectors are increasingly avoiding passively stored wines in favor of professionally housed bottles, whose storage conditions are more tightly controlled.

While 55° F is the most widely agreed-upon temperature for wine storage, some of the greatest old Scottish wine collections sold at auction (like the Glamis Castle consignment of nineteenth-century Lafite Rothschild offered at Christie's in the 1970s) were housed in cellars in which the thermometer never rose much above 48° F. Many seasoned contemporary collectors have become enamored of the cooler-is-better concept for very old wines because the slightly cooler temperature helps to retard the aging process. Veteran New Jersey collector Charles Klatskin cellars a portion of his collection at the standard 55° F, but places older, rarer bottles in a separate room at 48° F. Prominent Ohio collectors Frank and Mary Wall Komorowski also store their wine at 48° F. While their approach cannot be verified scientifically, I've sampled fifty-year-old rare wines from Klatskin's collection and have found them to be in remarkable condition.

If you cannot maintain high humidity levels in your cellar, there's a compelling contrarian view worth considering. Seasoned wine writer Matt Kramer feels that the notion of preserving high humidity levels is a throwback to the days when wine was stored in wooden barrels that needed to be kept moist in order to maintain their seals. "I think it's a canard for the home cellar, an unthinking leftover from a time when home and restaurant wines were still stored in wood," he told me. Winemaker John Kongsgaard agrees. "Humidity is far less important than temperature control. Lack of humidity will ultimately dry out a cork, but that would take decades, especially if the wine is stored cork down or cork sideways." Kongsgaard notes.

INTERNATIONAL WINE ACCESSORIES, PETER MELTZER

Standing storage units for wine. The Avanti 54-bottle unit (left) costs about $600. A unit this size can be useful if you must store the bulk of your collection at a separate location. If you're storing all your wine in one place, I recommend starting collectors with something like the 170-bottle EuroCave Compact 170 Wine Cellar (about $1,800, right), which fits snuggly into a typical closet.

In the short run, Kramer and Kongsgaard are probably right. Their advice is meant to assuage the fears of anyone who does not have access to a storage space with proper humidity levels. But if you are planning to keep your wines for decades, or pass them along as a legacy, why not err on the safe side? All prefab wine storage units come with both temperature and humidity controls.

If space is at a premium, consider storing the bulk of your wine in a professional wine warehouse (the going rate is $1.50 to $2.00 per case per month). Purchase a small wine storage unit (about 5' × 2' × 2') to accommodate fifty to one hundred bottles for short-term consumption, which you can replenish from storage as needed. Obviously, this method will deprive you of full access to your collection, and won't allow you to spontaneously uncork that special bottle reposing miles away in a refrigerated warehouse.

If you have the floor space to devote to your wine collection, you'll find freestanding temperature- and humidity-controlled wine storage units that can accommodate anywhere from fifty to seven hundred bottles. (The largest will measure approximately 7' × 5' × 2.5'.) Purchase a unit with a capacity that exceeds your existing cellar to give yourself room to expand. For example, a budding collector with a 250-bottle collection might consider a unit with a 450-bottle capacity. During the past twenty years, I have stored my wines in units manufactured by EuroCave and Traulsen without ever encountering a problem. Other highly rated brands include Breezaire, Le Cache, Vinocraft, Avanti, Haier, Danby, and Marvel. Established refrigerator manufacturers like Sub-Zero and Wolfe have also ventured into the wine storage market.

Whatever size you settle upon, you'll definitely want to do some comparative shopping, because the disparity between brands of storage units can be considerable. Exterior and interior finishes and the specific type of cooling unit employed are some reasons for the price spread; it's almost like buying a car. For example, a 286-bottle unit from Le Cache runs about $3,400, whereas a 700–bottle unit from Vinothèque sells for just $400 more. The popular but diminutive Marvel unit stores only fifty bottles yet costs about $1,700.

At the upper reaches of the climate-controlled cabinet hierarchy is a brand called Chambrair, whose ultradeluxe models, replete with multizone temperature controls, start at about $13,000. They can be further customized according to a client's wishes. Aesthetic factors, such as brushed stainless steel or tinted glass doors, further affect the price of a unit.

Larger collections may necessitate the purchase of several wine units, or the dedication of a basement or unused bedroom to house a climate controlled modular wine room. They come framed and insulated, with a cooling unit and wire racks tailored to the capacity of the collection. Simple modular cellars that accommodate one to two thousand bottles range in price from $3,000 to $8,000 and in size from 7' × 7' × 4' (roughly 200 cubic feet) to 7' × 7' × 10' (roughly 500 cubic feet). Usually, a company

Understand that all cooling units have a shelf life, and that repairing the refrigeration component can prove problematic. For that reason, check out the warranties, which may range from one to five years on all vital parts. And ask to *listen* to a store model. The noise factor is important, especially if you intend to place the unit in your dining or living room. The mechanics of storage are also worth examining. Some models come with racks that can only accommodate 750-ml bottles, leaving owners of magnums and other large-format bottlings in the lurch. Others are configured for back-to-back placement, which saves space but makes retrieval a problem. Still others have racks that are designed specifically for Bordeaux- or Cabernet Sauvignon–shaped bottles, and can damage Burgundy or Pinot Noir labels because the shelves are too tight.

representative will assemble and install the unit for a nominal fee. Two good suppliers are IWA (International Wine Accessories; iwawine.com) and Wine Enthusiast (see page 185). Having a modular wine room also means you'll be able to allot space to stack unopened cases of wine, something I suggest if you have any intention of reselling part of your collection: they command a premium over bottles that have been binned.

No matter what, be sure to install the unit in a space that accommodates proper drainage. Like an air conditioner, the unit's cooling mechanism may dribble water. If you opt to place it aboveground, you may have to reinforce the floor to support the weight of your collection (one hundred cases of wine weighs approximately 2,500 pounds). You might want to check with a contractor first.

If security is a concern, look for a unit with a sturdy Medeco-style lock, or wire your cellar door to a preexisting burglar alarm. More sophisticated still are heating, ventilating, and air conditioning (HVAC) security systems that constantly monitor the climate control of your wine cellar. In the event of a temperature or humidity malfunction, they will inform you

or a caretaker via an electronic pager. According to Tronarch, a Lisle, Illi-
nois-based company that pioneered the technology, the system costs anywhere from $500 to $5,000 to install, depending upon specifics.

If the sky's the limit, there are now a host of architects and designers
who create custom wine cellars with every imaginable embellishment—
from wrought iron fixtures to cedar-trimmed redwood racks to elaborate
tasting rooms and dine-in facilities replete with wine-related antiques,
murals, and even chandeliers. Building a custom wine cellar is expensive
because of the craftsmanship, the sophisticated engineering, and the materials involved (mahogany and marble can be pricey). Costs can run from
$400 to more than $1,000 per square foot—which translates to $200,000
to $500,000 for an average designer cellar.

WINE INSURANCE

Like any valuable, a wine collection should be separately insured against fire,
breakage, and theft if you want to receive full coverage in the event of a dis-
aster. Contrary to what you might assume, just because you have a homeowner's policy doesn't mean your wine cellar is fully covered against all risks.
Most homeowner's policies are subject to a deductible clause, which can
range anywhere from several hundred to several thousand dollars.

If you have a collection worth several thousand dollars or more, there
are two options worth considering: a blanket policy or a stand-alone wine
insurance policy. Both cost the same and either one gives you better coverage than your homeowner's policy. A blanket policy insures your wine
under one lump sum and is appropriate for bottles valued at less than
$10,000 each, the maximum per-bottle limit under most blanket policies.
All you do is total the amount to be insured. No documentation is required. A stand-alone policy itemizes and insures your wines individually,

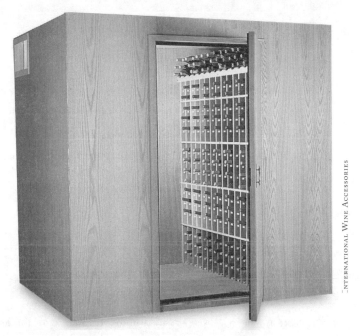

Modular wine unit. This freestanding modular wine cellar is 80.5 × 80.5 × 45.5 inches and holds up to 900 bottles. It's also useful for storing stacks of unopened cases of wine.

127

A basement outfitted for wine storage. Jacques Bergier built his 2,000-bottle capacity wine cellar in an unused storage room in his basement. He started from scratch, insulating the walls, installing racks and bins, and a cooling unit and humidification system. Jacques prudently designed space for individually racked bottles, bins for case lots, and room for unopened cases.

Top Custom Cellar Designers

Professionally designed custom wine cellars come replete with elaborate finishes and flourishes and are not for the average collector. Nor are they particularly cost efficient if you own fewer than 1,500 bottles. But as the trend toward bigger and more costly houses becomes more entrenched in the American lifestyle, the desire to have an extravagant space to showcase a wine collection is becoming more prevalent.

Design Build Consultants Inc.
100 Melrose Avenue, Suite 200, Greenwich, CT 06830
800-820-9463; 203-861-0111
customwinecellars.com
Owner Evan Goldenberg is a licensed architect and builder who began constructing custom wine cellars in 1993. Although he focuses on the Tri-State area, Goldenberg's client list is national. He says that over the past ten years, his projects have gotten bigger and bigger, both in square footage and price. "The decision to build a custom cellar stems from a desire to have a beautiful space to showcase the customer's passion for wine," he says. Although Goldenberg can still produce a two-thousand-bottle custom cellar for around $30,000, it is not uncommon for him to receive commissions for cellars larger than twenty thousand bottles costing in excess of $350,000. Apart from size, differences in price result from the incorporation of elaborate details, shelving, custom finishes, and plastering. A lot of people request an adjacent space to the wine cellar for a tasting or dining room. "I usually set up the area with all the necessary ducting to eventually convert the room into additional cellar space in case the client exceeds the original cellar's capacity."

Apex Wine Cellars & Saunas
15540 Woodinville-Redmond Road, Suite A800, Woodinville, WA 98072
800-462-2714; 888-999-9749; 425-644-1178
apexwinecellars.com

Doug Smith has been in the business of making custom wine cellars for twenty years. His company now has seventeen offices across the country and produces several thousand cellars annually. "When I got started," Smith says, "all a customer would request was a functional, below-ground, temperature- and humidity-controlled cellar without many extras. Nowadays, clients want bigger, more dramatic spaces with windows or glass doors, arches, and pedestals to display a prized bottle." However, Apex can still transform a small closet into a temperature- and humidity-controlled wine cellar for about $3,000 to $5,000. Smith says his average customer owns a one-thousand- to fifteen-hundred-bottle collection that may cost $10,000 to $30,000 to house in a custom environment. At the upper end, Apex has created twenty-five-thousand-bottle custom cellars priced in the six-figure range. "Depending on size, they take anywhere from a day to a week to install," says Smith.

TIXA CUSTOM WINE CELLARS

1265 North Sweetzer Avenue, West Hollywood, CA 90069

323-650-1829

tixawinecellars.com

Owner Jean-France Mercier has been designing custom wine cellars for twenty years. In the eighties, he would typically be approached by collectors who already had a three- to four-thousand-bottle collection. Today, he still gets commissions from seasoned collectors, yet frequently gets inquiries from beginners with only fifty to sixty bottles who intend to make a major commitment to creating a wine cellar. "My client base tended to be older twenty years ago—well into their fifties. Now they are in their mid-forties or younger." There are several Hollywood stars in his client roster (including Sharon Stone and Jason Priestley), but he says their needs are no different than any other serious collector's. Mercier remarks that no wine room he builds is ever the same, whether it's a deluxe, $350,000 model or one that costs one-tenth that amount. "Every situation is different. I am partial to hard redwood racks and often order rare wood from Chile. However, I try to explain that if you own less than fifteen hundred bottles, a custom cellar is not cost efficient. You'll need all the same cooling equipment and ducting as you would for a three-thousand-bottle cellar. Probably the biggest mistake a collector can make is when he tries to build a cellar himself," Mercier cautions. "It rarely works."

CHRISTINE HAWLEY DESIGNS, INC.
155 West 70th Street, New York, NY 10023
212-721-0705, cell 917-750-2224
chawley@optonline.net

Christine Hawley is an accomplished interior designer whose first exposure to wine cellars came in the form of visits to the great chateaus of Bordeaux with her husband, Michael Aaron, CEO of Sherry-Lehmann, the Manhattan wine merchant. She admits to being influenced by the antique French look, and likes to incorporate arches and vaults into her designs, along with wrought-iron racks and bins. Where appropriate, she will employ antique hardware and distressed wooden doors. As an additional flourish, she might surround a stone floor in gravel, which serves to trap humidity as well as add another authentic period touch. Hawley's cellars don't come cheap. They average $1,500 per square foot, and range in price between $250,000 to $1 million. What does a client get for a seven-figure cellar? It might come complete with a dining room and glass doors overlooking the racks, accented by an oversize gilded wood mirror carved with a grape motif that enables guests on the other side of the table to see the cellar's reflection. The most over-the-top request came from a six-foot-six client who insisted the ceiling in his cellar be high enough to accommodate his full height when wearing a cowboy hat and boots!

130

and is suited to collections of expensive items. Individual appraisals are only required for bottles worth $10,000 or more. Many collectors opt for a blended policy, "With a stand-alone for more expensive bottles and a blanket for the less expensive ones." It's incumbent to notify your insurance company of any significant increase in value of your wine collection. If a case of wine is on the books for $2,000 yet has a current value of $6,000, you will still end up underinsured in the event of a loss.

The premium you pay and the exact coverage you get is a function of your specific insurer. Most policies fully cover theft and fire. But what happens if you inadvertently drop and break a magnum of Château Lafite Rothschild 1982 (worth about $1,500) on the way from the cellar to the dining room? Chubb, AIG, and AXA are among the few insurers who cover their policyholders against accidental breakage. No deductibles apply against a covered claim.

When it comes to storage-related insurance, Chubb will provide up to $5,000 in spoilage coverage due to equipment failure. AXA will completely cover damage incurred as a result of mechanical breakdown caused by fire or lightning, but not poor maintenance or equipment malfunction. AIG provides full coverage due to equipment malfunction.

Wine insurance premiums are fairly standard across the country. They run between 42 and 50 cents per $100 of coverage, which means the maximum premium on a $50,000 cellar will be about $250. (Policy holders in California may pay an additional premium of up to 20 percent for earthquake coverage.) However, few insurance companies will issue a blanket or stand-alone or blanket policy for under $500 unless the applicant already has a homeowner's, or automobile policy with the company in question.

Note that most companies require that the insured have a pre-existing central station alarm system for fire and theft.

There is no insurance coverage for a corked or Madeirized bottle.

Wine insurance policies are best taken out through your local broker. For additional information:

AIG: (877) 638-4244 or www.aig.com/gateway/home

AXA: (877) AXA-4-ART or www.axa-art.com/site/contact_ci.html. See also: www.axa-art.co.uk/cwh/cwh010.asp

CHUBB: (908) 903-2000 or email: gdamiano@chubb.com. See also: www.chubb.com/international/canada/englishnf/protecting/wine_protection.html

THOMPSON & PRATT: (877) 334-6327 or e-mail: fineartguy@aol.com

ORGANIZING YOUR CELLAR

∿∿∿∿

No matter whether your cellar takes the form of a 250-bottle, climate-controlled cabinet or an elaborate walk-in storage facility, it is essential to devise a plan for storing, retrieving, and tracking your bottles. There's nothing more disappointing than coming upon an overlooked vintage classic, only to realize that it should have been consumed years ago.

There are bar-coding devices on the market that can record and track the status of every bottle in your collection from acquisition through depletion, such as the one legendary collector and industrialist Bill Koch installed in his cellar. Unless you have a monumental collection, however, a simple spiral notebook, or, better still, a Palm Pilot or laptop computer equipped with a spreadsheet program, will enable you to oversee your inventory. You can sort a database in many different ways—alphabetically, by price, quantity, producer, varietal, location, etc. You can even append your own tasting notes, or cross-reference them against professional scores.

There are also sophisticated wine storage software programs worth considering. Some come packed with user-friendly fields for information retrieval. Others contain vintage ratings, tasting notes, and suggested maturity dates, like the web-based storage guide offered by Vinfolio (vinfolio.com), or Robert Parker's Wine Advisor & Cellar Manager Software, which retails for about $150. A more expensive alternative to cellar management is the sophisticated eSommelier Wine Management Server (esommelier.net). No matter which route you take, it is essential to keep the information current, which means updating your data on a regular basis. Otherwise, the software is of no use to you.

While there is no unequivocal way to lay out your wine cellar, it's essential to have a systematic scheme so specific wines can be readily located. Common sense dictates that you assemble your cellar by place of origin,

wine	vintage	original quantity	remaining	cellar location	cost–date	current replacement cost
Château Léoville-las-Cases	1986	12	8	B – 7	$684–10/95	$2,676

tasting notes

12/1995   Extremely tannic and concentrated. Great potential—needs much more time. Best after 2000? (1 btl. opened)

2/1998   Still very youthful and full-bodied, with pronounced flavor. (1 btl.)

5/2001   Intense and powerful, very rich with a good finish. Approaching drinkability. (1 btl.)

8/2005   Starting to soften up. Great structure. Very smooth. Best to hold off until 2006. (1 btl.)

Organizing your cellar: A sample wine entry. It is essential to record the details of your wine purchases. Keep track of the current and original quantity of each wine, its location in your cellar (the B refers to bin number), the price paid, and date purchased. Where applicable, periodically note the replacement cost of your wine. Individual tasting notes are an important record of a wine's maturation process, and serve as a guideline for future consumption. My Château Léoville-las-Cases is verging on maturity, so I don't think I'll hold back on it much longer.

producer, varietal, and vintage—in just the same way you might organize your computerized inventory. If you are starting from scratch, it's fairly easy to map out what to place in each sector of your cellar. Conversely, if you've neglected to record the details and placement of your purchases, one expedient is to take a pocket tape recorder into the cellar and dictate the names and locations of the wines in your racks, then transfer the information to a spreadsheet. You can then re-sort the bottles accordingly.

Bin labels, which are available at wine specialty stores or online outlets such as IWA (iwawine.com) and the Wine Enthusiast (wineenthusiast.com) allow you to delineate an individual row, rack, or column of wines with a name, number, or letter that corresponds to a particular region, varietal, or vintage. For example, if you have a significant quantity of Napa Valley Cabernet Sauvignons in a particular corner of your cellar, you could designate those sections with appropriate bin labels and then jot down which individual wines are located there.

For smaller cellars fitted with racks, *neck labels* (plastic rings that fit over a bottle's neck) are convenient retrieval devices. You write the wine's name and vintage on the label and then hang it around the bottle's neck so that you can identify it easily without removing it and disturbing the contents each time you want to determine what it is.

It's incredibly easy to forget about an individual bottle stashed away in a large cellar unless you have organized your wines according to their projected consumption date. Keeping a bottle too long is far worse than drinking it too soon. Depending on the size of your cellar, you might want to allocate a rack, a bin, or an entire wall to wines that should be consumed in the short term. You can then subdivide them according to their place of origin, grape type, or producer.

THE BASICS OF TASTING

~\\\\\\~

Stories abound about venerable wine merchants sitting around a dining table tasting wines *blind*—with the labels masked by a brown paper bag. The goal is to see who among them will correctly identify the greatest number of the bottles. While the practice sounds somewhat sadistic, professionals insist that the only objective way to evaluate a wine is without knowing its identity, because such knowledge can prejudice opinions. Most professional wine tastings are conducted blind for this purpose—not to encourage guessing games.

For the home taster, conducting a blind tasting is a great way to focus one's tasting skills, but it's not essential if your objective is simply to learn about the wine. It's better to first grasp the salient characteristics of different varietals and vintages by sampling a series of related bottles in a pressure-free environment in order to develop personal preferences. While there's nothing wrong with comparing Bordeaux to Burgundies, or Petite Syrahs to Zinfandels, most tastings are either *horizontal* (different wines of the same vintage from a specific region or varietal) or *vertical* (different vintages of the same wine). You can also organize a tasting by varietal across several regions, tasting Pinot Noirs from different wine growing regions around the world, for example.

Ultimately, you will build a mental taste bank that will enable you to make intelligent choices—corresponding to your tastes, not someone else's—either at a wine store, at auction, or at a restaurant. It's not that different from an experienced art lover who can roam through a museum or a gallery and identify different paintings at a glance.

The mechanics of tasting are fairly straightforward. Basically, wine is evaluated in the context of its color, bouquet, palate, and aftertaste. You'll want to taste white wines at cellar temperature (about 55° F) and reds at about 65°–70° F. To avoid compromising the wine aromas and flavors, no cologne or perfume should be worn to the tasting.

Take the wineglass by its stem (grasping it by the bowl creates smudges that will obscure the color and warm the wine unnecessarily) and hold it against a white backdrop to examine the color. Assess its faults, if any. Check for clarity or cloudiness. Is the hue bright or flat? Does it show considerable intensity, or is it thin? As red wine ages, it devolves from bright red or purple into brick or mahogany, browning around its edges. White wine will turn progressively golden as it matures. Wines that are the product of a less than perfect harvest will be less intense than those picked under ideal conditions.

Next, rest the glass on the table and swirl it. Once the wine subsides, you'll perceive a clear film that materializes on the side of the glass commonly known as *tears* or *legs*. While much has been made about the significance (and symbolism) of legs, they are simply a measure of the alcoholic content of the wine. The more you see, the higher the volume of alcohol.

Now swirl the glass rigorously and inhale deeply. There's practically no end to the number of aromas you might detect. As with color analysis, first determine whether you sense any *off* odors. Probably the most important taint to recognize is that of a *corked* bottle. A moldy, musty flavor that some say is redolent of wet cardboard is a sure sign that a bottle has been tainted with a chemical called trichloroanisole (TCA). There's no telling when this will happen, and some debate whether a corked wine results from a chemical substance (usually chlorine) in which a fresh cork is washed before bottling or for other reasons altogether.

Corked bottles are fairly common, which explains why there is a growing movement toward twist-off or synthetic corks. It has been estimated that as much as 10 percent of worldwide wine production is affected by spoiled corks. Unfortunately, the corkiness rarely disappears, even after decanting. Your only recourse is to open another bottle (or to send it back, if you're at a restaurant). By the way, sniffing the cork is unlikely to tell you much about the taste of the wine itself, so you can skip this once-revered ritual of wine service.

Oxidized (also know as *Madeirized*) wine results from undue exposure to the air, either during vinification or because the cork has dried out, allowing oxygen to enter the bottle. An oxidized wine will smell somewhat like Sherry or Madeira. Other odors that should function as warnings are barnyard smells that derive from a yeast commonly referred to as *brett*; volatile acidity, which smells a bit like nail polish remover, and is the result of ambient bacteria; and sulfur, which is used as a preservative when harvesting and fermenting grapes and is somewhat redolent of boiled eggs.

On the positive side, there are hundreds—even thousands—of pleasant aromas and scents that you may discern by sniffing a glass of fine wine. So if a red wine is said to possess complex fruits, that might mean blackberry, raspberry, black currant, or cassis, to name just a few. The vocabulary of a professional taster may seem daunting or eccentric (common descriptors like "wet hay," "lead pencil," and "petrol" prove this point) yet such expressions are nonetheless evocative of clearly identifiable smells.

Ultimately, any descriptive that accurately conjures up your impressions of a wine's flavor will do. For starters, try to recall the scents of your spice rack, vegetable garden, and flowerbeds in order to pinpoint the aromas contained in a wine. (There are now even commercially bottled scents to assist the aspiring taster.) There's no need to be nervous if you get confused. Harry Waugh, the famed English wine writer, was once asked whether he ever mistook a Bordeaux for a Burgundy. "Not since lunch," he quipped.

Your nose will actually tell you more about a wine than your mouth, because our sense of taste is actually restricted to four categories: sweet, sour, salty, and bitter. To maximize the impact of a wine on your palate, slosh it around in your mouth, aerating it by taking in deep breaths at the same time. Ideally, keep the wine in your mouth for at least ten seconds before expelling it into a spittoon or slop bowl. (There are no taste buds in the back of your throat, and if you wish to remain level headed during the tasting, it's smart to spit.)

137

Assessing body is best done by analogy. Think of the differences between skim milk, regular milk, and cream when you determine whether a wine is light-, medium-, or full-bodied. To evaluate a wine's length or finish, see how many flavors remain in your mouth five, ten, and fifteen seconds after you have expelled the wine. A wine with a short finish will dissipate fairly quickly, whereas one with a long finish will linger—even up to a full minute.

Wine tasting is an exhaustive subject that has filled scores of books. English wine writer Jancis Robinson is one of the greatest authorities on the subject, and her two tomes, *How to Taste: A Guide to Enjoying Wine* and *Jancis Robinson's Wine Course: A Guide to the World of Wine*, are well worth adding to your library. Kevin Zraly's *Windows on the World Complete Wine Course: A Lively Guide* and Andrea Immer's *Great Wine Made Simple: Straight Talk from a Master Sommelier* are also worth reading.

138

Tasting for the Cellar: Evaluating Your Best Wines

Wine collectors arrive at the tasting table with a specific set of goals. Initially, they taste to learn about different wine regions, grape varieties, and styles. Once they have mastered the ropes, they start tasting to identify complex, cellar-worthy vintages that have a potential for longevity—as opposed to pleasant, everyday bottles that have no shelf life. Cellar-worthy qualities could include a bouquet that gains in nuances as it develops, or a combination of balance, length, concentration, and depth of flavor that only a limited number of wines are capable of delivering. Don't go by price or ratings alone.

A slightly different set of criteria applies to tasting older wines. Evaluating young wines for cellar-worthiness is mainly about potential. With older vintages, the question becomes how much time the wine has left, or whether it is still worth buying. Instead of fruitiness, the pronounced characteristics of older wines may include tobacco, mushrooms, or cedar, compounded by traces of seductive sweetness. Now that the tannins have

No matter what kind of tasting you organize, make sure you have the right equipment. Ideally, you should have enough glasses (and decanters when necessary) so that you don't have to stop the proceedings to wash them. Don't forget to place cocktail napkins around the table, as well as pitchers and water glasses. Make sure your table is topped with a white tablecloth or white placemats against which you can properly assess a wine's color. Guests will need spittoons so that they can spit out the wine once they have tasted it. Bowls containing unsalted crackers or a freshly sliced baguette will enable them to clear their palates. Supply the tasters with a tasting sheet that lists the wines in the order in which they will be tasted, with room for comments.

How many wines to taste is a function of your guest list and your budget. You can count on approximately fourteen pours from the average bottle (fewer if you are serving older wines that have developed sediment). I have attended tastings at which more than one hundred wines were examined over a two-day period (palate fatigue will eventually set in if you get too ambitious and attempt to cover a large array in just one sitting), and others with only ten wines that were wrapped up in a little more than an hour. It's a good idea to hire a wine waiter to assist in the proceedings if you are serving a large number of bottles. At trade tastings there may be as many as five hundred guests; intimate gatherings of about a dozen friends can be far preferable. If you know the participants well, you may also suggest that each one chip in for a portion of the costs.

THE HORIZONTAL TASTING: Strictly speaking, a horizontal tasting is an examination of different wines from the same vintage and wine-producing district. Since vintage quality varies dramatically from region to region, there is no point in comparing a 1994 Napa Valley Cabernet Sauvignon with a counterpart from Margaux or Mendoza unless all you are trying to ascertain is differences in regional style. There's nothing wrong with comparing labels from Napa with Sonoma, or, separately, Pauillac with St.-Estèphe, however, as long as they share the same vintage. Whether you taste a wine blind or with its label exposed is up to you.

There are no rules regarding which vintages or wines to choose. However, most horizontal tastings focus either on classics or new releases. You might want to concentrate on an older vintage of California Cabernet Sauvignon, like 1985, 1987, or 1994, or on a relatively new release, like 2002 Pinot Noir from Burgundy or 2003 from Bordeaux. There's no reason why you cannot examine an off-vintage in the hopes of discovering a sleeper, but generally speaking, it's not worth the bother. Similarly, there's not much point pitting a $20 wine against a $200 bottle, either, so make sure each grouping is similarly priced.

For example, if you want to compare high-ranking bottles of 1997 California Cabernet Sauvignon, your short list might include David Arthur, Diamond Mountain Vineyard, Mount Veeder, Robert Mondavi Oakville, Pride, Spottswoode, and Cornerstone. You will want to assess the wines according to the criteria established in the "Basics of Tasting" and decide on a score (either out of 20 or 100) for each bottle. The fun part is sharing your scores and opinions with your fellow tasters, and eventually stocking up on the wines you like best.

THE VERTICAL TASTING: A vertical tasting is more focused than its horizontal counterpart because it examines only different vintages of the same wine. Yet the purpose of a vertical tasting is similar—to discover personal preferences with the possible aim of laying away a favorite vintage. In addition, it shows how a specific wine evolves over time, which characteristics a particular vintage shares with another, and whether there have been major stylistic changes over the years.

There is no unequivocal way to go about a vertical tasting, but, as with horizontal tastings, there is not much point in examining mediocre wine that does not have significant aging potential. Similarly, unless you are planning a definitive examination of a particular winery, don't include average and below-average vintages: you are better off selecting an array of vintages that fall within predetermined price points that you potentially want to acquire more of or simply want to learn about.

For instance, you could analyze bottlings of Antinori Tignanello from the past decade, a selection of Château Gruaud-Larose from 1975 through 1990, or 1995 to the present. If the sky's the limit, you could set your sights on stellar vintages of legendary Bordeaux first growths like Château Latour 1961, 1966, 1970, 1982, and 1990 (in this instance, you might very well need to pool your resources with your fellow tasters).

A note on purchasing these wines: you can sometimes pick up a mixed lot at auction whose contents will serve as an instant vertical or horizontal tasting. More often, you will have to source retail outlets for relatively recent releases and auction houses that favor small lots of vintage wines so you don't have to acquire a whole case of a specific wine just so you can serve one bottle at your tasting.

Here's an example of a vertical Pétrus tasting I attended in 1985 at a gala event hosted by veteran collector Lloyd Flatt. The notes and ratings are my own, after comparing impressions with fellow tasters.

1945 Bright color, browning edges. Deep, rich bouquet. Very powerful. Hints of cedar on palate. Incredibly complex and rich. 95/100.

1947 Caramel-like bouquet. Pronounced sweetness on the palate. Rich and opulent with considerable ripeness. Still has a long way to go. 98/100.

1948 Good color, rich and round, but falls off quickly. Short after-taste. 85/100.

1949 Good color, big nose with traces of tobacco, velvety palate. Good finish. 95/100.

1950 Best color of the group. Still incredibly youthful, and fresh. Good berry flavors. Full-bodied. Long finish. 98/100.

subsided, does the wine still display evidence of fruit and length? How fresh is it? What about its longevity? An excellent way to learn more about the nuances of older wines is to take advantage of the tastings conducted by auction houses, where you may be able to sample vintage classics before they go on the block. On occasion, fine wine retailers also host vintage retrospectives.

A word about tannins: they are derived from grape skins and seeds as well as from the oak barrel in which wine is aged, and are germane to a red wine's longevity because they act as a preservative. You can detect the presence of tannins on the side of your tongue (think of the puckering sensation created by strong tea). Wine expert and educator Kevin Zraly says that if a wine is overly tannic, you can detect it throughout your mouth—on the sides, on the gums, and on the palate. Typically, a young California Cabernet Sauvignon or Bordeaux is loaded with tannin, which may initially give it a harsh taste. Over time, the tannins dissipate, rendering the wine more harmonious. However, tannins alone are not always a guarantee of quality, because they can mask fruit flavors or the absence of them. Certain vintages of classified Bordeaux, like 1975 (which was initially heralded as one of that decade's greats), never delivered on their initial promise. Their harsh flavor never disappeared, and with few exceptions, 1975s remain a less than stellar drink.

Over the past decade, viticultural research has yielded new solutions to taming tannins' harshness. "The simplest answer lies in delaying the harvest until the grape tannins have ripened," explains vintner John Kongsgaard. "Now, at last, many winemakers are looking at tannin maturity. Ripe tannin is a good idea, and relatively new in the California winemaking consciousness. It's something you have to learn to recognize, as there is no machine to detect it. As they mature, the tannins, and the flavor of the grapes in general, change from something rather vegetable-like to a ripe fruit or even dessert-like flavor.

"With notable exceptions, like the Nebiollos of Piedmont, and maybe Diamond Creek Cabernet Sauvignon in Napa, most wines that are a misery of tannin when young do *not* grow out of their toughness with bottle age," Kongsgaard says. "I believe the really great wines that will have long lives in bottle actually begin as beauties. The idea that they have to be painful as youngsters in order to be great when they are old is nonsense."

Age-Worthiness: The Measure of a Fine Wine

The concept of an age-worthy wine has undergone close scrutiny and reevaluation over the years. In the nineteenth and early twentieth centuries, most classified Bordeaux were aged in wood for as long as five years, which gave them a very high tannin content by today's standards and meant they were generally unapproachable until they had matured another decade or two in bottle. Today, winemakers have reduced the time red wine spends in wood to about twenty-four months or less, making the wine more accessible in its youth. However, modern winemakers tend to age their wines in new oak (their nineteenth-century counterparts did not), which itself has a high tannin content.

The dialectic over how long specific wines should age once bottled continues. I have been lucky enough to sample several vintages of nineteenth-century Château Lafite Rothschild that were still remarkably intact, including an 1864, an 1865, and an 1870. The 1870 Lafite was so tannic in its youth that it was said to be undrinkable until the early twentieth century. Served at a dinner party in 1983, it was remarkably bright, fresh, and complex—no historical curiosity there. In contrast, some 1966 first growths that I mistakenly held on to until 2005 were definitely past their peak when uncorked, despite proper storage.

Based on his extensive experience, James Laube, a senior editor at *Wine Spectator*, has evolved a simple formula for aging: don't overdo it. "For the most part, you're better off drinking your wines young and fresh and on their way up, instead of aging them too long and hoping for a miracle to occur in the bottle," he writes. "I must confess that some of my greatest disappointments have come from buying spanking new wines and then cellaring them too long. . . . Experience tells me most wines are best drunk in their youth. Age wines too long and you're setting yourself up for disappointment. I'd much rather make conservative recommendations than suggest you hold them for too long."

Laube says that sooner is usually better than later with wine because nobody really knows how a given wine or vintage will age. "There are plenty of educated guesses, and if you choose the right wines, the odds may be in your favor. I'm sure that Bordeaux 2000 will be phenomenal. Yet there will be surprises. The longer you wait on a wine, the greater the expectations and the greater the odds that it will turn out to be a dreaded bomb." If you have several wines from the same vintage in your cellar, one foolproof approach is to open a bottle periodically to see how it is showing.

Uncorking and Decanting

There are hundreds of different corkscrews worth considering, and seasoned collectors develop favorites over time (see page 185 for a discussion of some of the best).

When uncorking older wines, be sure to first remove the top of the capsule completely and clean the lip of the bottle with a damp paper towel. If by chance the cork breaks in the process of removing it (a not uncommon occurrence with older wines and vintage ports), the best recourse is to remove the corkscrew and penetrate the cork again at a 45° angle: there is no point in inserting it into the original hole. If, after repeated attempts, you fail to extract the cork, then slowly push it into the bottle and decant the wine with the assistance of a funnel lined with cheesecloth. Alternatively, you can widen the hole in the cork until it is large enough to pour from.

Decanters should be used with caution, attractive as they may be. It was once assumed that all mature wines should be decanted well in advance of serving. Now opinions on the subject are mixed. A young wine may benefit from extra aeration, but not all older wines can safely withstand the additional exposure to the air because the process triggers oxidation. Simply opening a bottle to let it breathe won't accomplish very much, because you cannot properly aerate an entire bottle through such a small opening. You are better off pouring the wine directly into a glass, where there is more surface-to-air contact. If a large amount of sediment has accumulated in the bottle, pour with a very sturdy hand to avoid disturbing it.

You should decant a wine that has thrown a deposit (visible in the bottom of the bottle, often only with the aid of a flashlight). If the wine is no more than twenty to twenty-five years old, it is unlikely that it will suffer from the decanting process. To be on the safe side, decant the wine about one half hour before your guests arrive—no longer. If you are opening a large-format bottle like a magnum or double magnum, you may increase the lead time. Older wines should be decanted just before serving them. Decanting remains a trial-and-error process. If you are planning to open two identical vintage treasures, wine writer Jancis Robinson suggests you decant one and not the other, or open them at different times, as an experiment. That way you'll have a more definitive rule of thumb to go by in the future.

Be sure to stand a bottle upright twenty-four hours ahead of time so that any sediment falls to the bottom. To decant, raise the bottle until it is at a right angle to the lip of the decanter (or, alternatively, place both the bottle and the decanter at right angles to one another) and pour very slowly until the sediment approaches the neck of the wine bottle. Stop. I use an upright flashlight for illumination rather than a candle, because it casts more light. If it appears that a bottle contains a significant amount of sediment, you might want to use a wine funnel equipped with a sieve, or even a plastic kitchen funnel fitted with cheesecloth, to further cut down on the precipitate matter that enters the decanter. Funnels have the added advantage of providing a wider opening to pour through, cutting down on spillage.

Rinse out the decanter with warm water as soon after dinner as possible to avoid stains. For tough stains, use distilled white vinegar. If that doesn't work, try bleach. Either way, remember to thoroughly wash out any residue left by the cleansing agent.

145

PAIRING WINE WITH FOOD

∿∿∿∿

The rules of pairing have been relaxed substantially since the old adage *white wine with fish, red wine with meat* was first prescribed. (For a thorough examination of the subject, see David Rosengarten and Joshua Wesson's book, *Red Wine with Fish: The New Art of Matching Food with Wine*.) Examine your recipe and find a wine of comparable attributes to complement it. Full-bodied wines tend to go best with full-bodied foods; delicate wines generally go best with lighter dishes. And unless your point is to show off the quality of your wine collection, remember there are certainly occasions when a rosé is preferable to Romanée-Conti.

I often serve a Pinot Noir with meaty grilled fish like swordfish, tuna, and halibut. In contrast, I usually find Cabernet Sauvignon and Bordeaux to be too tannic for most seafood, whereas the tannins and complexity are a good match to most cuts of beef, pork and lamb. Devotees of Sauternes suggest that the wine goes well with a larger variety of foods than you would imagine, including lobster, blue cheese, and foie gras.

The spicy flavors of Mexican or American Southwest cooking may call for a quality Zinfandel, like one of the many exciting labels from Helen Turley, or a hearty Tuscan red like Tignanello. Rieslings also work well with intense flavors. Châteauneuf-du-Papes are great palate pleasers that appeal to both dedicated Cabernet Sauvignon and Pinot Noir drinkers. One of the great pleasures of having a diverse collection of wines lies in the ability to match a variety of labels with different foods until you achieve the perfect wedding.

Pairing older wines with food can sometimes be tricky. Notwithstanding the superb 1870 Lafite served with a roast of beef at a gathering of wine collectors in Napa back in 1983, I've often found that most older wines are often best served on their own as an intermezzo—between courses. That's because the delicate flavors of a vintage classic can easily be overpowered by many contemporary recipes. When I served an 1890 Château Lafite on New Year's Eve 1990, I decanted it quickly and poured the wine on its own after the main course and before dessert. Interestingly, in the nineteenth century, classic Bordeaux was most often served after a meal, not with it. The late Baron Edward de Rothschild (a partner in Domaines Barons de Rothschild) told me he preferred very simple foods— roast beef, sliced ham—with fine and rare wines because they don't compete with what's in the bottle.

But his cousin, the late Baron Philippe de Rothschild, owner of Château Mouton-Rothschild, had the final word on wine tasting dinners: "Remember," he told me, "it's the guest list, not the wine list, that counts the most."

147

505

Get him started on the topic of wine collecting, and you'll instantly see how profound an influence Rob Rosania's avocation has had on him. This thirty-five-year-old Manhattan real estate investor reverently views wine as one of the few elements in our society that improves with age. And he has a five-thousand-bottle collection of vintage classics to prove it. "Most things deteriorate over time, or are rendered obsolete by new technology. In contrast, wine equals patience rewarded," he muses. "A well-made, properly aged bottle inevitably makes you contemplate the vintner's art, which, unlike a painting, can be appreciated with several senses—sight, smell, and taste."

The fact that Rosania has assembled a major wine collection in a very short period of time (five years) attests to his passion for fine wine and his determination to acquire the best examples from Bordeaux, Burgundy, and Italy. As with many collectors, it was an exceptional bottle served at dinner that first sparked his interest. In his case, a Tenuta San Guido Sassicaia 1985, one of Tuscany's greatest estate-bottled reds from an extraordinary vintage, made him want to learn more about fine wine.

CREATING HIS CELLAR: Thanks to his Italian heritage, Rosania had a casual exposure to wine from childhood. But Lambrusco and the homemade varieties his family consumed had nothing in common with Italy's best. So he started tasting a broad range of Italian reds in the $30 to $40 range, and then progressed to bottles costing $80 to $90. His first major purchase was a case of the highly rated 1997 Tenuta dell'Ornellaia, which cost about $1,200. Then he started buying other "super-Tuscan" labels like Solaia and Solengo with the idea of laying them down and overseeing their aging process.

Few collectors start off by acquiring Italian wines. Yet like many beginners, Rosania also branched out to explore California Cabernet Sauvignons and experimented with classified Bordeaux. "I couldn't believe what I was tasting," he recalls. When the celebrated 2000 vintage of Bordeaux was offered as a future, he unhesitatingly bought ten to fifteen cases of high-end labels like Château Lafite Rothschild, Mouton-Rothschild, Léoville Las Cases, and Pavie. He stored them in a professional wine warehouse. Then, as now, he keeps the bulk of his collection in storage and has a five-hundred-bottle temperature- and humidity-controlled unit in his home so he can organize impromptu wine events.

BEST BOTTLES: When John Kapon, president of Acker Merrall & Condit, the wine retailer and auctioneer, formed a tasting group, Rosania became an eager participant. Tastings included modern classics like 1982 and 1986 classified Bordeaux as well as vintage treasures such as 1961 and 1959 Latour, Haut-Brion 1955, and La Mission Haut-Brion 1955. When he first tasted the older giants, it was as if a light bulb went on. "They were more elegant, refined, and rounded than anything I had ever experienced," Rosania recalls. "They were also riskier acquisitions, as conditions can vary dramatically in older wines. Nevertheless, I went out on a limb and bought a bottle of 1959 Haut-Brion for $1,000. It was amazing—and amazingly expensive."

Rosania started buying vintage classics in dribs and drabs—a few bottles here, maybe a case there. "Few people come into the rare wine scene and immediately purchase a cellar outright. My collecting is for drinking. I only sell what I choose not to drink or have too much of." Somewhat surprisingly, Rosania admits he doesn't have a specific buying strategy. "My only business plan is to cellar the wines I love so I can drink them with friends. If I only have one bottle of Château Latour, I can only drink it once. So where possible—and affordable—I buy in multiples, so I can sample a wine several times and gauge my impression."

COLLECTING WISDOM: Rosania's advice to collectors at every stage is to follow what their senses tell them, not the score a wine happens to garner in the wine press. He is an advocate of an empirical approach to fine wine. "Experience as much as you can before buying in quantity. Bulking up on California wine is hardly a mistake if you have experienced everything else."

Having sampled many of the world's great wines, Rosania has decided that fine red Burgundy is the benchmark by which all wine should be judged. In the same breath, he admits Burgundies are also the most expensive and hardest to understand—a true challenge. Rosania hasn't abandoned his love of fine Italian bottlings, especially Barolos from renowned producers such as Giacosa, Conterno, and Moscarello. Top Rhône reds and vintage Champagne are also among his favorites.

And as much as Rosania admires fine Burgundies, he hasn't lost his reverence for vintage Bordeaux. "A Bordeaux that is seventy-five years old reaches a state of elegance that is unmatched in anything else," he intones. "It's an amazing amalgam of nature, God, and man."

COLLECTING:
A BRIEF BACKGROUND

〜〜〜〜〜

EVIDENCE OF WINEMAKING HAS VARIOUSLY BEEN TRACED TO ANCIENT
Turkey, Persia, and China, and is thought to have originated anywhere
from 6000 to 8000 BCE. Wine collecting, on the other hand, is a far more
recent phenomenon—largely the product of a newfound global affluence
beginning in the eighteenth and early nineteenth centuries. One could
even argue that today's notion of collecting—accumulating wine for future
drinking pleasure—is an altogether twentieth-century phenomenon.
While it is difficult to substantiate whether our ancestors actually collected wine per se, it is certain that they distinguished between the diverse
varieties and ages of wine available.

In *Vintage: The Story of Wine*, Hugh Johnson writes that as early as
2470 BCE, Egyptians recognized six different appellations of wine. One
thousand years later, when Tutankhamun went to his grave, his sarcopha-
gus was accompanied by thirty-six amphorae of wine, uncovered only in
1922 when his tomb was opened. "The labeling of wine jars was almost as
precise, say, as California labeling today—with the exception of the grape
variety. It specified the year, the vineyard, the owner and the head vintner,"
writes Johnson. More revealing, the amphorae were further differentiated
by vintage: Year Four, Year Five, Year Nine, and Year Thirty-One, suggesting the possibility of a primitive rating system.

In ancient Greece and Rome, select regions were renowned for the
quality of their wine, notably the islands of Chios and neighboring Les-
bos. In *The Romance of Wine*, H. Warner Allen writes with enthusiasm
about a famous banquet staged by Horace at which he served a superb

thirty-five-year-old wine called Massic. Allen also refers to a sumptuous dinner given by Julius Caesar in 46 BCE at which the emperor served four wines at the same repast: Falernian, Chian, Lesbian, and Mamertine Cato.

In the ruins of Pompeii, there is evidence that as many as two hundred bars once flourished in the city, and that different prices were charged according to the quality of the wines. According to Johnson, the Roman equivalent of a first growth was "the miraculous Opimian vintage of 121 BCE. It came from the Falernum vineyard and Amineum vine. It was said to be drinkable even 100 years after the harvest. It was most likely white and sweet."

Insofar as cellar-worthy wine is concerned, one can virtually fast forward from the fall of the Roman Empire in 476 CE to the seventeenth or early eighteenth century, when wines were first bottled in cork-stoppered vessels, allowing the contents to age and to develop more profound nuances of flavor for the very first time. Prior to then, wines were shipped in barrels and decanted as needed. In the absence of a hermetically sealed environment, most wine spoiled within a year, which is why young, "fresh" wine actually cost considerably more than older wine.

According to Stephen Brook, author of *Bordeaux: People, Power and Politics*, the draining of the Médoc marshes in the late 1600s by Dutch engineers, and technical advances such as the use of sulfur dioxide to prevent wine from oxidizing and to inhibit bacteria growth, paved the way for fine French wine as we know it today. Brook adds that by the early eighteenth century, the leading estates of Bordeaux—Châteaux Haut-Brion, Latour, Lafite, and Margaux, "were all established in London as reliable, if costly brands." Other coveted labels included Chambertin from Burgundy and Hermitage from the Rhône.

The wines of that era differed significantly from their contemporary counterparts. Most clarets (the name is derived from the French *clairet*, a rosé-colored wine whose juice had only brief contact with the grape skins) were quite delicate, and they were often blended with Syrah from the Côtes du Rhône or Alicante from Spain to provide body. The process was known as *hermitagé* and the practice, although it diminished in popularity, continued until the 1940s. The doctored Bordeaux sold in England and the Bordeaux consumed in Bordeaux probably did not have much in common. Originally, there was no stigma attached to ameliorating a wine in this way, though by the twentieth century it was cause for scandal.

Until the outbreak of the Civil War, Americans remained avid buyers of Bordeaux. During the 1850s, the United States was said to be Bordeaux's principal client. Excavations performed in 1984 in lower Manhattan have unearthed remnants of a prominent wine merchant's shop belonging to Anthony Winan, Esq. (it was destroyed in the Great Fire of 1835). Archeologists discovered wine bottles that bore glass seals embossed with the word LEOVILLE (a highly celebrated vineyard and the progenitor of Châteaus Léoville Las Cases and Léoville-Barton), still packed in crates imported from England.

A study of the meaning of the French word *sommelier* tells us that by 1690, important households in France engaged a servant who was in charge of the place settings and who prepared the wine. However, the French Revolution took its toll, largely eliminating the primary clientele for fine wines. Although the French remained extremely proud of their vinous patrimony, it was the English who assembled the great wine cellars of the nineteenth century.

By the early 1800s, drinking had become quite fashionable in Regency London. Venetia Murray, author of *An Elegant Madness: High Society in Regency England*, writes that "a three-bottle man was not an unusual guest at table. It was considered rather dashing to spend the better part of life in a state of semi-intoxication, a proof of masculinity. The only thing that saved them was drinking very slowly and out of very small glasses."

British monarchs were particularly partial to Champagne, which fast became the drink of preference at garden parties, picnics, and racing events. The Russian Czars became devotees of Roederer Cristal, primarily because it was packaged in a crystal bottle. It was initially produced for the

The collecting process was greatly enhanced by the 1855 Bordeaux Classification, which ranked sixty-one chateaus according to their historical sales performance (though not necessarily their quality) during the previous twenty years. For the *Exposition Universel de Paris*, Napoleon III instructed Bordeaux *négociants* and merchants to undertake a classification system, which broke down the leading French *châteaux* into first, second, third, fourth, and fifth "growths." Within each of the five rankings, the wines were listed—not alphabetically, but rather by performance.

The classifications amounted to an officially sanctioned hierarchy, and wineries in the upper echelons of the grading system felt empowered to charge more for their products than those at lower levels. While today select chateaus have outperformed their original ranking, the 1855 classification remains very much intact. Only Château Mouton-Rothschild has managed to elevate itself from its original position as a second growth to first growth status. In 1932, a classification listing of nearly two hundred *crus bourgeois* was also prepared, which was further divided in 2003 into *Cru Bourgeois Exceptionnel* (the top ranking group), *Cru Bourgeois Superior*, and basic *Cru Bourgeois*.

The 1855 listings were primarily comprised of wines from the Médoc, with the exception of Château d'Yquem, a *premier grand cru* from Sauternes, and Château Haut-Brion, a first growth from Graves. Otherwise, the chateaus of Pomerol, Graves, and St.-Emilion were excluded from the ranking. Since then, the latter two regions have created their own classifications in 1959 and 1996, respectively.

Premiers Crus Classés (First Growths)	*Deuxièmes Crus Classés* (Second Growths)
Château Lafite-Rothschild, Pauillac	Château Rauzan-Ségla, Margaux
Château Latour, Pauillac	Château Rauzan-Gassies, Margaux
Château Margaux, Margaux	Château Léoville Las Cases, St. Julien
Château Haut-Brion, Pessac, Graves (since 1986, Pessac Leognan)	Château Léoville-Poyferré, St. Julien
Château Mouton-Rothschild, Pauillac (since 1973)	Château Léoville-Barton, St. Julien
	Château Durfort-Vivens, Margaux

Château Gruaud-Larose, St. Julien
Château Lascombes, Margaux
Château Brane-Cantenac,
  Cantenac-Margaux
Château Pichon-Longueville Baron,
  Pauillac
Château Pichon Longueville-
  Lalande, Pauillac
Château Ducru-Beaucaillou,
  St.-Julien
Château Cos d'Estournel,
  St.-Estèphe
Château Montrose, St.-Estèphe

Troisièmes Crus Classés
(Third Growths)

Château Kirwan, Cantenac-
  Margaux
Château d'Issan, Cantenac-
  Margaux
Château Lagrange, St.-Julien
Château Langoa-Barton, St.-Julien
Château Giscours, Labarde-
  Margaux
Château Malescot St. Exupéry,
  Margaux
Château Cantenac-Brown,
  Cantenac-Margaux
Château Boyd-Cantenac, Cantenac-
  Margaux
Château Palmer, Cantenac-
  Margaux
Château La Lagune, Ludon-Haut-
  Médoc
Château Desmirail, Margaux
Château Calon-Ségur, St.-Estèphe
Château Ferrière, Margaux

Château Marquis d'Alesme-Becker,
  Margaux

Quatrièmes Crus Classés
(Fourth Growths)

Château St. Pierre, St.-Julien
Château Talbot, St.-Julien
Château Branaire-Ducru, St.-Julien
Château Duhart-Milon, Pauillac
Château Pouget, Cantenac-Margaux
Château La Tour-Carnet, St.-
  Laurent-Haut-Médoc
Château Lafon-Rochet, St.-Estèphe
Château Beychevelle, St.-Julien
Château Prieuré-Lichine,
  Cantenac-Margaux
Château Marquis-de-Terme,
  Margaux

Cinquièmes Crus Classés (Fifth
Growths)

Château Pontet-Canet, Pauillac
Château Batailley, Pauillac
Château Haut-Batailley, Pauillac
Château Grand-Puy-Lacoste,
  Pauillac
Château Grand-Puy-Ducasse,
  Pauillac
Château Lynch-Bages, Pauillac
Château Lynch-Moussas, Pauillac
Château Dauzac, Labarde-Margaux
Château Mouton-Baronne-Philippe
  (now Château d'Armailhac),
  Pauillac
Château du Tertre, Arsac-Margaux
Château Haut-Bages-Libéral,
  Pauillac

Château Pédesclaux, Pauillac

Château Belgrave, St.-Laurent-
Haut-Médoc

Château de Camensac, St.-Laurent-
Haut-Médoc

Château Cos-Labory, St.-Estèphe

Château Clerc-Milon-Rothschild,
Pauillac

Château Croizet-Bages, Pauillac

Château Cantemerle, Macau-Haut-
Médoc

Cru Bourgeois Exceptionnel

Château ChasseSpleen, Moulis

Château Haut Marbuzet, St-
Estèphe

Château Labegorce Zédé, Margaux

Château Les Omles de Pez, St-
Estèphe

Château de Pez, St-Estèphe

Château Phélan-Ségur, St-Estèphe

Château Potensac, Médoc

Château Poujeaux, Moulis

Château Siran, Margaux

Cru Bourgeois Superieur
87 Châteaus, including these
standouts

Château D'Angludet, Margaux

Château Coufran, Haut-Médoc

Château Glana, St. Julien

Château Meyney, St-Estèphe

Château Pibran, Pauillac

Cru Bourgeois
151 Châteaus

SAUTERNES-BARSAC

Grand Premier Cru
(Great First Growth)

Château d'Yquem

Premiers Crus Classés
(First Growths)

Château La Tour-Blanche

Château Lafaurie-Peyraguey

Château Clos Haut-Peyraguey

Château de Rayne-Vigneau

Château Suduiraut

Château Coutet

Château Climens

Château Guiraud

Château Rieussec

Château Rabaud-Promis

Château Sigalas-Rabaud

Deuxièmes Crus Classés
(Second Growths)

Château de Myrat

Château Doisy-Daëne

Château Doisy-Dubroca

Château Doisy-Védrines

Château d'Arche

Château Filhot

Château Broustet

Château Nairac

Château Caillou

Château Suau

Château de Malle

Château Romer-du-Hayot

Château Lamothe

Château Lamothe-Despujols

1959 GRAVES CLASSIFICATION

Château Bouscaut, Cadaujac
Château Haut-Bailly, Pessac-
    Léognan
Château Carbonnieux, Pessac-
    Léognan
Domaine de Chevalier, Pessac-
    Léognan
Château de Chevalier, Pessac-
    Léognan
Château de Fieuzal, Pessac-Léognan
Château d'Olivier, Pessac-Léognan
Château Malartic-Lagravière,
    Pessac-Léognan
Château La Tour-Martillac, Martillac
Château Smith-Haute-Lafitte,
    Martillac
Château Haut-Brion, Pessac-
    Léognan
Château La Mission-Haut-Brion,
    Talence
Château Pape-Clément, Pessac
Château Latour-Haut-Brion, Talence

Classified White Wines of Graves

Château Bouscaut, Cadaujac
Château Carbonnieux, Pessac-
    Léognan
Domaine de Chevalier, Pessac-
    Léognan
Château d'Olivier, Pessac-Léognan
Château Malartic-Lagravière,
    Pessac-Léognan
Château La Tour-Martillac,
    Martillac
Château Laville-Haut Brion,
    Talence

Château Couhins-Lurton, Vilenave
    d'Ornan
Château Couhins, Vilenave d'Ornan
Château Haut-Brion Blanc, Pessac-
    Léognan

ST. EMILION 1996 CLASSIFICATION

Premiers Grands Crus Classés (A)

Château Ausone
Château Cheval-Blanc

Premiers Grands Crus Classés (B)

Château Angélus
Château Beau Séjour Bécot
Château Beauséjour-Duffaut La
    Garrosse
Château Belair
Château Canon
Clos Fourtet
Château Figeac
Château la Gaffelière
Château Magdelaine
Château Pavie
Château Trottevieille

Grands Cru Classé

Château l'Arrosée
Château Balestard-La-Tonnelle
Château Bellevue
Château Bergat
Château Berliquet
Château Cadet-Bon
Château Cadet-Piola
Château Canon-la-Gaffelière
Château Cap-de-Mourlin
Château Chauvin

Château la Clotte
Château la Clusière
Château Corbin
Château Corbin-Michotte
Château la Couspaude
Couvent des Jacobins
Château Curé-Bon
Château Dassault
Château la Dominique
Château Faurie-de-Souchard
Château Fonplégade
Château Fonroque
Château Franc-Mayne
Château Grand-Mayne
Château Grand-Pontet
Château les Grandes-Murailles
Château Guadet St.-Julien
Château Haut-Corbin
Château Haut Sarpe
Clos des Jacobins
Château Lamarzelle
Château Laniote
Château Larcis-Ducasse
Château Larmande
Château Laroque
Château Laroze
Château Matras
Château Moulin du Cadet
Clos de l'Oratoire
Château Pavie-Decesse
Château Pavie-Macquin
Château Petit Faurie de Soutard
Château le Prieuré

Château Ripeau
Château St.-Georges-Côte-Pavie
Clos St.-Martin
Château la Serre
Château Soutard
Château Tertre-Daugay
Château La Tour-Figeac
Château la Tour-du-Pin-Figeac
   (Giraud-Bélivier)
Château la Tour-du-Pin-Figeac
   (Moueix)
Château Troplong-Mondot
Château Villemaurine
Château Yon-Figeac

Grand Cru: Approximately
Six Hundred Chateaus

POMEROL

159

The wines of Pomerol have never
been classified. However, its top
performers are

Châteaux Pétrus
Le Pin
Châteaux La Conseillante
Gazin
Lafleur
Lafleur-Pétrus
Latour-à-Pomerol
Petit-Village
Trotanoy
Vieux-Château-Certan

royal court on an exclusive basis, and Russia remained the principal export market for Cristal until the 1917 Revolution.

According to Hugh Johnson, "Then as now, there was a good deal of snobbery about wine, and connoisseurs were willing to pay comparatively high prices. At a sale of the Duke of Queensberry's effects in 1811, a particularly fine Tokay was sold for £84 per dozen quarts—or £7 per bottle. The Duke of Cumberland's cellar proved that good wine was a major expense: Champagne 11 to 12 guineas per dozen, Hermitage 14 guineas, and Port between £4 10s and £5 5s."

The naturally cool and damp cellars of England's landed aristocracy provided ideal conditions for the storage and longevity of fine wine. Perhaps the most extraordinary legacy of nineteenth-century wine collecting is the quantity of superb bottles that have survived into the twenty-first century—often in great condition. One of the most famous collections to go on the block was the cellar of Glamis Castle in Scotland (the family home of the Earls of Strathmore and Kinghorne), first offered at Christie's in 1971. Among the highlights were forty-one magnums of Château Lafite Rothschild 1870 (out of an original cache of forty-six). During the past decade, more than a dozen Glamis magnums have resurfaced at auction at prices ranging from $20,700 to $32,000 each. Thirty-five years ago, they each cost about $100.

It is still a matter of debate whether the great collections of the late nineteenth and early twentieth centuries were ever viewed as such by their creators. In an interview with Michael Broadbent, chairman emeritus of Christie's wine department (who oversaw the disposition of numerous nineteenth-century classics), he told me there is not much evidence to suggest their owners were actually buying to collect. "Rather, they bought simply in order to drink. Aristocrats and the moneyed elite who entertained on a grand sale wanted to serve top-quality wine.

"Some individuals, like Lord Rosebery, whose mother was a Rothschild, may have been involved in the selection process," he says. "Others probably deferred to their butlers. One reason they may have left so much wine behind is that they accumulated more wine than they could possibly drink. And like many of us, they didn't open their very best bottles except for special occasions or special guests, creating an overage."

Much as California wines are increasingly commanding center stage in today's world wine markets, it's worth noting that even a century ago, select American wines already had a strong international following. At a global wine competition held in Paris in 1889, California wines won twenty out of thirty-four medals. At the Paris exposition of 1900, wineries such as Gundlach-Bundschu and Beringer were showered with critical acclaim.

Unfortunately, America was the source of a destructive influence on the world wine scene: phylloxera, an aphid that attacks the roots of a grapevine to devastating effect. While American rootstalks were generally immune to the disease, their European counterparts were not. American vine cuttings exported to France started an outbreak in 1878 that became epidemic. Thousands of acres of vineyards in France were destroyed, many never to be replanted again. Ultimately, vintners grafted their vines onto American rootstocks in order to protect their vineyards from phylloxera.

It has been suggested that, from a collecting standpoint, wines produced in the post-phylloxera era have never achieved the same heights as their predecessors. In 1920, the famed British wine writer and scholar George Saintsbury wrote that post-phylloxera wines mature more quickly and have a shorter lifespan than their pre-phylloxera counterparts. He cites the examples of great pre-phylloxera vintages such as 1875 and 1878, and the finest of them all, 1864.

I have sampled several examples of pre-phylloxera Lafite more than a century after the wines were produced, and there is no question that these mid- to late-nineteenth-century vintages are outstanding. But it remains to be seen whether, as Sainsbury suggests, modern clarets have lost their polish. We may have to wait another fifty years for the answer. It is still possible to find pre-phylloxera wines at auction (notably from Châteaux Lafite

Rothschild, Margaux, and Latour), although they tend to cost a minimum of $2,000 per bottle.

From an American standpoint, access to fine wine virtually ground to a halt with the enactment of Prohibition in 1919. Shipments of wine from Europe and domestic wine production were both declared illegal. Ironically, the consumption of alcohol (as opposed to its procurement) was not deemed a crime. In anticipation of the Volstead Act, which gave the Eighteenth Amendment (which established Prohibition) legislative teeth, some followed writer H. L. Mencken's lead: he allegedly sold his Studebaker and invested the proceeds in a wine cellar. Otherwise, the only recourse for anyone who wished to partake in fine wine was to frequent posh speakeasies like the 21 Club in Manhattan, which had invested in a legendary wine cellar.

In the post-Prohibition era, celebrated merchants like Sam Aaron, Frank Schoonmaker, and Alexis Lichine preached the gospel of wine, striving to convince their clients of the virtues of creating a personal wine cellar. Anyone prepared to listen would have made a windfall with vintages like 1929, 1937, 1945, 1947, and 1949, which were laughably cheap compared to recent releases. In those days you didn't have to be rich to buy Château Pétrus; you simply had to know what it was.

The 1959 and 1961 harvests in Bordeaux were eye openers, heralded for the first time by the popular American press and awakening the public to the potential drinking pleasure of spectacular French vintages. Meanwhile in California, a new breed of vintners led by Robert Mondavi, Jamie Davies, Mike Grgich, and Warren Winiarski trail-blazed the creation of boutique wineries that emphasized concentrated flavors. Some say the Paris Tasting of 1976 (at which American Chardonnays and Cabernet Sauvignons bested their French counterparts) was a clarion call to investment bankers and entrepreneurs, some of whom traded in their briefcases for pruning sheers. Today, there are 2,500 wineries in California, ten times the number there were just twenty-five years ago.

It's easy to take wine auctions for granted now that they have become so ingrained in the fine wine distribution system. Christie's debuted its

London wine department in 1966 under the aegis of Michael Broadbent, whose genius for marketing and flair in the salesroom generated serious interest for what had hitherto been a somewhat arcane pastime. Sotheby's followed suit in 1970. Those early auctions attracted a small coterie of American buyers who ultimately became some of the country's top collectors: Lloyd Flatt of New Orleans, Lenoir Josey of Houston, Tawfiq Khoury of San Diego, Dr. Marvin Overton of Dallas, and Barney Rhodes of Napa, California. Drawn together by their common passion for wine, they have, over the years, staged definitive tastings of priceless Bordeaux from Châteaux Pétrus to Haut-Brion, which they offered gratis to their guests.

"At the time," recalls Lloyd Flatt, "We had nothing to go by other than our own palates. It was a great way to learn about fine and rare wine." Michael Broadbent had yet to write *The Great Vintage Wine Book*, Marvin Shanken had yet to buy the *Wine Spectator*, and Robert Parker was still in law school.

Between 1990 and 2005, commercial U.S. auction revenues rose from just under $11 million to $166 million. Nine firms currently conduct upwards of forty sales per year. As recently as 1980, however, total auction proceeds for the year amounted to only $618,000—and that all derived from a single sale conducted in San Francisco by Heublein, Inc., the wine and spirits conglomerate.

Billed as the "Premiere National Auction of Rare Wines," the legendary annual auction was conducted in major American cities between 1969 and 1983. Orchestrated by Heublein executives Sandy McNally and Irving Dobrow and presided over by Christie's U.K. wine director Michael Broadbent, it was the only exposure domestic wine collectors had to the auction process until Christie's settled in Chicago in 1982.

The annual Heublein auction presented an opportunity not only to acquire collectible wines, but also to learn about them. Their dazzling pre-sale tastings resembled a fine wine road show that traveled around the country, with prominent wine authorities officiating. The auctions themselves drew a joyful mixture of knowledge-thirsty neophytes and seasoned collectors. In retrospect, the sales engendered a sense of camaraderie notably absent from today's business-like affairs.

"We were pioneering, and it was a good time," recalls the peripatetic Broadbent (now a global wine lecturer and senior consultant to Christie's since handing over the reigns to the wine department). "The sales were very serious, but much more fun and creative because there weren't any models to follow." Sandy McNally produced illustrated catalogs based on Christie's prototypes, which grew more and more elaborate as the years passed. For an extra touch of theater, Broadbent would appear on the podium wearing a morning suit with a crisp red carnation in his lapel.

My overriding recollection of the four Heublein sales I attended, in Atlanta, Chicago, Boston, and Los Angeles, was the undercurrent of electricity the well-dressed crowd seemed to exude. In an era before faxes and cell phones, absentee bidding was less of a factor than it is today. Big-time collectors attended a sale in person and didn't shy away from media attention. In fact, Broadbent would usually identify bidders by name (not by paddle number) as they openly vied for Heublein's well-cellared treasures. Equally revealing was the crowd's adulation for Broadbent himself. At a sale's conclusion, successful bidders rushed the podium for a brief audience with the exhausted auctioneer (Broadbent would conduct the entire auction without backup), many clutching Heublein catalogs or copies of his *Great Vintage Wine Book* and hoping for an autograph.

Broadbent recalls occasional show-stopping moments, like when André Tchelistcheff, the doyen of Napa Valley winemakers, decanted a bottle of Château Lafite 1899 before a hushed Heublein crowd. Not realizing his microphone was connected, he blurted out his now infamous assessment: "Appreciating an old wine is like making love to an old lady; it is possible . . . but requires a bit of imagination." Risqué for 1971.

The 1970s were also a time when many of the great U.K. cellars went on the block. Some of these wines were eventually consigned to Heublein, commanding record prices that have never been exceeded. In 1978, a jeroboam of Lafite Rothschild 1864 was snapped up by Memphis

Michael Broadbent presiding over a Christie's London wine auction in the mid-1980s. Note the formal composition of the salesroom and the attire—a sea of suits, typical of auctions at that time.

restaurateur John Grisanti for $18,000, and a year later, Charles Mara, a wine merchant from Syracuse, bid an unprecedented $28,000 for a single bottle of Lafite 1806. The record $2,100 paid in 1983 for a bottle of Beaulieu Vineyards Private Reserve Cabernet Sauvignon 1946 still stands.

Although detractors complained that Heublein's estimates were inflationary and its prose hyperbolic, most lots were rather accessible, especially when compared to today's prices. In 1971, a case of six magnum of Château Pétrus 1947 commanded $740, and Château Mouton-Rothschild 1945 was $610 per dozen (the former now sells for $14,950 per magnum, while the latter routinely commands about $60,000 to $100,000 per case).

The Heublein auctions demonstrated a real demand for an alternative means of acquiring fine and rare wine, a fact that was not lost on Broadbent, who, by the advent of the 1980s, was surveying the landscape for Christie's. Along the way, he helped launch Robert Mondavi's pet project, the Napa Valley Wine Auction, which debuted in 1981 with an augury: a staggering $32,000 hammer price for a barrel of "Napamedoc" Cabernet Sauvignon 1979 (soon to be rechristened Opus One).

In 1982, Christie's established its first full-time wine department in the United States, situating it in Chicago primarily because prominent members of Manhattan's retail wine trade had obtained injunctions preventing Christie's from auctioning wine in New York State. Recalls Michael Davis, who joined Christie's wine department soon after its inception, "The early auctions were as exciting as any wine event could be. The sales became instant destinations, and people flew in from all over to attend them."

Davis nostalgically recollects gala pre-sale dinners organized with the Chicago Wine Company. The wine list for one 1983 fete included DRC Romanée-Conti 1970, Beaulieu Vineyards Private Reserve Cabernet Sauvignon 1968, Château Cheval-Blanc 1947, Château d'Yquem 1967, and Taylor Vintage Port 1927—all for $195. Such dinners have gone the way of $100 bottles of Mouton-Rothschild 1982.

Davis's assessment of his early sales is more measured. "There were some phenomenal collections, but also some marginal ones. Bidders were less sophisticated and discerning than today. The vast majority of the wines on offer were French—including some outstanding old Bordeaux—but also some off-vintages. Vintage port was a much bigger phenomenon, and California lots were virtually nonexistent: at most, there was an occasional case of Mondavi Private Reserve," he recalls.

It wasn't long, however, before collectors intent on bolstering their cache of California Cabernets found a new suppplier. Butterfield & Butterfield, the San Francisco auction firm (now known as Bonhams & Butterfields) inaugurated a wine department in 1985. Bruce Kaiser joined the following year. "Historically," Kaiser remembers, "we offered twice the amount of California wine as the competition. Over the years, we tried to change the way people looked at California wines by getting them to think of Heitz or Ridge in context of Château Latour or Palmer."

THE NEW AUCTION

~\\\\\\~

Once the euphoria surrounding the country's first wine auction ventures had subsided, events moved swiftly. Late in 1993, New York State finally passed legislation permitting commercial wine auctions. Some of the first licenses were issued to the very retailers who had blocked the legislation a decade before. (Under New York State law, wine can only be auctioned in conjunction with a licensed retailer of ten years' standing.) Today's collectors haven't lost their passion for the pursuit—and the sales statistics prove it. It is remarkable how seamlessly wine auctions have integrated themselves into the fine wine pipeline. Live wine auctions are a monthly event in the United States, a biweekly occurrence in England, and a daily phenomenon online.

When Morrell & Company, the Manhattan retailer, held New York's first wine auction in 1994, a crowd of five hundred packed the ballroom of the Pierre Hotel to witness the 944-lot sale generate an unprecedented $516,000. Legalization couldn't have been timelier. In 1994, America was emerging from a recession, and as financial markets began to recover, an army of cash-rich collectors descended on Manhattan auction houses to spend their disposable incomes on prestigious case-lots of wine.

The arrival of Sotheby's, Christie's, and their retail affiliates in the American wine market energized what had been a sleepy process elsewhere in the country and transformed a relatively arcane avocation into a glamorous pastime. Sotheby's entered the fray that fall with Manhattan retailer Sherry-Lehmann and garnered $1.5 million, only to be eclipsed by Zachys-Christie's $1.8 million auction the following spring.

Approximately $35 million worth of fine and rare wine was auctioned worldwide in 1994, most of it in England. By 2005, America accounted for $106 million, nearly 75 percent of the international total. The *Wine Spectator* Auction Index, which tracks more than 150 commonly traded collectible wines on a semi-annual basis, rose from a base of 100 in 1994 to 221 by the end of 2005. The average hammer price per bottle listed in the index increased from $135 to $250 during the same time frame.

Record prices that seemed preposterous in the early 1990s— $112,500 for a case of Mouton-Rothschild 1945, $24,150 for a dozen bottles of Beaulieu Vineyards Private Reserve Cabernet Sauvignon 1951, or $16,425 for twelve bottles of DRC La Tâche 1990 (sold on the Internet, no less)—became benchmark statistics by decade's end.

In May 1997, Sotheby's sale of Sir Andrew Lloyd Webber's collection raked in a record $6 million. Five cases of Pétrus, Cheval-Blanc, and Latour-à-Pomerol from the highly acclaimed 1947 vintage fetched a staggering $57,730 each. The impact of celebrity sellers drew similar consignments out of the cellar. Just four months later, Christie's rewrote the record book. Its $11 million "*Grands Crus*" sale featured two of the most expensive wines ever sold at auction: a jeroboam of Mouton-Rothschild 1945 for $114,614 and an imperial of Cheval-Blanc 1947 for $109,324.

By the third quarter of 1997, the *Wine Spectator* Auction Index had soared from its 1994 base rate of 100 to 194. But an October collapse in world financial markets that struck Far Eastern economies most severely would soon have a devastating effect on the fine wine market. Buyers in Hong Kong and Singapore (who had represented as much as 30 percent of the wine collecting public) simply vanished.

Although the Dow Jones soon recovered its equilibrium, the Auction Index continued a downward slide, bottoming out at 146 in the third quarter of 1998. Prices for first growths from stellar vintages such as 1990, 1989, and 1982 in particular underwent a major correction, dropping by as much as 50 percent from the 1997 peak. In retrospect, it was a buyer's market, and astute bidders who took advantage of the opportunities broadened their positions at a discount.

Bordeaux hit a slump, but a new breed of California wines (popularly referred to as *cults* because of the worshipful following they spawned) soon became the darling of the auction salesroom. Limited-production, high-quality labels like Screaming Eagle, Colgin, Harlan, and Bryant Family soon vied in popularity—and price—with even the most sought-after vintages of Domaine de la Romanée-Conti and Pétrus. Some collectors scoffed at the instant acclaim these upstart wines achieved, not to mention their extravagant prices, but the cult wine category has continued to flourish.

The cults' dramatic potential was underlined at Zachys-Christie's inaugural "California Only" sale in June 1998, when a dozen bottles of Colgin Cabernet Sauvignon Herb Lamb Vineyard 1994 sold for a record $16,100. At the same auction, Screaming Eagle Cabernet Sauvignon 1994 commanded $1,225 per bottle. "Cult wines have become trophies that you buy to brag about," observed behavioral economist Richard Thaler at the time.

The momentum established by the cults and select Burgundies seemed to have a trickle-down effect on the rest of the wine auction market as 1999 came to a close. Millennium madness was also a major factor in the upturn, and it produced an outpouring of impeccable consignments. The $14.4 million total Sherry-Lehmann achieved at Sotheby's "Millennium Sale," held in November 1999, still stands as the highest wine auction total to date. The sale was rife with record prices; some of them—like a case of Henri Jaboulet's legendary Hermitage La Chapelle 1961 procured for $41,400—sold at nearly double their estimates. It demonstrated that exceedingly rare wines, like great works of art, could still provoke feverish bidding. The "Millennium Sale" also proved that collectors were prepared to pay a huge premium provided the provenance was right, a trend that has continued ever since.

Unlike 1997, when trade buyers tended to corner most of the parcels, few of the large lots on offer today go to a single buyer. Instead, they are offered case by case (often to the chagrin of auctioneer) to disparate individuals. "The speculating party is over," says New Jersey collector Charles Klatskin. "Prices are already high, making the prospect of a quick turnover a virtual impossibility. There is no major sign of inflation in sight to fuel expectations. Now if you are playing the fine wine game it's for drinking, not investing."

Compeition for product has become fiercer as more auctions are now conducted by a greater number of houses. That's a major benefit for consignors of important cellars, who are now in a preferred position to negotiate commissions.

Another challenge to traditional firms is coming from dot-coms, which are luring personnel and collectors away from the brick-and-mortar variety. Sophisticated software makes it easier to research wines online and to receive instant notification when outbid at auction. Lower commissions, automated incremental bidding, and the option of purchasing partial lots make the process potentially less expensive. Dozens of auction websites compete for the wine collector's attention (see page 103, "Wine on the Web"). It's worth noting, however, that several auctioneers who left brick-and-mortar firms for Internet careers have since returned to their former venues.

THE AUCTION SCENE TODAY

~\\\\\\~

As the wine auction market has matured, its structure has polarized. Unprecedented supply—and demand—for the finest and rarest bottlings has essentially produced two separate markets: a high-end forum for collectors with very deep pockets who duel over trophy bottles, and a more accessible arena in which bidders can snap up decent, everyday wines at more reasonable prices. That's good news for collectors looking to make purchases for around $40 to $60 per bottle.

Two dramatic illustrations of the current mania for rare bottlings occurred early in 2006. Acker Merrall & Condit conducted a $10.64 million auction—the highest sum ever generated by a single-owner cellar belonging to an American. Six magnums of DRC Romanée-Conti 1971 sold for a record $136,275, 12 bottles of DRC Romanée-Conti 1962 fetched $118,500, and a case of Château Latour à Pomerol 1961 also brought $118,500.

Barely a month later, NYWinesChristie's conducted a "finest & rarest" sale, where the average price per lot was $22,000—about ten times the average hammer price at a typical wine auction. Five lots surpassed the $100,000 mark, notable six magnums of DRC Romanée-Conti 1985, which commanded $170,375—the highest price ever paid for a case of wine at a commercial auction.

Young Burgundies generally remain a tough sell and, in turn, a potential buying opportunity for the collector. But with an onslaught of highly anticipated new releases from Bordeaux, Burgundy, and California soon to enter the market, these friendly buying conditions are unlikely to persist. The rise in the value of the euro against the dollar means that higher replacement costs for French wines may ultimately impact auction prices. For the budget-conscious, the consensus among auction experts is that 1995 and 1996 Bordeaux represent relatively good value—for now.

Proof of the ongoing strength of the American auction market was the phenomenal reception achieved by the country's newest auction firm, Hart Davis Hart in Chicago, which debuted with a $2 million sale in January 2004. Hart Davis Hart Wine Company's inaugural wine auction drew a crowd of 250 people to its salesroom at the Chicago Athletic Association. "That's more than I've seen for years either here in Chicago or in New York," enthused Michael Davis, the firm's president and CEO. What's more, bidding from the floor was very active. "The real importance of this sale is that it puts Chicago back on the map as a wine auction center," he observed. "I think a lot of collectors were waiting in the wings to see what would happen."

Wine has always played a prominent role in White House dinners, but only a handful of presidents have involved themselves in the actual selection process. George Washington's fondness for Madeira is well documented. His personal correspondence contains more than one hundred references to wine and its acquisition, including a sardonic letter written in 1785 to merchants Lamar, Hill, and Bisset over the cost of a pipe of Madeira, which he complained was £7 more expensive than his previous purchase. John Adams was also a connoisseur, ordering five hundred bottles before setting off for London as minister to the court of St. James.

No other president's passion for wine came close to Thomas Jerfferson's. Thomas Jefferson was a compulsive consumer of expensive French wines, a passion he developed as America's emissary to France. His papers are full of orders placed with importers and *négociants*, in which he often requested "the finest old wines ready for use." Not content with the existing White House wine cellar, he designed an ingenious new one in 1801. It was sixteen feet deep with a platform floor elevated over a bed of ice (replaced monthly) packed in sawdust. He called it the ice house.

Jefferson also served as a wine adviser to Presidents Washington, James Madison, and Monroe. During the period 1784–89, he penned a primer on the wines of France, citing his own favorites. He showered praise on Hermitage Blanc, which he described as the "finest wine in the world," along with Châteaux Margaux and La Tour de Ségur, and, variously, Hautbrion and Obrion [*sic*] and de la Fite [*sic*].

In 1784, the forty-one-year-old Jefferson departed for Paris as America's commissioner to France, a position that made him responsible for negotiating commercial treaties. "He would acquire a depth of knowledge and an appreciation of wines that no American of his time would rival," observed James M. Gabler, author of *The Wines and Travels of Thomas Jefferson*. Jefferson immediately went on a wine-buying spree, purchasing 276 bottles of wine. He visited Benjamin Franklin, who lived in France at the time (having originally come there to obtain support for the American Revolution) and had a 1,100-bottle wine cellar. For Christmas in 1794, Jefferson bought himself 36 bottles of first growths (Margaux, Haut-Brion, Lafite Rothschild, and Latour).

Jefferson especially liked Château Léoville (as the wine was known before it was split into its various components) from the 1784 vintage. He thought Chambertin was the best of Burgundy, followed by Vougeot and Vosne, "because they are the strongest and will bear transportation." According to Gabler, Volnay ultimately became Jefferson's favorite red Burgundy because it cost a quarter as much as Chambertin and Vougeot and it was ready to drink in a year.

Jefferson ordered his wine shipped to him directly in bottle (rather than in cask), which reduced the chances of fraud. In effect, he wanted—and received—his wines chateau-bottled, a practice that did not become standard in Bordeaux or Burgundy until the early 1930s.

In 1985, a bottle of Lafite 1787 engraved with Jefferson's initials and purportedly from his private collection, went on the block at Christie's London. It sold for a staggering $155,242—the highest price ever paid for a single bottle of wine—to the late Malcolm Forbes, publisher of *Forbes* magazine. For Forbes, the provenance of the wine took precedence over its contents, and he subsequently placed the bottle on display alongside other presidential memorabilia at his in-house museum.

When Jefferson became president in 1801, he chose Honoré Julien, a Frenchman, as his chef and Étienne Lamare, another Frenchman, to administer the White House. As president, Jefferson found that food— and fine wine—were an expedient means to meet informally. In one of his early years in office, White House food bills totaled $6,000—and wine expenditures $7,597. During his presidency, he purchased over twenty thousand bottles of wine from Europe. Generally, he dined at 4:00 P.M. and talked until nightfall. As was the custom in eighteenth-century America, beer and cider was served during the meal, and wine was served afterward.

Jefferson allotted one bottle of wine per three guests. "I am not a *bouveur* [drinker]" he once wrote. "My measure is a perfectly sober three to four glasses at dinner and not a drop at other times." Based on the size of glasses then in use, that equates to nine to twelve ounces of wine daily.

Sarah Polk, the wife of President James Polk (1845–1849), wouldn't allow dancing at the White House, and apparently held liquor in disdain as well. (Strong whiskey had been introduced into the White House during the Madison administration and apparently people had sometimes drunk too much and misbehaved.) Mrs. Polk banned whiskey. In its place, she stocked more table wines (bought by the barrel), and, consequently, wine was among the Polks' biggest expenses. An 1845 diary tells of how, at a dinner for forty at the White House, glasses for six different wines "formed a rainbow around each plate."

By Abraham Lincoln's time, as many as six different wines were customarily served at official White House dinners. However, barely a decade later, under Rutherford B. Hayes's administration, wine was eliminated from the presidential table altogether, partly due to a change in values and a movement toward more moderate drinking. The banishment of alcohol from the White House would earn First Lady Lucy Webb Hayes the nickname "Lemonade Lucy."

There were exceptions, however. For an 1877 dinner in honor of Grand Duke Alexis of Russia, wine was poured in abundance. But soon after, no liquor of any kind was served. William Seale, author of *The President's House*, observed: "The Hayes style at the White House conformed to the new moral ideas of the age. It exemplified President Hayes's determination to conform White House entertaining to society's new moral ideals following the [financial] Panic of 1873. The flamboyance of the Grant era had ended."

Between World War I and Prohibition, wine shipments to America slowed to a trickle. President Herbert Hoover (1929–1933) felt obliged to observe Prohibition, a decision that did not prevent him from routinely stopping by the Belgian Embassy (as a foreign outpost it was unaffected by the Eighteenth Amendment) for a 6:00 P.M. cocktail.

When King George VI and Queen Elizabeth paid a visit to the White House in 1939, President Franklin D. Roosevelt went to considerable lengths to ascertain their majesties' preferences in wines and spirits. In the president's official file on Great Britain, there are several letters advocating serving American wine to the royal couple. However, Mrs. Henrietta Nesbitt, the White House major-domo, insisted foreign wines should be served on state occasions with the king and queen.

An explanation came in a four-page letter from Ambassador William C. Bullit to Roosevelt, which revealed that their majesties' preferences "do not go much beyond Veuve Clicquot and Pommery-Greno Champagne from the best years." Roosevelt ordered one hundred bottles from the 1928 vintage. Ambassador Bullit further communicated that the king's footman would need "a tray with sets of glasses, lump and crushed ice, decanters of lemon and orange juice, and everything necessary for the preparation of cocktails and various drinks."

A considerable amount of white wine and Champagne was poured during the Harry S. Truman years, but regrettably, the White House records do not list either the producers or the vintages.

The contrast between the Eisenhower and Kennedy administrations could not have been more pointed. In *Lady, First: My Life in the Kennedy White House and the American Embassies of Paris and Rome,* author Letitia Baldridge recounts the impressions of pianist Leonard Bernstein, who performed for both presidents. "During the Eisenhower era," he said, "the food was ordinary, and the wines were inferior. Under JFK [who expressed a personal preference for Château Pétrus] dinner turns out to be not at a horseshoe table but many little tables, seating about ten people apiece, and these tables are laid in three adjacent rooms so that it's all like having dinner with friends. The food is marvelous, the wines are delicious. People are laughing out loud, telling stories, jokes, enjoying themselves, glad to be there."

John F. Kennedy initially served top-quality French wines at state occasions. References to Château Haut-Brion 1955 with roast spring lamb,

Piper Heidseick 1955 with *bombe glacée,* and Château Gruaud-Larose 1955 with grouse *à l'Américaine* abound in the administration's archives. But in response to criticisms that the menus and wines were too French, the food description was anglicized, and American wines became more prominent around the table. By June 1963, Inglenook Pinot Chardonnay was served with salmon, and at a dinner for the cellist Pablo Casals, Almaden Cabernet Sauvignon was poured with a filet of beef.

President Richard M. Nixon was said to have been a wine aficionado and partial to Château Margaux from the famed 1959 vintage. In *The Final Days,* the infamous final word on his administration by Watergate reporter Carl Bernstein, it is reported that at formal dinners, Nixon would open a bottle of Margaux for his own consumption and have it wrapped in a linen napkin in order to cover the label, while guests were poured a lesser growth or a California Cabernet.

According to one newspaper clipping, President Gerald Ford's early choices of some Michigan and Ohio wines were so heavily criticized he switched to more popular California offerings. President and Mrs. Lyndon Johnson entertained prolifically, but there is no list of White House dinner wines—just the entertainments. Both President Jimmy Carter and his wife Rosalynn were light drinkers and seemed to prefer an occasional highball to wine or beer. Though not teetotalers, the Carters often held events like concerts on the White House lawn at which no alcohol was served. Curiously, since leaving the White House, Carter has since taken to bottling his own vintages.

President Ronald Reagan was an exponent of wines from his native state, and was not above functioning as its cheerleader. When entertaining an important French delegation in 1982, he quipped, "I hope you all realize that we know, of course, France has great appreciation for fine wines, and that's why we decided to treat you to some California wine tonight."

President George H. W. Bush's major pronouncements on wine came in the form of an oft-repeated joke. He would relate that his dog Millie's celebrity status (she featured prominently in a book written by his wife,

177

Barbara) had gone to her head. "Last night, I gave her a bowl of Alpo, and she asked to see the wine list there at the White House."

According to Dee-Dee Myers, who was President Bill Clinton's White House secretary, the former president enjoys wine, but doesn't drink it often because he's allergic to it. He was well advised, however, serving wines from top California and Oregon estates such as Newton Chardonnay "Unfiltered" 1996, Swanson Sangiovese "Estate" 1995, and Mumm Napa Valley "DVX" 1993 at a state dinner in February 1998, and, in 1997, Cuvaison "Carneros" Chardonnay 1995, Ponzi "25th Anniversary" Pinot Noir 1995, and Iron Horse Blanc de Blanc L.D. 1991.

————— ⁄⁄⁄⁄⁄⁄ —————

"Wine collecting is much easier today," insists Lloyd Flatt, a veteran collector who started acquiring world-class wines in the late 1960s and remains an active buyer today. When Flatt, an Alexandria, Virginia, based aerospace consultant, began amassing what would become a fifteen-thousand-bottle wine cellar, there were no reference guides to depend on: no *Wine Spectator*, no *Wine Advocate*, no classic books like Michael Broadbent's *Great Vintage Wine Book*, and certainly no Internet. Instead, collectors like Flatt relied on the occasional advice of an expert palate and embarked on a largely empirical acquisition process.

CREATING HIS CELLAR: Very much the engineer, Flatt began to accumulate wines systematically, focusing on First Growth Bordeaux, then branching out into lesser growths, Burgundies, and old Champagnes. He also collected Port and Cognac. "I would never do it that way again," he says, "nor would I need to. There's so much more information about fine and rare wine in the public domain. Consequently, I'd be more selective and wouldn't acquire the breadth nor the quantity of wines I did."

BEST BOTTLES: At its peak, Flatt's cellar was almost exclusively French, heavily weighted toward classified Bordeaux, with a considerable stash of hard-to-come-by Burgundy—including rare bottlings of Bouchard Père et Fils from the 1800s. It was all stored in a stunning temperature- and humidity-controlled "wine house" in New Orleans' French Quarter, where Flatt then resided. Breadth was matched by depth. Nineteenth-century bottlings and twentieth-century classics figured prominently. There were virtually priceless jeroboams, such as 1929 Mouton-Rothschild, double magnums of 1953 Pétrus, and even Lafite-Rothschild 1806.

Flatt's acquisitiveness seemed boundless. He only bought wines of the finest provenance and condition—criteria that remain paramount for him today. But even so, he stresses that his was always a working cellar, not a showcase. He collected in order to learn about his finds, to drink them, and to share them. He never hesitated to uncork a rare bottle if a guest expressed interest. Throughout the 1980s, Flatt hosted many a wine extravaganza, complete with marching bands and black-tie dinner dances. His celebrated megatastings included a 115-vintage examination of Château Lafite back to the 1784 vintage, and vast vertical forays into Châteaux Pétrus, Mouton, Ausone, and Cheval-Blanc. They were all conducted gratis for the edification of his wine buddies.

Flatt was forced to reconstruct his collection in 1990 when his cellar was auctioned off at Christie's in the wake of his divorce. Since then, he has rebuilt a (comparatively) more modest, four-thousand-bottle collection comprised of some classic clarets and with a new emphasis on Burgundy. Yet Flatt's underlying philosophy remains constant. "I never buy for resale. I always mentally expense the value of my wine at the time of purchase," he explains, "so that the adjusted cost never becomes an obstacle in uncorking a bottle.

"In a way, the divorce was the best thing that happened to my collection, as it forced me to rethink my tastes," he says. "I started buying selectively, and attended and conducted tastings. I actually learned a lot more about wine. I've become particularly interested in food and wine pairings. I relish drinking great bottles with friends who share my passion. In some instances, it's a matter of my playing the role of patriarch and saying, 'I think you'll be interested in this.'"

BEST BUYS: Flatt admits that at this point in his life (he's in his late sixties), his tastes are fairly set, and he is less adventuresome than he once was. "I am very selective about what I buy," he says. "I would not chase after an old bottle of wine just to taste it unless I'm familiar with it and for some reason crave it. I'm not buying too many young vintages for aging. However, there are some very fine current vintages of white Burgundy that I still buy at auction. I'm quite selective about growers and only seek out the best. I continue to be fond of vintage Champagne."

Flatt says it's a myth that Champagne doesn't have longevity, believing a well-stored vintage Champagne can be more stable than a fine old white

Burgundy. "I have tasted Bollinger Champagne 1911 and it was still showing beautifully," he remembers. However, he warns that if you see a bottle that has low fill levels, or is discolored around the foil and the cork, to beware of oxidation. He recommends focusing your buying strategy on vintages from the 1970s and 1980s to be on the safe side, and then experimenting with the occasional 1959, 1947, or 1945.

COLLECTING WISDOM: Asked to compare current market conditions to those when he first began collecting, Flatt says he doesn't find today's hefty prices out of hand, particularly when he takes into account how other collectibles have appreciated. He feels that compared to the real estate and fine arts markets, rare wines remain approachable. Although he admits that prices for truly great Burgundy are out of sight, he thinks that lesser growths of Bordeaux and Burgundy still represent good value. "Let's face it," he concedes, "having a wine collection has become chic, and the only way to accumulate a serious cellar is to go out there and buy it." Flatt believes the process hasn't changed all that much over the years; only the participants are different. "There's a new generation of aggressive collectors out there who are becoming major players. I think that's one of the big drivers in the present market.

"My advice to anyone contemplating a wine collection today is to focus," Flatt says. "Find something that you enjoy. Don't try to explore everything. Starting collectors should form groups that share a mutual interest in wine tasting to hone their preferences. It's far better than attending a wine class."

Flatt regards wine collecting as a relaxing and fulfilling pastime, with one major caveat: "Unlike an art collection, which is permanent, wine ultimately must be consumed. You shouldn't even contemplate a cellar if you cannot accept that fact."

BEYOND WINE:
THE ACCESSORIES

~/\\\\\\\~

~\\\\\\\~

AS WINE BECOMES AN INTEGRAL PART OF YOUR LIFESTYLE—AND AS
the quality of wine you drink improves—you may find that the stemware
and other accoutrements you've been using no longer do your wines jus-
tice. It's partly a matter of aesthetics: a crystal decanter can heighten the
experience of uncorking a Château Latour. But it's also a matter of practi-
cality. There are now several lines of glassware designed to enhance the attributes of specific varietals.

184

There are myriad sources online and specialty shops across the country that boast a wide inventory of wine-related objects. If you want functional tools for perfecting the wine-drinking experience—expressly shaped
blown stemware, fail-safe corkscrews—you will be able to find top-of-the-
line products for under $100.

For many enophiles, creating a wine cellar sparks a passion in collecting that extends beyond just the acquisition of bottles. If your goal is to
complement your wine collection with objects that are as rare as the wines
in your cellar—that are works of art in themselves—then the world of
wine antiques is worth exploring. After all, what's the point of decanting
Pétrus with a rubber funnel?

ACCESSORIES TO MAXIMIZE YOUR DRINKING EXPERIENCE

∧\\\\\\∨

Strictly functional wine accessories can be found many places and at many different prices. In addition to wine shops, look for them in department stores, specialty outlets such as Williams-Sonoma, home design centers, antique shops, and, of course, online. For the largest array of accessibly priced wine accoutrements—from corkscrews to modular wine cellars—try Dallas-based International Wine Accessories (iwawine.com) and New York–based Wine Enthusiast (wineenthusiast.com). Many items sold at Wine Enthusiast are discounted from standard retail pricing. Both companies specialize exclusively in wine-related artifacts and equipment, making them ideal for one-stop shopping.

Corkscrews

One of the most attractive models is the Laguiole from France. Loosely based on the waiter's corkscrew, it ranges in price from $40 to about $100, depending on the materials used in its construction. Design considerations notwithstanding, the most important thing about a corkscrew is that it works efficiently and effectively, without shredding the cork or pushing it into the bottle.

Two of the most popular corkscrew designs on the market are the screw-pull (with a Teflon-covered *worm*, the section of the corkscrew that pushes into the cork) and the waiter's corkscrew (with a double-hinged lever). Both examples extract particularly well, with a minimum of disturbance to the bottle's contents. If you are entertaining large groups, the

Screwpull Lever Model, which uses a simple up-and-down motion, keeps the cork straight and removes it in seconds. It costs about $100, and similar brands, like the Rabbit from Metrokane, run about $60. The double-pronged Ahh-So model, based on a nineteenth-century design, is a favorite in California.

Gas-pressure openers are trendy, but they have been known to explode the occasional bottle. Avoid the once-popular double-handled corkscrew and the more expensive bar model that affixes to a tabletop, because both have a solid worm that can shred a cork or push it into a bottle. And with any corkscrew, if the worm is bent, it's time to shop for a new one.

Glassware

Anyone who has accumulated a collection of fine wine should consider owning stemware that shows off the aromas and flavors of each varietal to its best effect. Supermarket-issue wineglasses with small stems and bowls won't do the job, whereas expertly crafted and proportioned glassware by manufacturers such as Speigelau, Tritan, and Riedel will. The latter is the acknowledged industry leader, producing more than five million lead-crystal wineglasses a year in various shapes and at various price points. Riedel pioneered the concept of tailoring a glass to specific types of wine and has developed a loyal following among collectors and restaurateurs. Both Speigelau and Tritan also produce competitively priced glassware designed to enhance a varietal's characteristics.

It may seem improbable that a specially configured glass could enhance or alter a wine's performance. However, anyone who has attended a Riedel tasting (at which an identical wine is sampled both from a Riedel glass and a plain, off-the-shelf model) will most likely come away convinced of the Riedel's ability to enhance a wine's bouquet, aroma, and taste. Riedel now makes dozens of glasses for many different types of wine: Bordeaux and Burgundy, Champagne and Sauterne, Riesling and Eiswein. The

Vinum series is the company's workhorse. It's dishwasher safe and most models run $14 to $18 per glass. The more expensive, hand-blown Sommelier series is the firm's trophy line, suitable for owners of trophy wines who are prepared to spend upward of $65 for a lead-crystal glass that must be hand washed. The latter is more exquisite but also more prone to breakage. Riedel has also introduced a stemless, tumbler-style wineglass called the O series, with bowls designed to enhance specific varietals.

Decanters

Contemporary decanters can range from inexpensive models that cost under $100 to elaborately designed vessels from celebrated glassmakers such as Steuben or Lalique that cost ten times as much. They all do pretty much the same job. No matter which you buy, make sure that it is easy to grasp and, equally important, easy to clean. (Some fanciful designs with unnecessary appendages or extremities can be a nightmare.)

Wine Keepers

If you find yourself with a half-empty bottle of vintage Barolo at the end of a dinner party, or simply don't want to go through a whole bottle of Sauterne in one sitting, there are a number of products that retard the oxidation process. At the high end, the WineKeeper's products (winekeeper.com), which can cost around $1,400, use nitrogen to preserve up to four open bottles. Single-bottle models start at around $100. For just $30, the Rabbit Lever Vacuum Pump will extend a single bottle's shelf life. Products that simply create a vacuum seal (at the low end, you can buy a vacuum saver for just $3) are likely to be less effective than ones that supplant the oxygen with nitrogen.

Bin Labels

Bin labels were designed to help quickly identify the individual contents of a large cellar. Usually made of pottery or Creamware, they are often shaped in the form of a shield or a bell and tacked to a wall, rack, or bin with the salient information about the contents written in ink or pencil. They still play a practical role in a large cellar and can also double as novel place cards at a dinner party.

VINTAGE COLLECTIBLES

Ever since the introduction of the cork-stopped wine bottle in the 1700s, guilds of talented craftsmen have been engaged in the production of accessories to accommodate these "modern" wine vessels. Collectible corkscrews, decanters, coasters, cabinets, coolers, wine tables, and racks are all indirect products of the marriage of cork and bottle, and constitute a serious enhancement to any wine collection. There are numerous examples on the market ranging in price from well under $100 to in excess of $100,000.

Wine aficionados don't always collect vintage wine accoutrements, despite the obvious affinity. Yet a period wine cooler or *cellarette* (a free-standing cabinet used to store wine prior to serving it) can add a definitive aesthetic element to a room. Provided the objects are in good condition, they can prove just as functional today as they were originally. What's more, unlike a spent bottle of fine wine (or most contemporary wine accessories), antique collectibles are forever reusable, and they can boast considerable resale potential. They do, however, require a more substantial investment than most of their modern counterparts—and a more extensive search process.

Auction houses are a good venue for vintage collectibles, as are antique stores and the occasional high-end wine shop. Other sources include country fairs and tag sales. There are also a number of websites specializing in corkscrews and wine-related antiques: iCorkscrew.com, WineAntique.com, and Bacchus-Antiques.com. In addition to being a good source of supply, browsing an online inventory is an ideal way of learning the going rate for a variety of models.

Corkscrews

More than three hundred different patents for corkscrew designs were taken out during the late nineteenth century alone. The allure of collecting vintage corkscrews lies partly in the fact that no one really knows how many different types have been made. It's an enduring enigma.

Prototypes range from simple, straight-pull models made of wood or metal and outfitted with a screw (technically known as a *worm* or *helix*) to elaborate models crafted by silversmiths, metalworkers, and wood carvers. Collectible corkscrews can vary in price from as little as $10 to tens of thousands of dollars.

189

The most sought-after collectible examples fall into two distinct categories: corkscrews made out of precious metals or stones and those employing a mechanical process such as a lever or double-spring action for removing the cork. One of the most popular varieties is a pair of enamel "ladies' legs" made in Germany in the late nineteenth century. Once considered highly risqué because of their flesh-colored thighs and striped tights, "ladies' legs" typically sell for about $500 apiece.

The most expensive corkscrew sold to date is an eighteenth-century silver pocket model from the collection of Bernard Watney (the author, with Homer Babbidge, of *Corkscrews for Collectors*), auctioned at Christie's in 1997. The model was engraved on the handle and dated "November 1st, 1743." Its provenance was enhanced by the additional engraving "1910, A.R. Alexandra Regina, from the Queen" (the wife of King Edward VII). Estimated at $6,300 to $9,500, it brought in a whopping $29,000.

Condition is germane to a corkscrew's value, much in the same way the price of a good vintage wine will depend on the bottle's provenance. A bent or broken helix will seriously diminish a model's worth. But don't rush to uncork a contemporary bottle with any century-old corkscrew unless you're sure the worm is still up to the task.

Glassware

Antique glasses make a major statement at the dinner table, even if they are not in sync with every imaginable grape variety. Some of the most elegant examples, known as twisted stemware because of the brilliant spiral twists of opaque glass embedded in their stems, date from the mid-1700s. Like period decanters, many examples were engraved with grape motifs. Some glasses made during the Regency period in England boast an attractive geometrical form with large bowls, beaded stems, and a short, heavy base. Occasionally, they come embellished with enamel. Antique glassware usually has good resale value.

Decanters

Decanters as we know them are the product of eighteenth-century design. Earlier models tended to resemble jugs, and were used to decant wine straight from the wine barrel. The basic eighteenth-century model was patterned on a globe-and-shaft design, often embellished by a series of rings near the lip or engraved with a grape motif. Curiously, polished stoppers were a nineteenth-century innovation (before then, stoppers were left with a coarse matte finish), so any merchant claiming to sell an eighteenth-century decanter with a polished stopper is either uninformed, or foisting a "marriage" of two separate pieces on an unsuspecting buyer. Because of breakage, pairs of identical decanters are extremely rare, as are large-format pieces. Prices vary tremendously according to style and condition, but, like collectible glassware, antique decanters tend to have good resale value.

Wine Funnels

Usually made of silver, wine funnels were devised to facilitate the decanting process and reduce spillage. Some contained sieves or filters to trap the sediment contained in older wines. Others allowed for the insertion of a piece of cheesecloth. The earliest and rarest funnels, dating from the mid-1600s, were designed with a bent spout so that the wine would slowly trickle down the side of the bottle. But most examples found on the market date from the 1760s or later. Condition will largely dictate the value of a period funnel. Objects with dents or crooked spouts do not command a premium.

Glass funnels are particularly scarce because of their fragility, yet decorative examples that have managed to survive the centuries still tend to cost under $500, far less than silver models. In contrast, at Sotheby's, a rare Chinese Export wine funnel made of porcelain dating from 1700 sold for $8,400, seven times the pre-sale high estimate.

191

Decanter Wagons and Decanting Machines

Two curiosities that should appeal to the impassioned accessory collector are the decanter wagon and the decanting machine, both of which date from the early 1800s. The former was a highly whimsical object made of silver or silver-gilt patterned in the shape of a chariot, wagon, or boat. It was designed to hold one or two bottles of wine and set on wheels so that the wine could be moved effortlessly from one end of a dining table to the other without disturbing the wine's sediment. Museum-quality examples have been known to fetch tremendous sums. In April 2004, a pair of silver-gilt, double-coaster wine wagons sold for $265,100 at Christie's New York.

A decanting machine looks like a device left over from an enophile's science project. Made of nickel-plate, silver, or brass, it was meant to cradle a bottle of wine, then raise and tilt it to the appropriate angle with levers and screws so that the wine could be poured into a decanter or straight into a glass with a minimum of disturbance. Period decanting machines can cost several thousand dollars. Modern reproductions sell for $250 or less.

A variation on the decanting machine is the bottle holder, usually made of mahogany and mounted with a brass handle. Popular in Burgundy (where, strangely, some wine aficionados have an aversion to decanters), it is meant to hold a bottle at about a 30° angle so that the cork can be easily extracted and its contents poured smoothly.

Bottle carriers were meant to facilitate the transport of bottles from the wine cellar to the dining table without shaking up the sediment. Designed to hold two to six bottles with a slot for each, the bottles would be placed upright in the container, where they would be firmly held. Usually crafted out of mahogany, more primitive examples were fashioned out of metal with a plain wooden handle.

Silver Collectibles

There are a host of silver wine collectibles ranging from museum-quality cisterns and coolers to more approachable *tastevins* and neck labels that can nicely accessorize a wine collection. At the high end, a rare German silver cistern and fountain made in 1710 for King George I of England and originally used to dispense wine and rinse glasses fetched $1.3 million at a Christie's New York auction in October 2000. "In the eighteenth and nineteenth centuries, grand objects like cisterns and coolers represented the ultimate in architectural display and utilitarian design," explains Jeanne Sloane, head of Christie's silver department. "Prominently centered on a buffet, they were brought out for special occasions and entertainments."

At auction, silver wine coolers (bucket- or trophy-shaped receptacles that were filled with iced water to chill white wine) can fetch anywhere from several hundred dollars to upward of one million dollars, depending on age, design, materials, provenance, and the reputation of their makers. One of the most expensive examples to go on the block was a pair of coolers given by Catherine the Great of Russia to her lover and political ally, Count Gregory Orloff, which sold at Christie's New York in April 2002 for $933,500.

Wine coasters are as practical today as they were two hundred years ago. Circular with a wooden or silver base intricately banded in silver, they serve as bottle or decanter holders that protect the surface of a dining table or bar from inadvertent spills and drips. A set of four early nineteenth-century examples made of silver sold at Christie's for $9,650, but you could probably find a pair of very handsome examples for one-tenth the price in an antique shop. Some silver coasters come engraved with a coat of arms on the base. Other fine examples were made from lacquered papier-mâché.

Christie's Sloane says that both wine and silver collectors share an equal interest in claret jugs (a name coined in Victorian England for practically any decoratively fashioned decanter). "But there's an interesting twist," she notes. "Whereas the silver collector will seek out an example made of solid silver, the wine collector looks for one with a clear glass body mounted on a silver base, which is better for evaluating or admiring the wine's color."

Silver-mounted antique claret jugs can be found for less than $2,000, but prices escalate dramatically for top-quality examples. A pair of important claret jugs made in London in 1871 (embossed with flutes and silver mounts engraved with stylized foliage) brought $19,120 at Christie's.

Tastevins began life as a professional tool for wine merchants and *négociants*, who would sample newly released wines in the *chais*, or cellars of France. Resembling a small bowl about three to five inches in diameter, they came into widespread use in the seventeenth century. *Tastevins* were usually made from multifaceted silver that would amplify available light in the cellar and aid in determining the character of a wine's color. More elaborate models were decorated with grape vines or bunches of grapes. Antique *tastevins* can range from several hundred to several thousand dollars depending on age, design, condition, and provenance, but modern reproductions cost only a fraction of that amount.

Neck labels (known as *bottle tickets* in the eighteenth century) were escutcheon-shaped pieces of silver or ivory that bore a description of a decanter's contents set on a small chain so that they could be easily transferred. Neck labels were first manufactured in the early 1700s. Typical examples were designed for fortified wines that would remain in a decanter for some time: Port, Madeira, Sercial, and Sherry. However, Champagne, Burgundy, and claret labels were also produced. Prices will depend on the reputation of the silversmith and the label's design and condition, and can run from under $100 to in excess of $1,000.

Wine Furniture

One of the most common objects found in affluent eighteenth-century homes was the *cellarette*, or wooden wine cooler. It was intended to chill bottles of white wine or Champagne that were placed in a lead liner (about two feet in diameter) filled with ice water. The cellarette varied in design from an oval or hexagon-shaped wooden basin atop tripod legs to highly ornate versions carved out of mahogany with intricate embellishments such as grape clusters or lions' masks or paws.

Simple antique cellarettes start at about $3,000 at auction, with finer versions commanding upward of $15,000. (The very best examples, crafted in the late eighteenth century by American cabinet makers, can cost as much as $250,000.) Anyone who intends to use a wine cooler for its original purpose (as opposed to furniture collectors, who buy them as decorative side tables or planters) should check to see that the metal liner is leakproof, and that the drain for emptying the ice water still works.

One of the most unusual objects designed especially for drinking was the wine table—a horseshoe-shaped piece of furniture that measured about seven feet wide, four feet deep, and about two and one half feet high. The wine table was usually placed in front of a fireplace, where guests could both warm their feet and enjoy a glass of Port. Wine tables generally date from the 1820s to the 1840s. They were usually equipped with a swiveling brass arm and a coaster (upon which a bottle or carafe was placed) that could be swung around the table for self-service. Antique wine tables can range from about $7,000 to well over $40,000, depending upon design, provenance, and the reputation of the cabinetmaker.

Wine tables may be objects of intense curiosity, but they also take up a considerable amount of space. Fred Imberman, co-owner of Kentshire Antiques in New York, says, "Before you contemplate buying one, be sure that you have enough room to display it, and check that the swiveling brass arm is still in working condition." As with any collectible, condition is germane to the asking price. Legs or bases that have been replaced diminish the overall worth of the piece.

French artisans also produced a variety of handsome, wine-related furniture during the eighteenth and nineteenth centuries. The most common example is the *rafraichissoir*, which, like the English wine table, came in particularly handy on the butler's day off. Placed in a corner of the dining room, it resembled a side table, except that it had a false front into which two or three small removable buckets were sunk. It could be filled with ice water to chill or simply hold the evening's wines. Often decorated with a banded rim and reeded legs, it had slots for corkscrews and drawers for other wine paraphernalia. At auction, they can sell for upward of $10,000: a hefty price for a self-service device, but worth it.

Sometimes, the right object at the wrong auction will yield a tremendous bargain for the savvy collector. A few years ago at Sotheby's, a handsome French wine cabinet dating from 1780 sold below estimate. Made of mahogany, it was fitted with a metal-lined well for storing bottles on their sides. Estimated at $10,000 to $20,000, it was snapped up at the low estimate for just $10,800 (inclusive of the 17.5 percent buyer's fee), possibly because it was one of the few pieces of foreign furniture at a predominately American sale.

195

By modern collecting standards, my cellar is not very large (about one thousand bottles), nor extraordinarily valuable (probably worth less than $100,000). That's because for most of the past fifteen years, in addition to my wine writing, I was editor and publisher of *Passport to New York Restaurants* (the Manhattan restaurant guide) and, therefore, dined out as many as six nights a week, obviating the need for an enormous wine collection. Yet that's not to suggest my collecting urges were altogether restrained.

I was extremely fortunate to have befriended a group of prominent American wine collectors in the early 1980s, men like Lloyd Flatt, Tawfiq Khoury, Marvin Overton, and Stacey Childs, who were a profound influence both on my vocation and avocation. Over the years, they hosted benchmark vertical tastings of Châteaux Lafite Rothschild, Mouton-Rothschild, Pétrus, and Haut-Brion, as well as horizontal examinations of the acclaimed 1974 California Cabernet Sauvignons and the highly celebrated 1945 and 1959 vintages of classified Bordeaux, to mention a few. These tastings exposed me to and instilled in me a taste for older wines, an appreciation of their nuances in style, and, above all, the importance of provenance. Drinking a wine that is older than you are, or one that commemorates a long-gone historical event, can impart an almost ethereal dimension to the tasting experience.

CREATING MY CELLAR: I started collecting wine seriously in 1982. During that year, I installed three temperature- and humidity-controlled wine cabinets in the basement of my apartment and amassed a fairly broad-based selection of new releases and vintage classics. I purchased the former at retail and the latter primarily at auction, all the while keeping a revolving stash of more reasonably priced wines for everyday drinking.

My collecting debut also coincided with futures offerings from the 1982 Bordeaux vintage—then hailed as the vintage of the century. At that time, first growths averaged about $390 a case. They now sell for about $9,000. I picked up three cases of first growths (Latour, Mouton-Rothschild, and Lafite) along with Léoville Las Cases, Lynch-Bages, and Gruaud-Larose. At auction, I remember buying case-lots of Grand-Puy-Lacoste 1966 and Mouton-Rothschild 1966, Beaulieu Vineyards Private Reserve Cabernet Sauvignon 1968, Remoissenet Clos de Bèze 1969, and Château Suduiraut 1967.

Today, I continue to pursue a similar mix, investing in futures, buying recent releases, and bidding on the occasional vintage classic. My current collection is fairly representative of the contents of a typical auction catalog: fine Bordeaux, Burgundy, Rhône, California, and a smattering of estate bottlings from Italy and Spain. Its major weakness is a lack of depth in fine white wine.

BEST BOTTLES: In my kitchen in my house in the country, I have a large antique bottle rack dating from the pre–World War II era, when bottles were washed, dried, and reused. It's filled with my favorite empties—a Lafite Rothschild 1890 opened on New Year's Eve 1990, a Château Margaux from 1906 consumed at a charity event I co-hosted, a magnum of Mouton-Rothschild 1949 from another New Year's dinner, a Barbi Brunello di Montalcino 1970 opened when I became engaged, and a 1955 Latour drunk on my fiancée's birthday. It gives me enormous pleasure to gaze upon the bottles, to conjure up their salient characteristics, and, above all, to recall the people who shared them with me, or the events at which they were uncorked.

For my fortieth birthday, instead of place cards, I dug into my cellar and arranged thirty bottles spanning 1955 through 1990 on the dining tables. Each guest pulled a card out of a bowl corresponding to the year of a bottle, then sat by the appropriate wine, which also served as a take-home souvenir of the evening. Some lucky individuals went home with the likes of Léoville Las Cases 1961, Château Talbot 1982, and Lynch-Bages 1985. I arranged a mini-tasting of 1951s that evening as well (a dreadful vintage in France, but a wonderful one in California).

I also enjoy donating wine to worthy causes. At a recent benefit for the Pasteur Foundation, I contributed a bottle of Château d'Yquem 1967, which sold for $4,500 (about triple its market value). A more unusual gift was a

197

In the pre-World War II era, when glass was at a premium, many wineries (particularly in outlying regions of the French countryside) washed out used bottles and set them to dry on a rack such as this one before being refilled with another vintage. I use my bottle tree as a repository of favorite bottles consumed with close friends.

PETER MELTZER

198

magnum of Korbel Cuvée Inaugural 1993, the sparkling wine that was served at one of President Clinton's inaugural lunches. Why I held on to it all these years I don't know, but when I discovered that Clinton was the guest of honor at the gala, I urged one of the event organizers to have him sign it. He did, and the bottle sold for a whopping $2,500. Its true worth was under $25.

BEST BUYS: While I've sold my first growth 1982 bottles, I have kept my 1982 lesser growths and am still enjoying the fruits of that spectacular harvest today. Meanwhile, I have continued buying small quantities of Bordeaux futures from 1986 through 2003. I am on the mailing list for Arietta and Harlan, two top limited-production Napa Valley wines and I always enjoy bottom-fishing for well-made Burgundies such as Corton Chandon de Briailles from off-vintages such as 1997 and 1998. Another favorite is Le Vieux Donjon, a Châteauneuf-du-Pape that sells for about $30—when you can find it.

I love buying at auction, but I tend to be a rather conservative bidder because, as custodian of the *Wine Spectator* Auction Index, I know what a wine is worth and am reluctant to pay much more than its recent index average. However, I am always prepared to be aggressive when I'm buying wines for tasting purposes, as I was when purchasing recent releases of Robert Foley Vineyards Claret, Sloane (a limited-production Cabernet blend from Napa Valley), and Switchback Ridge Peterson Family Vineyard Cabernet Sauvignon on WineBid.com for an average price of about $200 per bottle.

I don't own many very large-format bottles because I find them unwieldy. I think I have donated more jeroboams and imperials to charity than I have consumed. I have also learned the folly of serving overly elaborate wines at festive dinner parties. I once made the error of decanting magnums of Léoville Las Cases 1962 for a group of twelve. The wine was totally lost on the guests, and I won't make that mistake again. After all, it's the guest list, not the wine list, that makes the evening.

My favorite wines change regularly. Right now, I'm partial to a hard-to-come-by red Burgundy called Les Gaudichots, which was once part of Domaine de la Romanée Conti La Tâche. My stash hails from the 1990s, although I was able to sample a remarkable 1929 at a Christie's tasting. For everyday drinking, Macon Milly, produced by the Domaine Comtes Lafon, represents excellent value at $13. (Lafon's Montrachet sells for about $1,500 a bottle.) Then there's the 1914 Croizet Cognac, which I bought at auction fifteen years ago (there are only two bottles left from the original case). I dole it out with an eye-dropper.

COLLECTING WISDOM: I have always maintained that almost every collector has a ceiling above which he or she feels uncomfortable uncorking a bottle, no matter what its original cost. For some that may be $1,000; for another, it could be $100. When the auction price for my first growths from the legendary 1982 vintage soared to $600 per bottle, I decided it made more sense to cash in my profits and place the proceeds elsewhere.

TOP AUCTION HOUSES

∿∿∿∿∿

ACKER MERRALL & CONDIT

Phone: (877) ACKER 47

Fax: (877) ACKER 24

ackerauctions.com

2005 sales: $21 million

Contact: John Kapon

ackerbids@aol.com

Acker Merrall & Condit charges no consignor's fee and levies an 18.5 percent buyer's premium—and has snared many important collections as a consequence. It also features a variety of smaller mixed lots catering to the collector who does not wish to buy by the case-load. The catalogs display considerable wit. Acker sells a lot of California wine.

AULDEN CELLARS-SOTHEBY'S

Phone: (212) 606-7050

Fax: (212) 606-7880

sothebys.com

2005 sales: $19 million

Contact: Jamie Ritchie

jamie.ritchie@sothebys.com

A founding member of the wine auction establishment (Sotheby's began offering wines at auction in London in 1970 and in New York in 1994), the firm is known for big-time consignments from collections of impeccable provenance. Their "Millennium Sale" in 1999, which realized $14.4 million, still stands in the record books as the most valuable collection ever offered. The buyer's premium is 19.5 percent.

BONHAMS & BUTTERFIELDS

Phone: (323) 436-5431

butterfields.com

2005 sales: $6 million

Contact: Frank Martell

frank.martell@bonhams.com

Under the tenure of Frank Martell (who arrived at Bonhams in 2002), the firm has witnessed an upswing in serious consignments. It auctions more California wines than its competitors. The buyer's fee is 17 percent.

THE CHICAGO WINE COMPANY

Phone: (847) 647-8789

Fax: (847) 647-7265

tcwc.com

2005 sales: NA

Contact: Simon Lambert

info@tcwc.com

This auction veteran, launched in 1974, offers Internet, mail order, and live auctions. There is no buyer's premium.

CHRISTIE'S LONDON

Phone: (011) 44 (0)20 7752 3366

christies.com

2005 sales: $13 million

Contact: David Elswood, international head

delswood@christies.com

Founded in 1766, the wine department, revitalized by Michael Broadbent in 1966, has been the scene of spectacular single-owner, ex-chateau sales. Christie's consistently offers a choice selection of rare Burgundy and claret. The buyer's premium is 10 percent.

Christie's Los Angeles

Phone: (310) 385-2600

christies.com

2005 sales: $5 million

Contact: Scott Torrence

Phone: (310) 385-2603

Fax: (310) 385-9292

storrence@christies.com

Christie's Los Angeles offers a mix of classic French and California wines. The buyer's premium is 17.5 percent.

NYWinesChristie's

Phone: (212) 636-2266

Fax: (212) 636-4954

christies.com

2005 sales: $11 million

Contact: Richard Brierley, head of North American wine sales

Phone: (212) 636-2266

rbrierley@christies.com

Contact: Michael Troise, auction director, NYWines

Phone: (212) 463-8600

NYWinesChristie's sells an unusually wide range of fine Burgundy, along with rare claret and California labels. In 2004, it auctioned the private American wine collection from the estate of Doris Duke, which grossed $3.8 million. In March 2006, NYWC sold a case of DRC Romanée-Conti for a record $170,375. The buyer's premium is 17.5 percent.

Edward Roberts International (Chicago)

Phone: (847) 295-8696

Fax: (847) 295-8697

eriewine.com

info@eriwine.com

2005 sales: $2 million

Contact: Edward Brooks

ebrooks@eriwine.com

A boutique auction house with many treasures presided over by the former head of Christie's New York wine department. The buyer's premium is 15 percent.

HART DAVIS HART (CHICAGO)

Phone: (312) 482-9996

Fax: (312) 335-9096

hdhwine.com

2005 sales: $10 million

Contact: Michael Davis

mdavis@hdhwine.com

Michael Davis and Paul Hart (formerly joint-heads of Sotheby's North American wine department) have teamed up with veteran fine wine merchant John Hart to offer a focused, personalized auction service and a wide array of enticing collections. The buyer's premium is 17 percent.

MORRELL & CO.

Phone: (212) 307-4200

Fax: (212) 207-5242

morrellwineauctions.com

2005 sales: $3 million

Contact: Nikos Antonakeas

Contact: Kimberly Janis

Morrellvin@aol.com

info@morrellwineauctions.com

Morrell & Co. was the first firm to auction wine in New York after the legalization of auctions. It offers appealing mixed lots as well as smaller parcels and classic private collections. There is no consignor's fee; the buyer's premium is 17 percent.

203

SOTHEBY'S LONDON

Phone: (011) 44 (0) 7293 5727

sothebys.com

2005 sales: $11 million

Contact: Serena Sutcliffe, senior director, head of

Sotheby's International Wine Department

Contact: Stephen Mould, senior director, head of European Wine Department

Phone: (011) 44 (0) 7293 5046

Fax: (011) 44 (0) 7293 5961

stephen.mould@sothebys.com

Serena Sutcliffe has breathed new life into the firm since taking over the department in 1990. Sotheby's is known for celebrated single-owner sales and rarities, such as the famed $6 million sale of Sir Andrew Lloyd Webber's collection. The buyer's premium is 15 percent.

ZACHYS, NEW YORK

Phone: (914) 448-3026

Fax: (914) 206-4544

zachys.com

2005 sales: $28 million

Contact: Jeff Zacharia, president

Contact: Linnea Housewright, auction director

lhousewright@zachysauctions.com

Since going independent in 2002, Zachys has aggressively carved a niche in the upper echelons of the auction arena, and now reigns as the auction leader in America. Two of the country's most esteemed auctioneers, Fritz Hatton and Ursula Hermacinski, conduct the sales. It is known for its strong prices and its high percent sold rates. The buyer's premium is 18 percent.

Zachys with Wally's (Los Angeles)

Phone: (310) 446-6622

Fax: (310) 446-6172

wallywine.com

2005 sales: $6 million

Contact: Amanda Keston, LA manager

Alternatively, contact Zachys (above)

A new joint venture that shattered commercial California auction records with a $4.2 million sale in October 2004. The buyer's premium is 18 percent.

Seller's fees at all the houses are often subject to negotiation depending on the size and value of the cellar, and may range from zero to 10 percent or higher. The buyer's premiums are accurate as of this writing but do change; you should confirm them with the auction house.

AUCTION RECORDS

~~~~~~

FRANCE

$170,375	DRC Romanée-Conti 1985	6 magnums	NYWines Christie's	2006
$155,242	Château Lafite Rothschild 1787	1 bottle	Christie's	1985
$118,500	Château Latour-à-Pomerol 1961	6 magnums	Acker Merrall & Condit	2006
$114,614	Château Mouton-Rothschild 1945	1 jeroboam	Christie's London	1997
$109,324	Château Cheval-Blanc 1947	1 imperial	Christie's London	1997
$100,725	DRC Romanée-Conti 1990	1 methuselah	Acker Merrall & Condit	2006
$100,300	Château Mouton-Rothschild 1945	6 magnums	Zachys with Wally's	2005
$91,691	Château Pétrus 1961	12 bottles	Christie's London	1997
$88,125	Château Cheval-Blanc 1947	24 half-bottles	NYWines Christie's	2005
$85,188	DRC Romanée-Conti 1989	12 bottles	Aulden Cellars-Sotheby's	2005
$76,375	DRC Romanée-Conti 1996	12 bottles	Aulden Cellars-Sotheby's	2005
$70,800	DRC Romanée-Conti 1971	1 methusaleh	Zachys	2005
$63,000	Château La Mission-Haut-Brion 1949	1 jeroboam	Sherry-Lehmann with Sotheby's	1999
$53,100	Château Lafleur 1947	1 magnum	Zachys with Wally's	2005

$53,100	Château Latour 1959	6 magnums	Zachys	2005
$52,875	Château Mouton-Rothschild 1947	6 magnums	NYWines Christie's	2005
$51,750	Château d'Yquem 1921	12 bottles	Sherry-Lehmann with Sotheby's	1999
$44,062	DRC Romanée-Conti 1966	12 bottles	Aulden Cellars-Sotheby's	2004
$41,400	Jaboulet Hermitage La Chapelle 1961	12 bottles	Sherry-Lehmann with Sotheby's	1999
$36,687	Château Lafite 1811	1 tappit hen (1 magnum)	Christie's London	2000
$35,650	Château Lafleur 1959	5 magnums	Zachys-Christie's	2000
$34,500	Château Latour 1945	12 bottles	Sherry-Lehmann with Sotheby's	1999
$30,810	Château Pétrus 1989	12 bottles	Acker Merrall & Condit	2005
$30,680	DRC Montrachet 1990	12 bottles	Hart Davis Hart	2006
$29,500	Château Pétrus 1921	1 magnum	Zachys with Wally's	2005
$26,019	DRC La Tâche 1985	12 bottles	Sotheby's London	2004
$22,923	Château Palmer 1961	12 bottles	Christie's London	2000
$22,235	Château Cheval-Blanc 1947	1 magnum	Aulden Cellars-Sotheby's	2005
$21,330	A. Rousseau Clos de la Roche 1962	12 bottles	Acker Merrall & Condit	2005
$18,975	G. Roumier Bonnes Mares 1971	12 bottles	Bonhams & Butterfields	2004
$18,975	Château Calon-Ségur 1947	12 bottles	Zachys-Christie's (Los Angeles)	2000

$16,425	DRC La Tâche 1990	12 bottles	WineBid.com	2000
$12,925	Krug Collection 1953	1 magnum	Aulden Cellars-Sotheby's	2005
$12,285	Château l'Evangile 1947	1 magnum	Acker Merrall & Condit	2004
$11,700	Château Trotanoy 1961	1 double magnum	Acker Merrall & Condit	2004
$11,115	Château d'Yquem 1816	1 bottle	Zachys	2004
$10,281	Domaine Leflaive Chevalier-Montrachet 1996	12 bottles	Aulden Cellars-Sotheby's	2005
$6,490	Heidsieck Monopole Gout American Champagne	1 bottle	Zachys	2005

ITALY

$10,063	Sassicaia 1985	12 bottles	Sherry-Lehmann with Sotheby's	1999

CULTS AND CALIFORNIANS

$112,500	Colgin Cellars Cabernet Sauvignon Herb Lamb Vineyard 1992–1995	4, 18-liter bottles	Zachys-Christie's (New York)	1998
$71,100	Screaming Eagle 1992	6 magnums	Acker Merrall & Condit	2005
$30,680	Beaulieu Vineyards Private Reserve Cabernet Sauvignon 1951	12 bottles	Zachys with Wally's	2005
$23,100	Dominus 1991	1 imperial	Davis & Company	1997
$21,850	Araujo Eisele Vineyards Cabernet Sauvignon 1991–1995	5 double magnums	Zachys-Christie's (Los Angeles)	1999
$17,250	Inglenook Cabernet Sauvignon 1941	3 bottles	Sherry-Lehmann with Sotheby's	1999
$15,340	Heitz Martha's Vineyard Cabernet Sauvignon 1974	12 bottles	Zachys	2005

$15,340	Harlan Estate 1994	12 bottles	Zachys	2006
$11,500	Screaming Eagle Cabernet Sauvignon 1994		Zachys-Christie's (Los Angeles)	2000
$10,350	Bryant Family Cabernet Sauvignon 1994	12 bottles	Zachys-Christie's (Los Angeles)	1998
$9,775	Dalla Valle Maya 1994	1 imperial	Zachys-Christie's (Los Angeles)	1999

THE WINE SPECTATOR
AUCTION INDEX

~/\/\/\/\~

Every serious wine drinker soon comes to realize that there is no unilateral price for any label, whether found at retail or at auction. One of the biggest challenges of the collecting process, therefore, is being able to determine a given bottle's true worth. The *Wine Spectator* Auction Index, created in 1995, is one of the best gauges of the current or going rate for wines sold at auction in the United States.

Catalog estimates don't necessarily provide all the answers. Although established auction houses base their estimates on recently realized prices, they don't always take into account prices realized by their competitors. One house's high price for a specific wine could theoretically be another house's low, unbalancing both of their estimates. When it comes to extreme rarities that crop up infrequently, the estimate is sometimes just an educated guess of where the gavel will fall.

A perfect example is the celebrated Leroy La Romanée 1953, a classic Burgundy shipped directly from the domaine that sold well above estimate for $49,350 at a NYWinesChristie's auction in October 2004. Just a month later, a similar case of La Romanée 1953 commanded $19,975 at NYWinesChristie's, and then at Acker Merrall & Condit, another case in seemingly identical condition brought just $17,550. Even accounting for the pristine provenance of the first example, the extreme disparity in sales shows how imprecise auctions can be. The dynamic at every auction (and for every lot) can vary widely, causing significant price disparities.

In order to recognize such disparities and snare a bargain, you first have to know how to spot one. The *Wine Spectator* Auction Index—excerpted over the following pages—can be an efficacious tool for analyzing current auction estimates and results. It tracks the performance of thousands of the most frequently traded wines at all of the major commercial American auction houses, records average prices per bottle and percentage price changes, along with the high and low bids calculated from realized price lists. It also tracks the number of bottles sold per quarter.

The following charts are adapted from the *Wine Spectator* Auction Index, and compare results from the first half of 2005 with the first half of 2006 (minus sales for June 2006). In the first column, wines are listed by winery name, designation, and vintage. They are followed by their respective prices in the two selected halves, the percent change in their prices, and the high and low prices as designated by auction house. These prices include the buyer's premium (see page 78).

The price averages serve as a barometer of a wine's going rate. If you can snap up a wine at its current average price, you are getting good value. The high price can be used to determine your maximum bid or simply to note the recent ceiling for a wine. If a wine in an auction catalog is estimated at $1,500 to $2,000 per case, and the recent high price listed in the Auction Index was the equivalent of $1,975 per case, you'll probably have to pay top dollar in order to snare it. Conversely, if the bidding stops on the same wine at $1,400, then you are getting a relative bargain. By studying the charts in detail, you'll know when to raise or lower your paddle.

While past performance is no guarantee of future results, by closely examining the percentage change data, it's possible to gauge whether the price of a wine is currently ascending or descending. Regular increases in price are an indication of strong demand, whereas sustained declines show waning interest. (In the case of older vintages, however, variations in a wine's condition may also account for a hike or a drop in price.)

The low-price data serves as a reality check. For starters, it is unlikely that you will be able to pick up that wine much below its recent low. If you do, you are getting a steal. In contrast, if the low estimate printed in the catalog is higher than the wine's recent low price in the Auction Index, then it's likely that the seller has placed an aggressive reserve on the consignment and is unwilling to part with it at a discount.

Michael Troise, the auction director for NYWinesChristie's, says he always focuses on a wine's recent low price rather than its average or its high. "If a wine has sold for as little as $50 per bottle, that says to me it may do so again. I'm willing to hold out until that happens." A contrarian view is taken by Christie's Richard Brierley, who suggests that if you really want a specific wine, you should be prepared to go one extra bid-step in order to secure it.

To keep up to date over the long term, you can refer to a shortened index of the top 150 most frequently traded wines which is printed in *Wine Spectator* magazine. Or visit winespectator.com for a far more extensive index of over 16,000 listings (accessible to *Wine Spectator* subscribers for $49.95 annually). All you need to do is select a winery, vintage, or bottle size, and the search engine provides the average price, high and low spreads, and the percentage change in the wine's price. There is an additional link to tasting notes (where they exist) compiled by the *Wine Spectator* magazine's tasting panel.

wine	1h2006$	1h2005$	06 v. 05%	high $	low $
BORDEAUX					
Château Angélus 2000	165	147	12%	209	120
Château Angélus 1995	121	106	14%	128	108
Château Angélus 1990	267	234	14%	318	199
Château Angélus 1989	220	176	25%	257	176
Château Angélus 1982	64	77	-17%	64	64
Château Beychevelle 2000	40	59	-32%	40	40
Château Beychevelle 1995	40	37	8%	41	40
Château Beychevelle 1990	61	63	-3%	64	59
Château Beychevelle 1989	80	69	16%	110	58
Château Beychevelle 1982	126	128	-2%	154	108
Château Calon-Ségur 2000	77	70	10%	93	69
Château Calon-Ségur 1995	74	69	7%	79	69
Château Calon-Ségur 1990	95	100	-5%	98	91
Château Calon-Ségur 1989	71	61	16%	74	69
Château Calon-Ségur 1982	130	113	15%	167	98
Château Certan de May 2000	71	83	-14%	74	69
Château Certan de May 1995	64	73	-12%	NA	NA
Château Certan de May 1990	83	76	9%	93	73
Château Certan de May 1989	59	54	9%	59	59
Château Certan de May 1982	266	264	1%	313	215
Château Cheval-Blanc 2000	684	572	20%	847	492
Château Cheval-Blanc 1995	193	179	8%	294	150
Château Cheval-Blanc 1990	753	639	18%	885	583
Château Cheval-Blanc 1989	225	212	6%	296	178
Château Cheval-Blanc 1982	866	750	15%	1567	652
Château La Conseillante 2000	165	150	10%	235	125
Château La Conseillante 1995	64	67	-4%	64	64
Château La Conseillante 1990	258	228	13%	343	200
Château La Conseillante 1989	244	210	16%	367	170
Château La Conseillante 1982	231	206	12%	275	216
Château Cos-d'Estournel 2000	113	103	10%	159	84
Château Cos-d'Estournel 1995	107	96	11%	127	83
Château Cos-d'Estournel 1990	162	129	26%	186	128
Château Cos-d'Estournel 1989	116	93	25%	143	83
Château Cos-d'Estournel 1982	248	219	13%	275	208

wine	1h2006$	1h2005$	06 v. 05%	high $	low $
Château La Dominique 2000	41	39	5%	41	41
Château La Dominique 1995	39	45	-13%	39	39
Château La Dominique 1990	67	72	-7%	77	60
Château La Dominique 1989	95	78	22%	95	95
Château La Dominique 1982	97	77	26%	127	79
Château Ducru-Beaucaillou 2000	112	97	15%	149	88
Château Ducru-Beaucaillou 1995	125	96	30%	138	98
Château Ducru-Beaucaillou 1990	91	88	3%	119	73
Château Ducru-Beaucaillou 1989	84	78	8%	100	64
Château Ducru-Beaucaillou 1982	194	192	1%	236	148
Château L'Evangile 2000	219	171	28%	257	167
Château L'Evangile 1995	111	90	23%	133	99
Château L'Evangile 1990	254	221	15%	318	215
Château L'Evangile 1989	136	152	-11%	168	118
Château L'Evangile 1982	353	318	11%	529	224
Château Figeac 2000	118	74	59%	118	118
Château Figeac 1995	91	67	36%	98	84
Château Figeac 1990	148	147	1%	148	148
Château Figeac 1989	79	79	0%	79	79
Château Figeac 1982	204	173	18%	236	167
Château Grand-Puy-Lacoste 2000	56	64	-13%	59	52
Château Grand-Puy-Lacoste 1995	87	65	34%	94	84
Château Grand-Puy-Lacoste 1990	111	102	9%	111	111
Château Grand-Puy-Lacoste 1989	81	62	31%	84	78
Château Grand-Puy-Lacoste 1982	171	137	25%	217	120
Château Gruaud-Larose 2000	89	87	2%	149	74
Château Gruaud-Larose 1995	49	44	11%	49	49
Château Gruaud-Larose 1990	117	105	11%	137	99
Château Gruaud-Larose 1989	73	68	7%	80	59
Château Gruaud-Larose 1982	223	195	14%	277	176
Château Haut-Brion 2000	467	364	28%	511	375
Château Haut-Brion 1995	232	180	29%	313	150
Château Haut-Brion 1990	388	327	19%	415	334
Château Haut-Brion 1989	857	599	43%	1282	590
Château Haut-Brion 1982	423	394	7%	514	325
Château Lafite Rothschild 2000	538	397	36%	642	435

wine	1h2006$	1h2005$	06 v. 05%	high $	low $
Château Lafite Rothschild 1995	227	212	7%	334	187
Château Lafite Rothschild 1990	294	267	10%	375	225
Château Lafite Rothschild 1989	238	224	6%	316	195
Château Lafite Rothschild 1982	808	672	20%	1095	508
Château Lafleur 2000	1234	1078	14%	1593	1062
Château Lafleur 1995	433	234	85%	639	296
Château Lafleur 1990	1007	867	16%	1007	1007
Château Lafleur 1989	905	575	57%	1037	751
Château Lafleur 1982	2456	1644	49%	2742	1967
Château Latour 2000	547	477	15%	642	417
Château Latour 1995	258	220	17%	354	215
Château Latour 1990	678	523	30%	1033	433
Château Latour 1989	260	232	12%	279	197
Château Latour 1982	962	711	35%	1273	751
Château Léoville Barton 2000	122	117	4%	167	98
Château Léoville Barton 1995	60	61	-2%	60	60
Château Léoville Barton 1990	93	87	7%	98	88
Château Léoville Barton 1989	81	84	-4%	89	73
Château Léoville Barton 1982	122	129	-5%	153	98
Château Léoville Las Cases 2000	235	244	-4%	325	215
Château Léoville Las Cases 1995	144	121	19%	157	118
Château Léoville Las Cases 1990	235	197	19%	285	176
Château Léoville Las Cases 1989	142	125	14%	177	92
Château Léoville Las Cases 1982	427	364	17%	593	313
Château Lynch-Bages 2000	122	107	14%	149	96
Château Lynch-Bages 1995	91	78	17%	110	75
Château Lynch-Bages 1990	174	146	19%	205	144
Château Lynch-Bages 1989	187	173	8%	257	133
Château Lynch-Bages 1982	241	223	8%	374	177
Château Margaux 2000	599	428	40%	691	429
Château Margaux 1995	311	269	16%	395	229
Château Margaux 1990	667	549	21%	881	496
Château Margaux 1989	278	236	18%	465	208
Château Margaux 1982	680	556	22%	881	475
Château La Mission-Haut-Brion 1982	471	461	2%	529	393
Château La Mission-Haut-Brion 2000	470	369	27%	566	354

wine	1h2006$	1h2005$	06 v. 05%	high $	low $
Château La Mission-Haut-Brion 1995	123	98	26%	138	93
Château La Mission-Haut-Brion 1990	243	207	17%	256	208
Château La Mission-Haut-Brion 1989	549	445	23%	639	472
Château Montrose 2000	120	100	20%	138	88
Château Montrose 1995	74	88	-16%	93	64
Château Montrose 1990	358	324	10%	553	250
Château Montrose 1989	167	144	16%	207	157
Château Montrose 1982	126	120	5%	153	119
Château Mouton-Rothschild 2000	449	362	24%	548	343
Château Mouton-Rothschild 1995	227	190	19%	295	158
Château Mouton-Rothschild 1990	217	208	4%	256	176
Château Mouton-Rothschild 1989	251	237	6%	299	183
Château Mouton-Rothschild 1982	795	646	23%	1077	567
Château Palmer 2000	193	171	13%	217	148
Château Palmer 1995	103	98	5%	108	93
Château Palmer 1990	136	130	5%	156	108
Château Palmer 1989	231	187	24%	257	176
Château Palmer 1982	174	148	18%	215	118
Château Pavie 2000	278	286	-3%	393	237
Château Pavie 1995	49	49	0%	NA	NA
Château Pavie 1990	124	121	2%	124	124
Château Pavie 1989	61	65	-6%	69	54
Château Pavie 1982	105	114	-8%	119	89
Château Pétrus 2000	2450	1842	33%	2765	1665
Château Pétrus 1995	1223	820	49%	2154	826
Château Pétrus 1990	2365	1923	23%	2742	1770
Château Pétrus 1989	2466	1655	49%	3133	1534
Château Pétrus 1982	2909	2458	18%	4700	2000
Château Pichon-Longueville-Baron 2000	103	97	6%	119	71
Château Pichon-Longueville-Baron 1995	69	49	41%	78	60
Château Pichon-Longueville-Baron 1990	171	158	8%	215	120
Château Pichon-Longueville-Baron 1989	178	159	12%	216	147

216

wine	1h2006$	1h2005$	06 v. 05%	high $	low $
Château Pichon-Longueville-Baron 1982	148	155	-5%	162	138
Château Pichon-Longueville-Lalande 2000	185	146	27%	256	157
Château Pichon-Longueville-Lalande 1995	145	110	32%	197	118
Château Pichon-Longueville-Lalande 1990	113	120	-6%	176	90
Château Pichon-Longueville-Lalande 1989	156	144	8%	259	108
Château Pichon-Longueville-Lalande 1982	409	377	8%	551	320
Château Le Pin 2000	2559	1764	45%	2742	2469
Château Le Pin 1995	649	735	-12%	649	649
Château Le Pin 1990	2739	1482	85%	2938	1645
Château Le Pin 1989	1302	1400	-7%	1410	1284
Château Le Pin 1982	4909	3956	24%	5875	2844
Château Sociando-Mallet 2000	49	43	14%	49	49
Château Sociando-Mallet 1995	44	35	26%	47	40
Château Sociando-Mallet 1990	86	89	-3%	94	78
Château Sociando-Mallet 1989	50	49	2%	57	44
Château Sociando-Mallet 1982	69	75	-8%	NA	NA
Château Talbot 2000	51	52	-2%	69	40
Château Talbot 1995	49	49	0%	NA	NA
Château Talbot 1990	72	68	6%	89	64
Château Talbot 1989	63	63	0%	110	49
Château Talbot 1982	120	111	8%	169	111
Château Trotanoy 2000	217	114	90%	217	217
Château Trotanoy 1995	114	111	3%	143	92
Château Trotanoy 1990	178	135	32%	219	142
Château Trotanoy 1989	108	110	-2%	108	108
Château Trotanoy 1982	295	292	1%	382	250
Vieux-Château-Certan 2000	131	138	-5%	157	118
Vieux-Château-Certan 1995	79	59	34%	79	79
Vieux-Château-Certan 1990	98	119	-18%	98	98
Vieux-Château-Certan 1989	69	69	0%	79	59
Vieux-Château-Certan 1982	137	156	-12%	168	118

wine	1h2006$	1h2005$	06 v. 05%	high $	low $
SAUTERNES					
Château d'Yquem 1997	245	196	25%	284	158
Château d'Yquem 1990	352	312	13%	416	285
Château d'Yquem 1989	366	285	28%	441	250
Château d'Yquem 1988	373	308	21%	570	240
Château d'Yquem 1986	367	311	18%	433	285
BURGUNDY					
Louis Latour Corton-Charlemagne 1996	106	88	20%	138	75
Louis Latour Corton-Charlemagne 1995	75	122	-39%	76	74
Louis Latour Corton-Charlemagne 1990	129	141	-9%	199	59
Louis Latour Corton-Charlemagne 1989	212	153	39%	NA	NA
Louis Latour Corton-Charlemagne 1985	79	142	-44%	79	79
Domaine Leflaive Chevalier-Montrachet 1996	749	538	39%	1278	415
Domaine Leflaive Chevalier-Montrachet 1995	443	532	-17%	443	443
Domaine Leflaive Chevalier-Montrachet 1990	451	573	-21%	767	315
Domaine Leflaive Chevalier-Montrachet 1989	707	527	34%	741	600
Domaine Leflaive Chevalier-Montrachet 1985	599	582	3%	780	511
Leroy Clos de Vougeot 1999	247	208	19%	296	236
Leroy Clos de Vougeot 1996	314	311	1%	375	255
Leroy Clos de Vougeot 1993	474	374	27%	474	474
Leroy Clos de Vougeot 1990	376	454	-17%	393	354
Leroy Clos de Vougeot 1985	332	332	0%	NA	NA
Jacques-Frédéric Mugnier Musigny 1999	353	356	-1%	395	288
Jacques-Frédéric Mugnier Musigny 1996	266	195	36%	266	266
Jacques-Frédéric Mugnier Musigny 1993	768	498	54%	830	724

wine	1h2006$	1h2005$	06 v. 05%	high $	low $
Jacques-Frédéric Mugnier Musigny 1990	535	438	22%	593	448
Jacques-Frédéric Mugnier Musigny 1985	593	830	-29%	593	593
Ponsot Clos de la Roche Vieilles Vignes 1999	155	136	14%	192	128
Ponsot Clos de la Roche Vieilles Vignes 1996	122	102	20%	137	89
Ponsot Clos de la Roche Vieilles Vignes 1993	561	640	-12%	751	431
Ponsot Clos de la Roche Vieilles Vignes 1990	650	570	14%	713	551
Ponsot Clos de la Roche Vieilles Vignes 1985	1103	952	16%	1180	1027
Ramonet Montrachet 1996	1525	1133	35%	1567	1273
Ramonet Montrachet 1995	1102	823	34%	1175	770
Ramonet Montrachet 1990	2448	1258	95%	2448	2448
Ramonet Montrachet 1989	1602	1293	24%	1763	1410
Ramonet Montrachet 1985	1968	1363	44%	2006	1778
Domaine de la Romanée-Conti La Tâche 1999	1448	874	66%	1672	1278
Domaine de la Romanée-Conti La Tâche 1996	1210	744	63%	1665	708
Domaine de la Romanée-Conti La Tâche 1993	969	603	61%	1185	590
Domaine de la Romanée-Conti La Tâche 1990	3232	2023	60%	4896	1888
Domaine de la Romanée-Conti La Tâche 1985	2854	1587	80%	4896	1250
Domaine de la Romanée-Conti Romanée-Conti 1999	4813	4179	15%	6373	4345
Domaine de la Romanée-Conti Romanée-Conti 19968	4737	2675	77%	5178	306
Domaine de la Romanée-Conti Romanée-Conti 1993	3550	2470	44%	3792	3304
Domaine de la Romanée-Conti Romanée-Conti 1990	9502	5665	68%	14100	5288
Domaine de la Romanée-Conti Romanée-Conti 1985	9789	5098	92%	22325	4000

wine	1h2006$	1h2005$	06 v. 05%	high $	low $
G. Roumier Bonnes Mares 1999	391	383	2%	393	385
G. Roumier Bonnes Mares 1996	432	300	44%	474	375
G. Roumier Bonnes Mares 1993	622	563	10%	622	622
G. Roumier Bonnes Mares 1990	876	767	14%	940	747
G. Roumier Bonnes Mares 1985	1254	1069	17%	1377	885
Armand Rousseau Chambertin 1999	340	331	3%	375	275
Armand Rousseau Chambertin 1996	395	303	30%	415	356
Armand Rousseau Chambertin 1993	547	579	-6%	553	543
Armand Rousseau Chambertin 1990	683	577	18%	734	622
Armand Rousseau Chambertin 1985	871	823	6%	1058	711
Comte Georges de Vogüé Musigny Cuvée Vieilles Vignes 1999	347	307	13%	454	320
Comte Georges de Vogüé Musigny Cuvée Vieilles Vignes 1990	609	473	29%	823	354
Comte Georges de Vogüé Musigny Cuvée Vieilles Vignes 1985	354	349	1%	415	329
RHÔNE					
Château de Beaucastel Châteauneuf-du-Pape 2000	60	48	25%	74	47
Château de Beaucastel Châteauneuf-du-Pape 1998	96	74	30%	133	79
Château de Beaucastel Châteauneuf-du-Pape 1995	63	63	0%	69	59
Château de Beaucastel Châteauneuf-du-Pape 1990	169	145	17%	217	129
Château de Beaucastel Châteauneuf-du-Pape 1989	170	162	5%	296	118
Château de Beaucastel Châteauneuf-du-Pape Hommage à Jacques Perrin Grande Cuvée 2000	286	294	-3%	NA	NA
Château de Beaucastel Châteauneuf-du-Pape Hommage à Jacques Perrin Grande Cuvée 1998	327	279	17%	330	325
Château de Beaucastel Châteauneuf-du-Pape Hommage à Jacques Perrin Grande Cuvée 1995	267	253	6%	267	267
Château de Beaucastel Châteauneuf-du-Pape Hommage à Jacques Perrin Grande Cuvée 1990	622	649	-4%	1185	511

wine	1h2006$	1h2005$	06 v. 05%	high $	low $
Château de Beaucastel Châteauneuf-du-Pape Hommage à Jacques Perrin Grande Cuvée 1989	593	773	-23%	593	593
Henri Bonneau Châteauneuf-du-Pape Cuvée Marie Beurrier 1998	207	224	-8%	237	177
Henri Bonneau Châteauneuf-du-Pape Cuvée Marie Beurrier 1995	128	89	44%	NA	NA
Henri Bonneau Châteauneuf-du-Pape Cuvée Marie Beurrier 1990	531	186	185%	NA	NA
Henri Bonneau Châteauneuf-du-Pape Cuvée Marie Beurrier 1989	130	151	-14%	130	130
Henri Bonneau Châteauneuf-du-Pape Réserve des Célestins 1999	208	229	-9%	217	187
Henri Bonneau Châteauneuf-du-Pape Réserve des Célestins 1998	425	383	11%	474	359
Henri Bonneau Châteauneuf-du-Pape Réserve des Célestins 1995	237	290	-18%	237	236
Henri Bonneau Châteauneuf-du-Pape Réserve des Célestins 1990	789	841	-6%	1121	705
Henri Bonneau Châteauneuf-du-Pape Réserve des Célestins 1989	452	460	-2%	1003	376
Lucien & André Brunel Châteauneuf-du-Pape Les Cailloux Cuvée Centenaire 2000	141	155	-9%	148	118
Lucien & André Brunel Châteauneuf-du-Pape Les Cailloux Cuvée Centenaire 1998	326	255	28%	346	296
Lucien & André Brunel Châteauncuf-du-Pape Les Cailloux Cuvée Centenaire 1995	148	170	-13%	NA	NA
Lucien & André Brunel Châteauneuf-du-Pape Les Cailloux Cuvée Centenaire 1990	528	345	53%	632	356
Lucien & André Brunel Châteauneuf-du-Pape Les Cailloux Cuvée Centenaire 1989	270	260	4%	296	216
Chapoutier Ermitage Le Pavillon 1999	138	120	15%	138	138
Chapoutier Ermitage Le Pavillon 1996	163	114	43%	200	118
Chapoutier Ermitage Le Pavillon 1995	157	172	-9%	157	157
Chapoutier Ermitage Le Pavillon 1990	324	307	6%	472	274

wine	1h2006$	1h2005$	06 v. 05%	high $	low $
Chapoutier Ermitage Le Pavillon 1989	271	188	44%	315	224
Jean-Louis Chave Hermitage 1999	204	184	11%	237	176
Jean-Louis Chave Hermitage 1995	174	137	27%	237	158
Jean-Louis Chave Hermitage 1990	428	379	13%	465	392
Jean-Louis Chave Hermitage 1989	252	200	26%	277	189
Jean-Louis Chave Hermitage 1985	166	149	11%	188	125
E. Guigal Côte-Rôtie La Landonne 1999	481	466	3%	629	367
E. Guigal Côte-Rôtie La Landonne 1995	287	267	7%	325	277
E. Guigal Côte-Rôtie La Landonne 1990	735	587	25%	764	593
E. Guigal Côte-Rôtie La Landonne 1989	494	478	3%	561	353
E. Guigal Côte-Rôtie La Landonne 1985	1199	879	36%	1371	682
E. Guigal Côte-Rôtie La Mouline 1999	485	484	0%	629	413
E. Guigal Côte-Rôtie La Mouline 1995	309	279	11%	316	296
E. Guigal Côte-Rôtie La Mouline 1990	860	602	43%	979	569
E. Guigal Côte-Rôtie La Mouline 1989	519	471	10%	543	472
E. Guigal Côte-Rôtie La Mouline 1985	942	765	23%	1003	901
E. Guigal Côte-Rôtie La Turque 1999	457	486	-6%	629	393
E. Guigal Côte-Rôtie La Turque 1995	332	341	-3%	517	296
E. Guigal Côte-Rôtie La Turque 1990	716	604	19%	735	682
E. Guigal Côte-Rôtie La Turque 1989	540	436	24%	551	533
E. Guigal Côte-Rôtie La Turque 1985	1200	847	42%	1567	744
Paul Jaboulet Aîné Hermitage La Chapelle 1999	67	32	109%	74	59
Paul Jaboulet Aîné Hermitage La Chapelle 1990	358	286	25%	541	273
Paul Jaboulet Aîné Hermitage La Chapelle 1989	192	126	52%	275	157
Paul Jaboulet Aîné Hermitage La Chapelle 1978	704	684	3%	885	593
Paul Jaboulet Aîné Hermitage La Chapelle 1961	4832	3484	39%	5875	3555
Domaine du Pégaü Châteauneuf-du-Pape Cuvée Réservée 2000	53	57	-7%	59	47

wine	1h2006$	1h2005$	06 v. 05%	high $	low $
Domaine du Pégaü Châteauneuf-du-Pape Cuvée Réservée 1998	60	76	-21%	60	60
Domaine du Pégaü Châteauneuf-du-Pape Cuvée Réservée 1995	62	63	-2%	64	59
Domaine du Pégaü Châteauneuf-du-Pape Cuvée Réservée 1990	195	128	52%	254	154
Domaine du Pégaü Châteauneuf-du-Pape Cuvée Réservée 1989	123	78	58%	123	123
Château Rayas Châteauneuf-du-Pape Réservé 1998	113	114	-1%	138	89
Château Rayas Châteauneuf-du-Pape Réservé 1995	467	308	52%	637	235
Château Rayas Châteauneuf-du-Pape Réservé 1990	855	651	31%	988	629
Château Rayas Châteauncuf-du-Pape Réservé 1989	571	443	29%	590	533
Château Rayas Châteauneuf-du-Pape Réservé 1985	381	410	-7%	435	354
Pierre Usseglio & Fils Châteauneuf-du-Pape Cuvée de mon Aïeul 2001	86	82	5%	93	79
Pierre Usseglio & Fils Châteauneuf-du-Pape Cuvée de mon Aïeul 2000	66	72	-8%	74	54
Pierre Usseglio & Fils Châteauneuf-du-Pape Cuvée de mon Aïeul 1999	42	49	-14%	44	39
Pierre Usseglio & Fils Châteauneuf-du-Pape Cuvée de mon Aïeul 1998	148	72	106%	148	148
Félicien Diffonty & Fils Châteauneuf-du-Pape Cuvée du Vatican Sixtine Réserve 2000	29	37	-22%	NA	NA
Le Vieux Donjon Châteauneuf-du-Pape 1998	67	51	31%	69	64
Domaine du Vieux Télégraphe Châteauneuf-du-Pape 2000	39	35	11%	NA	NA
Domaine du Vieux Télégraphe Châteauneuf-du-Pape 1998	53	49	8%	44	NA
Domaine du Vieux Télégraphe Châteauneuf-du-Pape 1995	34	64	-47%	NA	NA
Domaine du Vieux Télégraphe Châteauneuf-du-Pape 1989	70	100	-30%	70	70

wine	1h2006$	1h2005$	06 v. 05%	high $	low $
Domaine du Vieux Télégraphe Châteauneuf-du-Pape 1985	85	56	52%	85	85
CHAMPAGNE					
Veuve Clicquot Brut Champagne La Grande Dame 1995	165	120	38%	168	158
Veuve Clicquot Brut Champagne La Grande Dame 1990	160	141	13%	216	127
Veuve Clicquot Brut Champagne La Grande Dame 1989	103	103	0%	NA	NA
Veuve Clicquot Brut Champagne La Grande Dame 1985	139	132	5%	142	138
Krug Brut Champagne 1990	230	248	-7%	NA	NA
Krug Brut Champagne 1988	162	184	-12%	162	162
Krug Brut Champagne 1985	234	246	-5%	266	163
Krug Brut Champagne 1982	239	184	30%	239	239
Krug Brut Champagne 1979	839	202	315%	839	839
Moët & Chandon Brut Champagne Cuvée Dom Pérignon 1996	151	151	0%	237	100
Moët & Chandon Brut Champagne Cuvée Dom Pérignon 1990	179	163	10%	256	122
Moët & Chandon Brut Champagne Cuvée Dom Pérignon 1985	245	161	52%	257	236
Moët & Chandon Brut Champagne Cuvée Dom Pérignon 1983	156	128	22%	156	156
Louis Roederer Brut Champagne Cristal 1996	224	194	15%	NA	NA
Louis Roederer Brut Champagne Cristal 1990	476	342	39%	588	356
Louis Roederer Brut Champagne Cristal 1982	332	310	7%	332	332
Pol Roger Brut Champagne Cuvée Sir Winston Churchill 1990	209	179	17%	296	168
Pol Roger Brut Champagne Cuvée Sir Winston Churchill 1988	353	94	276%	NA	NA
Salon Brut Blanc de Blancs Champagne Le Mesnil 1990	257	196	31%	257	257
Salon Brut Blanc de Blancs Champagne Le Mesnil 1988	256	105	144%	256	256

wine	1h2006$	1h2005$	06 v. 05%	high $	low $
Salon Brut Blanc de Blancs Champagne Le Mesnil 1985	257	145	77%	257	257
Salon Brut Blanc de Blancs Champagne Le Mesnil 1982	275	199	38%	275	275
Taittinger Brut Blanc de Blancs Champagne Comtes de Champagne 1990	197	171	15%	197	197
FRANCE MISC.					
Trimbach Riesling Alsace Clos Ste.-Hune 1999	173	188	-8%	201	158
Trimbach Riesling Alsace Clos Ste.-Hune 1997	168	138	22%	187	148
Trimbach Riesling Alsace Clos Ste.-Hune 1996	173	203	-15%	NA	NA
Trimbach Riesling Alsace Clos Ste.-Hune 1990	365	368	-1%	435	295
Trimbach Riesling Alsace Cuvée Frédéric Émile 1990	123	74	66%	123	123
Domaine des Baumard Quarts de Chaume 1998	40	40	0%	NA	NA
Domaine des Baumard Quarts de Chaume 1990	95	48	98%	95	95
S.A. Huët Vouvray Cuvée Constance 1995	107	77	39%	107	107
S.A. Huët Vouvray Cuvée Constance 1989	207	144	44%	207	207
S.A. Huët Vouvray Moelleux Clos du Bourg 1ère Trie 1959	237	209	13%	237	237
Château Montus Madiran Cuvée Prestige 1995	66	58	14%	69	64
CALIFORNIA					
Abreu Cabernet Sauvignon Madrona Ranch 1999	166	180	-8%	178	149
Abreu Cabernet Sauvignon Madrona Ranch 1997	532	472	13%	553	472
Abreu Cabernet Sauvignon Madrona Ranch 1996	270	284	-5%	316	236
Abreu Cabernet Sauvignon Madrona Ranch 1995	246	198	24%	257	236

wine	1h2006$	1h2005$	06 v. 05%	high $	low $
Abreu Cabernet Sauvignon Madrona Ranch 1994	259	235	10%	277	220
Araujo Cabernet Sauvignon Eisele Vineyard 1999	201	157	28%	273	158
Araujo Cabernet Sauvignon Eisele Vineyard 1997	227	211	8%	279	186
Araujo Cabernet Sauvignon Eisele Vineyard 1996	197	194	2%	256	138
Araujo Cabernet Sauvignon Eisele Vineyard 1995	275	270	2%	330	245
Araujo Cabernet Sauvignon Eisele Vineyard 1994	432	278	55%	2596	208
Bryant Family Cabernet Sauvignon 2002	379	356	6%	590	315
Bryant Family Cabernet Sauvignon 1999	385	325	18%	443	323
Bryant Family Cabernet Sauvignon 1997	913	711	28%	1298	649
Bryant Family Cabernet Sauvignon 1995	613	524	17%	885	454
Bryant Family Cabernet Sauvignon 1994	563	518	9%	764	472
Caymus Cabernet Sauvignon Special Selection 1999	132	124	6%	169	119
Caymus Cabernet Sauvignon Special Selection 1997	180	209	-14%	192	168
Caymus Cabernet Sauvignon Special Selection 1994	190	193	-2%	294	147
Caymus Cabernet Sauvignon Special Selection 1990	193	180	7%	215	177
Caymus Cabernet Sauvignon Special Selection 1985	206	237	-13%	206	206
Colgin Cabernet Sauvignon Herb Lamb Vineyard 2001	363	329	10%	470	283
Colgin Cabernet Sauvignon Herb Lamb Vineyard 1999	387	282	37%	647	277
Colgin Cabernet Sauvignon Herb Lamb Vineyard 1997	743	584	27%	930	553
Colgin Cabernet Sauvignon Herb Lamb Vineyard 1995	547	439	25%	629	421

wine	1h2006$	1h2005$	06 v. 05%	high $	low $
Colgin Cabernet Sauvignon Herb Lamb Vineyard 1994	565	499	13%	686	474
Dalla Valle Maya 1999	343	328	5%	371	295
Dalla Valle Maya 1997	640	478	34%	787	536
Dalla Valle Maya 1994	659	483	36%	734	413
Dalla Valle Maya 1990	344	334	3%	393	236
Dominus Estate 1999	95	82	16%	98	93
Dominus Estate 1997	129	130	-1%	158	83
Dominus Estate 1994	206	180	14%	275	162
Dominus Estate 1990	123	115	7%	138	106
Dominus Estate 1985	85	83	2%	93	78
Dunn Cabernet Sauvignon Howell Mountain 1999	61	64	-5%	69	50
Dunn Cabernet Sauvignon Howell Mountain 1997	104	99	5%	109	92
Dunn Cabernet Sauvignon Howell Mountain 1994	118	114	4%	119	118
Dunn Cabernet Sauvignon Howell Mountain 1990	98	101	-3%	128	64
Dunn Cabernet Sauvignon Howell Mountain 1985	106	98	8%	106	106
Harlan Estate 2001	669	573	17%	1180	429
Harlan Estate 1999	514	346	49%	885	351
Harlan Estate 1997	1156	771	50%	1573	652
Harlan Estate 1994	1000	749	34%	1377	711
Harlan Estate 1990	486	484	0%	531	454
Heitz Cabernet Sauvignon Martha's Vineyard 1997	157	116	35%	157	157
Heitz Cabernet Sauvignon Martha's Vineyard 1991	106	98	8%	106	106
Heitz Cabernet Sauvignon Martha's Vineyard 1990	118	122	-3%	118	118
Heitz Cabernet Sauvignon Martha's Vineyard 1985	258	255	1%	287	189
Heitz Cabernet Sauvignon Martha's Vineyard 1974	994	877	13%	1665	458
Marcassin Pinot Noir Sonoma Coast Marcassin Vineyard 2000	323	321	1%	413	274

wine	1h2006$	1h2005$	06 v. 05%	high $	low $
Marcassin Pinot Noir Sonoma Coast Marcassin Vineyard 1999	283	270	5%	341	217
Marcassin Pinot Noir Sonoma Coast Marcassin Vineyard 1998	398	321	24%	439	354
Marcassin Pinot Noir Sonoma Coast Marcassin Vineyard 1997	315	278	13%	472	237
Marcassin Pinot Noir Sonoma Coast Marcassin Vineyard 1996	274	356	-23%	326	236
Peter Michael Les Pavots Knights Valley 2002	200	186	8%	246	146
Peter Michael Les Pavots Knights Valley 2001	147	172	-15%	147	147
Peter Michael Les Pavots Knights Valley 1999	121	114	6%	127	108
Peter Michael Les Pavots Knights Valley 1997	163	164	-1%	177	153
Peter Michael Les Pavots Knights Valley 1994	141	112	26%	147	133
Robert Mondavi Cabernet Sauvignon Reserve 1999	59	59	0%	59	59
Robert Mondavi Cabernet Sauvignon Reserve 1997	79	77	3%	113	49
Robert Mondavi Cabernet Sauvignon Reserve 1994	117	118	-1%	148	89
Robert Mondavi Cabernet Sauvignon Reserve 1990	75	73	3%	79	69
Robert Mondavi Cabernet Sauvignon Reserve 1985	69	63	10%	79	56
Opus One 1999	155	140	11%	186	108
Opus One 1997	209	182	15%	275	167
Opus One 1994	209	203	3%	333	167
Opus One 1990	182	176	3%	196	177
Opus One 1985	180	156	15%	256	39
Joseph Phelps Insignia 1999	97	82	18%	106	89
Joseph Phelps Insignia 1997	157	138	14%	187	133
Joseph Phelps Insignia 1994	159	143	11%	215	133
Joseph Phelps Insignia 1990	70	74	-5%	70	70
Joseph Phelps Insignia 1985	127	96	32%	148	98
Pride Cabernet Sauvignon Reserve 2002	260	252	3%	295	203

wine	1h2006$	1h2005$	06 v. 05%	high $	low $
Pride Cabernet Sauvignon Reserve 2001	267	267	0%	374	217
Pride Cabernet Sauvignon Reserve 1999	148	134	10%	148	148
Pride Cabernet Sauvignon Reserve 1997	239	212	13%	250	222
Pride Cabernet Sauvignon Reserve 1994	296	243	22%	296	296
Ridge Monte Bello Santa Cruz Mountains 1999	79	83	-5%	79	79
Ridge Monte Bello Santa Cruz Mountains 1997	111	109	2%	138	98
Ridge Monte Bello Santa Cruz Mountains 1994	130	114	14%	176	104
Ridge Monte Bello Santa Cruz Mountains 1990	115	99	16%	137	106
Ridge Monte Bello Santa Cruz Mountains 1985	136	133	2%	157	118
Screaming Eagle Cabernet Sauvignon 2001	1576	1050	50%	1967	950
Screaming Eagle Cabernet Sauvignon 1999	1488	1133	31%	1888	1170
Screaming Eagle Cabernet Sauvignon 1998	1097	806	36%	1573	948
Screaming Eagle Cabernet Sauvignon 1997	2275	1943	17%	2832	1853
Screaming Eagle Cabernet Sauvignon 1996	1722	1347	28%	2056	1244
Shafer Cabernet Sauvignon Stags Leap District Hillside Select 1999	234	221	6%	257	198
Shafer Cabernet Sauvignon Stags Leap District Hillside Select 1997	407	368	11%	444	354
Shafer Cabernet Sauvignon Stags Leap District Hillside Select 1994	412	312	32%	494	274
Shafer Cabernet Sauvignon Stags Leap District Hillside Select 1992	207	198	5%	217	192
Shafer Cabernet Sauvignon Stags Leap District Hillside Select 1985	125	127	-2%	125	125
Spottswoode Cabernet Sauvignon 1999	65	72	-10%	79	59
Spottswoode Cabernet Sauvignon 1997	96	80	20%	98	93
Spottswoode Cabernet Sauvignon 1994	106	90	18%	118	94
Spottswoode Cabernet Sauvignon 1990	78	78	0%	84	68
Spottswoode Cabernet Sauvignon 1985	95	95	0%	96	94

wine	1h2006$	1h2005$	06 v. 05%	high $	low $
Sine Qua Non Pinot Noir Hollerin' M Shea Vineyard 2002	176	153	15%	216	148
Sine Qua Non Pinot Noir Yamhill County A-Cappella 2000	119	114	4%	119	11
Sine Qua Non Pinot Noir Yamhill County No. 6 2001	119	108	10%	119	119
Quilceda Creek Cabernet Sauvignon 2002	150	132	14%	158	138
Quilceda Creek Cabernet Sauvignon 2001	135	121	12%	143	119
Quilceda Creek Cabernet Sauvignon 2000	74	89	-17%	79	69
Quilceda Creek Cabernet Sauvignon 1999	104	87	20%	NA	NA
Quilceda Creek Cabernet Sauvignon 1998	107	92	16%	NA	NA
ITALY					
Aldo Conterno Barolo Granbussia Riserva 1996	108	107	1%	NA	NA
Aldo Conterno Barolo Granbussia Riserva 1995	138	147	-6%	138	138
Aldo Conterno Barolo Granbussia Riserva 1990	356	382	-7%	356	356
Aldo Conterno Barolo Granbussia Riserva 1989	375	385	-3%	448	367
Aldo Conterno Barolo Granbussia Riserva 1985	216	344	-37%	NA	NA
Giacomo Conterno Barolo Monfortino Riserva 1997	375	237	58%	375	375
Giacomo Conterno Barolo Monfortino Riserva 1990	491	535	-8%	514	384
Giacomo Conterno Barolo Monfortino Riserva 1985	647	732	-12%	686	531
Giacomo Conterno Barolo Monfortino Riserva 1964	657	1371	-52%	691	590
Giacomo Conterno Barolo Monfortino Riserva 1955	1138	756	51%	1138	1138
Gaja Barbaresco 1998	115	98	17%	118	108
Gaja Barbaresco 1997	158	184	-14%	177	137
Gaja Barbaresco 1990	228	265	-14%	236	221

230

wine	1h2006$	1h2005$	06 v. 05%	high $	low $
Gaja Barbaresco 1985	188	176	7%	212	164
Gaja Barbaresco 1978	186	214	-13%	NA	NA
Gaja Sorì San Lorenzo 2000	187	336	-44%	187	187
Gaja Sorì San Lorenzo 1997	309	274	13%	341	277
Gaja Sorì San Lorenzo 1996	193	181	7%	NA	NA
Gaja Sorì San Lorenzo 1990	308	306	1%	374	374
Gaja Sorì San Lorenzo 1985	312	423	-26%	NA	NA
Bruno Giacosa Barolo Falletto 1998	87	95	-8%	89	84
Bruno Giacosa Barolo Falletto 1997	118	118	0%	NA	NA
Bruno Giacosa Barolo Falletto 1996	117	168	-30%	NA	NA
Bruno Giacosa Barolo Falletto 1995	83	88	-6%	110	64
Bruno Giacosa Barolo Falletto 1982	178	284	-37%	NA	NA
Luciano Sandrone Barolo Cannubi Boschis 1998	97	82	18%	109	89
Luciano Sandrone Barolo Cannubi Boschis 1997	176	154	14%	193	167
Luciano Sandrone Barolo Cannubi Boschis 1996	184	252	-27%	236	158
Luciano Sandrone Barolo Cannubi Boschis 1990	624	661	-6%	869	468
Luciano Sandrone Barolo Cannubi Boschis 1989	348	376	-7%	415	296
Altesino Brunello di Montalcino Montosoli 1997	131	143	-8%	157	104
Altesino Brunello di Montalcino Montosoli 1995	95	79	20%	95	95
Altesino Brunello di Montalcino Montosoli 1990	154	300	-49%	167	128
Castello di Ama Vigna l'Apparita 1995	61	79	-23%	74	55
Castello di Ama Vigna l'Apparita 1990	105	137	-23%	NA	NA
Castello di Ama Vigna l'Apparita 1988	148	147	1%	NA	NA
Antinori Solaia 1999	128	140	-9%	128	128
Antinori Solaia 1997	292	305	-4%	354	236
Antinori Solaia 1990	261	247	6%	316	216
Antinori Solaia 1988	165	177	-7%	177	157
Antinori Solaia 1985	337	321	5%	374	283
Antinori Tignanello 1999	69	83	-17%	69	69
Antinori Tignanello 1997	133	130	2%	182	95

wine	1h2006$	1h2005$	06 v. 05%	high $	low $
Antinori Tignanello 1990	144	143	1%	148	138
Antinori Tignanello 1985	177	129	37%	207	158
Antinori Tignanello 1982	157	104	51%	NA	NA
Castello Banfi Brunello di Montalcino Poggio all'Oro Riserva 1997	118	109	8%	118	118
Castello Banfi Brunello di Montalcino Poggio all'Oro Riserva 1993	49	44	11%	NA	NA
Castello Banfi Brunello di Montalcino Poggio all'Oro Riserva 1990	133	127	5%	138	128
Castello Banfi Brunello di Montalcino Poggio all'Oro Riserva 1988	69	57	21%	NA	NA
Tenuta dell'Ornellaia Masseto 2001	400	490	-18%	629	375
Tenuta dell'Ornellaia Masseto 1999	244	215	13%	261	216
Tenuta dell'Ornellaia Masseto 1998	267	277	-4%	267	267
Tenuta dell'Ornellaia Masseto 1997	430	316	36%	518	316
Tenuta dell'Ornellaia Masseto 1995	266	262	2%	266	266
Tenuta dell'Ornellaia Ornellaia 1999	123	111	11%	128	119
Tenuta dell'Ornellaia Ornellaia 1997	196	164	20%	275	138
Tenuta dell'Ornellaia Ornellaia 1995	114	103	11%	157	79
Tenuta dell'Ornellaia Ornellaia 1990	190	178	7%	260	148
Tenuta dell'Ornellaia Ornellaia 1988	108	108	0%	108	108
Pieve Santa Restituta Brunello di Montalcino Rennina 1997	100	73	37%	162	73
Pieve Santa Restituta Brunello di Montalcino Rennina 1990	108	176	-39%	NA	NA
Pieve Santa Restituta Brunello di Montalcino Sugarille 1995	79	79	0%	NA	NA
Pieve Santa Restituta Brunello di Montalcino Sugarille 1990	144	144	0%	NA	NA
Castello dei Rampolla Sammarco 1997	83	131	-37%	102	74
Castello dei Rampolla Sammarco 1990	118	96	23%	118	118
Castello dei Rampolla Sammarco 1985	96	110	-13%	96	96
Castello dei Rampolla Vigna d'Alceo 2000	133	128	4%	138	128
Castello dei Rampolla Vigna d'Alceo 1999	150	165	-9%	NA	NA
Castello dei Rampolla Vigna d'Alceo 1998	79	77	3%	NA	NA

232

wine	1h2006$	1h2005$	06 v. 05%	high $	low $
Castello dei Rampolla Vigna d'Alceo 1997	138	137	1%	NA	NA
San Giusto a Rentennano Percarlo 1997	210	157	34%	237	197
San Giusto a Rentennano Percarlo 1990	230	150	53%	249	198
Tenuta San Guido Sassicaia 1999	132	158	-16%	133	129
Tenuta San Guido Sassicaia 1997	219	187	17%	259	166
Tenuta San Guido Sassicaia 1990	396	356	11%	490	215
Tenuta San Guido Sassicaia 1988	315	309	2%	413	237
Tenuta San Guido Sassicaia 1985	1371	996	38%	1567	1003
Livio Sassetti Brunello di Montalcino Pertimali 1997	108	111	-3%	109	108
Livio Sassetti Brunello di Montalcino Pertimali 1990	94	172	-45%	NA	NA
Lamborghini Umbria Campoleone 2000	85	83	2%	94	79
Lamborghini Umbria Campoleone 1999	89	89	0%	89	89
Lamborghini Umbria Campoleone 1997	151	176	-14%	187	128
Allegrini Amarone della Valpolicella Classico 1996	70	49	43%	70	70
Romano Dal Forno Amarone della Valpolicella 1998	293	406	-28%	293	293
Romano Dal Forno Amarone della Valpolicella 1997	553	601	-8%	553	553
Romano Dal Forno Amarone della Valpolicella 1996	433	551	-21%	433	433
Romano Dal Forno Amarone della Valpolicella 1995	433	380	14%	433	433
Romano Dal Forno Amarone della Valpolicella 1994	334	402	-17%	NA	NA
Feudi di San Gregorio Irpinia Serpico 2001	78	94	-17%	79	71
Montevetrano Colli di Salerno 1997	134	176	-24%	148	124
SPAIN					
Artadi Rioja Viña el Pison Reserva 1999	71	71	0%	NA	NA
Artadi Rioja Viña el Pison Reserva 1998	133	92	45%	133	133

wine	1h2006$	1h2005$	06 v. 05%	high $	low $
Artadi Rioja Viña el Pison Reserva 1996	128	128	0%	128	128
Artadi Rioja Viña el Pison Reserva 1995	187	211	-11%	187	187
Bodegas Alejandro Fernandez Ribera del Duero Pesquera Gran Reserva 1994	66	52	27%	69	64
Bodegas Alejandro Fernandez Ribera del Duero Pesquera Gran Reserva 1990	64	56	14%	64	64
Bodegas Alejandro Fernandez Ribera del Duero Pesquera Janus Reserva 1994	147	131	12%	207	118
Bodegas Alejandro Fernandez Ribera del Duero Pesquera Reserva 1994	59	65	-9%	NA	NA
Álvaro Palacios Priorat L'Ermita 1999	158	147	7%	158	158
Álvaro Palacios Priorat L'Ermita 1998	139	157	-11%	139	139
Álvaro Palacios Priorat L'Ermita 1997	111	147	-24%	NA	NA
Álvaro Palacios Priorat L'Ermita 1996	182	170	7%	NA	NA
Dominio de Pingus Ribera del Duero 2000	271	382	-29%	275	267
Dominio de Pingus Ribera del Duero 1998	176	190	-7%	NA	NA
Dominio de Pingus Ribera del Duero 1997	240	195	23%	NA	NA
Dominio de Pingus Ribera del Duero 1996	550	396	39%	NA	NA
Marqués de Riscal Rioja 1958	104	119	-13%	NA	NA
Marqués de Riscal Rioja 1953	98	103	-5%	126	89
Bodegas Vega Sicilia Ribera del Duero Unico Gran Reserva 1990	265	219	21%	313	216
Bodegas Vega Sicilia Ribera del Duero Unico Gran Reserva 1989	262	247	6%	293	256
Bodegas Vega Sicilia Ribera del Duero Unico Gran Reserva 1981	281	274	3%	281	281
Bodegas Vega Sicilia Ribera del Duero Unico Gran Reserva 1970	535	535	0%	783	323
Bodegas Vega Sicilia Ribera del Duero Unico Gran Reserva 1968	1016	826	23%	1175	797
Bodegas Vega Sicilia Ribera del Duero Unico Gran Reserva 1962	578	543	6%	593	568
Bodegas Vega Sicilia Ribera del Duero Unico Reserva Especial NV	189	190	-1%	217	176

wine	1h2006$	1h2005$	06 v. 05%	high $	low $
AUSTRALIA					
Clarendon Hills Astralis Clarendon 2003	296	196	51%	296	296
Clarendon Hills Astralis Clarendon 2002	228	235	-3%	235	216
Clarendon Hills Astralis Clarendon 2001	207	204	1%	266	197
Clarendon Hills Astralis Clarendon 1998	144	172	-16%	163	138
Clarendon Hills Astralis Clarendon 1997	151	177	-15%	216	106
Henschke Hill of Grace 1997	178	137	30%	178	178
Henschke Hill of Grace 1996	236	151	56%	NA	NA
Henschke Hill of Grace 1990	315	200	57%	NA	NA
Penfolds Shiraz South Australia Grange 1999	156	176	-11%	178	130
Penfolds Shiraz South Australia Grange 1998	331	281	18%	472	267
Penfolds Shiraz South Australia Grange 1997	168	151	11%	168	168
Penfolds Shiraz South Australia Grange 1996	185	197	-6%	190	164
Penfolds Shiraz South Australia Grange 1990	378	342	11%	465	313
Penfolds Shiraz South Australia Grange 1986	446	389	15%	511	411
Marquis Philips Shiraz Integrity 2002	125	195	-36%	125	125
VINTAGE PORT					
Dow Vintage Port 1997	44	41	7%	NA	NA
Dow Vintage Port 1994	62	70	-11%	79	54
Dow Vintage Port 1985	51	44	16%	54	44
Dow Vintage Port 1977	87	79	10%	104	71
Dow Vintage Port 1955	212	353	-40%	295	187
Fonseca Vintage Port 1997	56	55	2%	59	54
Fonseca Vintage Port 1994	118	137	-14%	137	100
Fonseca Vintage Port 1977	149	173	-14%	216	127
Fonseca Vintage Port 1970	139	163	-15%	207	92
Fonseca Vintage Port 1963	232	287	-19%	393	200

wine	1h2006$	1h2005$	06 v. 05%	high $	low $
Graham Vintage Port 1997	45	45	0%	NA	NA
Graham Vintage Port 1994	72	72	0%	79	67
Graham Vintage Port 1977	101	110	-8%	167	89
Graham Vintage Port 1970	100	127	-21%	108	88
Graham Vintage Port 1963	237	212	12%	237	237
Quinta do Noval Vintage Port Nacional 1997	577	522	11%	NA	NA
Quinta do Noval Vintage Port Nacional 1994	790	608	30%	882	608
Quinta do Noval Vintage Port Nacional 1985	315	264	19%	315	315
Quinta do Noval Vintage Port Nacional 1970	411	411	0%	NA	NA
Quinta do Noval Vintage Port Nacional 1963	2611	1464	78%	2938	2448
Taylor Fladgate Vintage Port 1997	61	73	-16%	69	59
Taylor Fladgate Vintage Port 1994	127	149	-15%	148	100
Taylor Fladgate Vintage Port 1977	125	131	-5%	165	98
Taylor Fladgate Vintage Port 1970	131	113	16%	197	108
Taylor Fladgate Vintage Port 1963	296	283	5%	393	200

WINE-COLLECTING
TERMS AND JARGON

〜〜〜〜〜

1855 classification: An official ranking of sixty-one Bordeaux chateaus prepared at the request of Emperor Napoleon III for the *Exposition Universel de Paris*. (See page 155.)

Absentee bid: A bid placed at auction by phone, fax, or e-mail, usually by someone who does not plan to attend the sale in person.

Age-worthy: A wine that has the potential to mature and develop complexity, as opposed to a simple table wine that has a limited shelf life.

Autobid: A feature available at online auction houses that automatically increases a bid up to a predetermined maximum in response to bids placed by competing bidders.

Balanced cellar: A cellar that contains wines for short-, mid-, and long-term consumption, especially one with equal depth and breadth.

Bid-steps: At an auction, the preset monetary increments required between bids.

Bidding off the chandelier: Nonexistent bids taken by auctioneers to gain some momentum until they arrive at one bid-step below the reserve.

Blind tasting: A wine tasting at which the identity of the wineries or the chateaus is intentionally withheld from the tasters to foster objectivity. Most professional tastings are conducted in this manner.

Blue-chip: A premium winery, usually referring to California.

Bottle Sizes:

Half bottle: 375 ml.

Regular bottle: 750 ml.

Magnum: Equal to two regular bottles, or 1.5 liters.

Marie-Jeanne: Equal to three regular bottles, or 2.25 liters.

Double magnum: Equal to four regular bottles, or 3 liters.

Jeroboam: For pre-1980 Bordeaux, equal to six regular bottles, or 4.5 liters. More recent jeroboams have been bottled in 5-liter containers. For Burgundy and Champagne, a jeroboam is equal to four regular bottles, or 3 liters.

Imperial: For Bordeaux, equal to eight regular bottles, or 6 liters.

Methuselah: For Burgundy and Champagne, equal to eight regular bottles, or 6 liters.

Bought in: A wine that fails to find a buyer at auction.

Breadth: The scope or amplitude of wines contained in a collection.

Brett: An unpleasant, barnyard-like smell in wine, derived from yeast.

Buyer's premium: The percentage an auction house levies on a buyer on top of the winning or final bid. It can range from zero to 18.5 percent.

Capsule: A lead or plastic foil that encircles the neck of a bottle.

Case-lot: At auction, a consignment consisting of a dozen bottles.

Cellar-worthy: A complex wine that has aging potential *(see also* Age-worthy).

Cellarette: A free-standing cabinet used to store wine prior to serving it.

Chais: French term for a winery's vat room or aging cellar.

Château bottled: A wine bottled on the premises of the wine-producing estate where it was made, and by the people who made it, giving it a guarantee of authenticity.

Claret: A term used primarily in England to refer to red Bordeaux.

Consignor: An individual selling his or her wine at auction.

Consignor's fee: A sliding scale fee charged to the seller by an auction house on the hammer price of the consignment *(see also* Hammer price). It can range from zero to 20 percent.

Corked: A moldy, musty flavor in wine caused by a tainted cork (see page 136).

Cru bourgeois: A category of Bordeaux wine that falls below the classified growths.

Cult wine: Highly concentrated (and expensive), limited-edition California wines that have developed a cult following.

Decant: To pour a wine from the bottle into a separate vessel in order to aerate the contents or to rid the bottle of sediment (see page 144).

Deposit: *See* Sediment.

Depth: Refers to the scope of vintages contained in a collection.

Domaine-bottled: *See* Chateau-bottled.

DRC: Domaine de la Romanée-Conti.

En primeur: French for "futures offerings." In the spring following the harvest in Bordeaux, many chateaus declare a preliminary case-price for delivery once the wines have been bottled, about two years hence *(see also* Futures).

Ex-Chateau: At auction, an offering of wines that have been consigned directly by the chateau or winery where they were made.

First growth: The highest ranking conferred on a Bordeaux chateau by the 1855 classification *(see also* 1855 classification).

Flight: A group of wines (usually no more than ten) in a vertical or horizontal tasting.

Futures: An initial offering of classified Bordeaux generally sold by the case, delivered after the wines have been bottled, about two years after the purchase date. Futures purchased from a reputable merchant guarantee a

239

fixed price and future availability. Infrequently, wines from California and Burgundy are marketed as futures (see page 155).

Garage wine: The French term for limited-edition cult wines, many of which were initially produced in ultra-small spaces no bigger than a garage.

Go one more: With a little bit of coaxing from an auctioneer, it may become apparent that if you "go one more" bid step you will secure the lot because you have exhausted the absentee bidder's maximum.

Hammer price: The price of a winning bid at auction excluding the buyer's premium, taxes, and delivery charges.

Helix: *See* Worm.

Hermitagé: A now-abandoned practice of adding robust wines to ameliorate thinner Bordeaux vintages.

Horizontal collection: A collection of different wines from the same vintage. *See also* Vertical collection.

Knocked down: At auction, an expression (used primarily in Britain) that refers to the final hammer price (e.g., *a case of Lafite Rothschild 1982 was knocked down for $7,500*).

Legs: A clear film that materializes on the sides of a wineglass once the wine has been swirled. Also known as *tears* (see page 136).

Lot: A specific wine or set of wines offered at auction. In a sale catalog, each lot is numbered separately.

Madeirized: Oxidized wine that is redolent of Maderia.

Négociant: A wine merchant who bottles and distributes wines (mainly used in Burgundy).

OWC: Original wooden case. An OWC wine has never been unpacked.

Order bid: At auction, an absentee bid.

Order book: At auction, a record book containing all the absentee bids.

Paddle: At auction, plastic-shaped paddles or cards inscribed with an identifying number that are issued to each registered bidder.

Parcel: Identical lots of the same wine that are offered as a package, or parcel, at auction. The winning bidder of the first of these lots has the option to buy the remainder at the same price.

Passed: At auction, a wine that fails to meet its reserve and is bought in.

Passive storage: Wines that are stored in a natural underground cellar without temperature and humidity controls.

Phylloxera: A tiny, root-feeding aphid responsible for devastating and ultimately uprooting French vineyards in the late nineteenth century (see page 160). Pre-phylloxera wines were made in the period predating the arrival of these plant lice. Some collectors believe their quality was better than that of their modern counterparts.

Provenance: The storage conditions and previous ownerships of a wine consigned to auction. Wines of pristine provenance (and, by implication, superb quality) command premium prices.

Reserve: At auction, a privately agreed upon sum between the consignor and the auction house below which the wine cannot be sold. The reserve is usually set somewhere between 80 and 100 percent of a lot's estimated low price.

Score: A wine's rating determined by a professional tasting panel or celebrated critic.

Sediment: A natural precipitate of tartrate matter and other elements that settles in the bottom of a bottle as it ages, visible when the bottle is stood upright (see page 145).

Six-pack: A six-bottle lot or case of wine.

Super-Tuscans: Highly complex, cellar-worthy wines produced in Tuscany that often contain a large percentage of nonindigenous varietals, such as Cabernet Sauvignon. Typical examples include Tenuta San Guido Sassicaia and Antinori Toscana Solaia.

Tannin: A substance found in grape skins, seeds, and stems, as well as in the wooden barrels in which red wines are aged. Tannins are important for balancing and aging wine.

Tears: *See* Legs.

Throw a deposit: Older Cabernet Sauvignons and Pinot Noirs may precipitate tartrate matter or some other pigment as they mature. While harmless, this matter will render a glass cloudy, and therefore the wine should be decanted to keep the liquid crystal clear.

Tranche: The first offering in a Bordeaux futures campaign.

Ullage: Also known as fill level, ullage refers to the distance in a wine bottle between the base of the cork and the start of the wine. Ullage increases as a wine ages or, sometimes, because of improper storage. Ullage is almost always described in an auction catalog. For a diagram depicting commonly occurring fill levels, see page 84.

Varietal: A specific grape type (e.g., Cabernet Sauvignon, Chardonnay, Pinot Noir, etc.).

Vertical collection: A collection of the same wine from different vintages. *See also* Horizontal collection.

Vintage: In general, the term refers to a wine produced in a specific harvest. However, Port producers only declare a vintage in harvests when conditions are exceptional, as do Champagne houses.

Volatile acidity: An unpleasant odor redolent of nail polish remover or old balsamic vinegar. Volatile acidity can result from a number of factors, including bacteria introduced to damaged grapes, grape juice, and wine. Other culprits can range from vinegar flies or contaminated winemaking equipment. Elimination of all air in wine barrels and the addition of sulfur dioxide will limit the growth of the bacteria. Also known by its initials, V.A.

Worm: The part of a corkscrew that is inserted into a bottle. (Also known as a helix.)

BIBLIOGRAPHY

~~~~~~~~

Allen, H. Warner. *The Romance of . . . Wine*. New York: E. P. Dutton & Co., 1932.

Asher, Gerald. *On Wine*. New York: Random House, 1982.

Asher, Gerald. *The Pleasures of Wine*. San Francisco: Chronicle Books, 2002.

Baldridge, Letitia. *A Lady, First: My Life in the Kennedy White House and the American Embassies of Paris and Rome*. New York: Viking 2001.

Bastianich, Joseph, and Lynch, David. *Vino Italiano: The Regional Wines of Italy*. New York: Clarkson Potter, 2002.

Broadbent, Michael. *Michael Broadbent's Vintage Wine: Fifty Years of Tasting Three Centuries of Wine*. New York: Harcourt, 2002.

Brook, Steven. *Bordeaux: People Power and Politics*. London: Mitchell Beazly, 2001.

Clarke, Oz, and Spurrier, Steven. *Clarke & Spurrier's Fine Wine Guide: A Connoisseur's Bible,* rev. ed. New York, San Diego, London: Harcourt, 2001.

Coates, Clive. *Grands Vins: The Finest Châteaux of Bordeaux and Their Wines*. Berkeley: University of California Press, 1995.

Dias Blue, Anthony. *American Wine: A Comprehensive Guide,* rev. ed. New York: Harper & Row 1988.

Diel, Armin, and Payne, Joel. *German Wine Guide*. New York: Abbeville Press, 1999.

Echikson, William. *Noble Rot: A Bordeaux Wine Revolution*. New York: W. W. Norton & Co., 2004.

Faith, Nicholas. *The Winemasters of Bordeaux: The Inside Story of the World's Greatest Wines*. 2nd ed. London: Prion Books, 1999.

Gabler, James M. *Passions: The Wines & Travels of Thomas Jefferson*. Baltimore: Bacchus Press, 1995.

Immer, Andrea. *Great Wine Made Simple: Straight Talk from a Master Sommelier*. New York: Broadway Books, 2000.

Johnnes, Daniel. *Daniel Johnnes's Top 200 Wines: An Expert's Guide to Maximum Enjoyment for Your Dollar*, 2004 ed. New York: Penguin Books, 2003.

Johnson, Hugh. *Vintage: The Story of Wine*. New York: Simon & Schuster, 1989.

Johnson, Hugh, and Robinson, Jancis. *The World Atlas of Wine, 5th ed*. New York: Barnes & Noble Books, 2003.

Juhlin, Richard. *2000 Champagnes*. New York: MT Train/Scala Books, 1999.

Kramer, Matt. *Making Sense of Wine*. New York: William Morrow, 1989.

Laube, James. *Wine Spectator's California Wine*, 2nd updated ed. New York: M. Shanken Communications, 1999.

Lichine, Alexis. *Alexis Lichine's New Encyclopedia of Wines & Spirits*, 5th Rev. ed. New York: Knopf, 1987.

Loftus, Simon. *Anatomy of the Wine Trade: Abe's Sardines and Other Stories*. New York: Harper & Row, 1985.

Lynch, Kermit. *Adventures on the Wine Route: A Wine Buyer's Tour of France*. New York: Farrar, Straus & Giroux, 1988.

MacNeil, Karen. *The Wine Bible*. New York: Workman Publishing Company, 2001.

McCoy, Elin. *The Emperor of Wine: The Rise of Robert M. Parker, Jr. and the Reign of American Taste*. New York: HarperCollins, 2005.

Morrell, Peter. *I'm in the Wine Store, Now What?!* New York: Silver Lining Books, 2000.

Murray, Venetia. *An Elegant Madness: High Society in Regency England.* New York: Viking, 1999.

Olney, Richard. *Yquem.* Boston: David R. Godine, 1985.

Parker, Robert. *Parker's Wine Buyer's Guide,* 6th ed. New York: Simon & Schuster, 2002.

Penning-Rowsell, Edmund. *The Wine of Bordeaux.* London: Penguin Books, 1985.

Redding, Cyrus. *A History and Description of Modern Wines,* 3rd ed. London: Henry G. Bohn, 1851.

Robinson, Jancis. *Jancis Robinson's Wine Course: A Guide to the World of Wine,* 2nd ed. New York: Simon & Schuster, 2000.

Robinson, Jancis. *How to Taste: A Guide to Enjoying Wine.* New York: Simon & Schuster, 2000.

Robinson, Jancis. *Tasting Pleasure: Confessions of a Wine Lover,* 2nd ed. New York: Penguin Books, 1999.

Rosengarten, David, and Wesson, Joshua. *Red Wine with Fish.* New York: Simon & Schuster, 1989.

Saintsbury, George. *Notes on a Cellar-Book.* New York: Mayflower Books, 1978.

Seale, William. *The President's House.* New York: White House Historical Association with Harry N. Abrams, 1986.

Suckling, James. *Vintage Port: The Wine Spectator's Ultimate Guide for Consumers, Collectors, and Investors.* San Francisco: Wine Spectator Press, 1990.

Watney, Bernard W., and Babbidge, Homer D. *Corkscrews for Collectors.* London: Sotheby Parke Bernet, 1981.

Waugh, Harry. *Diary of a Winetaster: Recent Tastings of French and California Wines.* New York: Quadrangle Books, 1972.

Wine Spectator's Ultimate Guide to Buying Wine, 8th ed. New York: Wine Spectator Press, 2004.

Zraly, Kevin. *Windows on the World Complete Wine Course,* 2005 ed. New York: Sterling Publishing, 2005.

INDEX

~\\\\\\~